# Israeli Politics and the First Palestinian Intifada

*Israeli Politics and the First Palestinian Intifada* investigates how the Palestinians in the occupied territories interpreted the deepening domestic Israeli divisions over the continuation of occupation as an opportunity to shake off the military occupation in 1987. In contrast to previous waves of confrontation during the deep-rooted Palestinian–Israeli conflict, the 1987 Intifada is distinguishable by both the social and political circumstances in which it coalesced. This is exemplified in the fact that over a million Palestinians had been put under Israeli military rule, and the unprecedented magnitude of contention Palestinian activists managed to mount and sustain.

Analyzing Palestinian print media articles published throughout the 1970s and 1980s, supported by data from interviews with Palestinian grassroots activists and Israeli journalists, this volume examines the reasons for the specific time context during which the Palestinian uprising crystallized. It also looks at:

- the military occupation of the West Bank and the Gaza Strip and the resulting profound socio-political changes to Israeli polity as well as to Palestinian society
- politicization of Palestinians' shared hardships and discontent, and their politics of resistance
- the consolidating Palestinian movement within the occupied territories and the ensuing capacity for a shared, collective framing of domestic Israeli divisions concerning the occupation
- the strategy and tactics of this moment which was based on its understanding of the opportunity presented by divisions in Israeli society concerning the occupation.

Eitan Alimi's use of unique sources, such as Palestinian activists and newspapers along with an analysis of the sources of the second Intifada allows him to provide an insightful and innovative understanding of the Israeli and Palestinian conflict and also the implications for the future of the conflict. *Israeli Politics and the First Palestinian Intifada* is essential reading for scholars and students with interests in Middle East politics and society and in the field of collective action.

**Eitan Y. Alimi** teaches on contentious politics, conflict resolution, and social movements at the Political Science Department, the Hebrew University and at the School of Political Sciences, University of Haifa, Israel. He received his Ph.D. from the Sociology Department at Boston College in 2004. He has researched and published articles on national insurgencies, the role of cognition in contentious politics, and the role of the news media during peace-building in *Mobilization, Conflict and Communication, Terrorism and Political Violence*, and *Studies in Conflict and Terrorism*.

# Routledge studies in Middle Eastern politics

# Israeli Politics and the First Palestinian Intifada

Political opportunities, framing processes and contentious politics

**Eitan Y. Alimi**

Foreword by William A. Gamson

Routledge
Taylor & Francis Group

LONDON AND NEW YORK

First published 2007
by Routledge
2 Park Square, Milton Park, Abingdon, Oxon OX14 4RN

Simultaneously published in the USA and Canada
by Routledge
270 Madison Ave, New York, NY 10016

*Routledge is an imprint of the Taylor & Francis Group, an informa business*

Transferred to Digital Printing 2009

© 2007 Eitan Y. Alimi

Typeset in Times by Wearset Ltd, Boldon, Tyne and Wear

*British Library Cataloguing in Publication Data*
A catalogue record for this book is available from the British Library

*Library of Congress Cataloging in Publication Data*
A catalog record for this book has been requested

ISBN10: 0-415-38560-1 (hbk)
ISBN10: 0-415-55885-9 (pbk)

ISBN13: 978-0-415-38560-2 (hbk)
ISBN13: 978-0-415-55885-3 (pbk)

To Nirit, Romi, and Omri
For being an endless source of support and joy

To Bill and Char
For showing me the value of teaching and research

# Contents

# Illustrations

## Figures

## Tables

# Foreword

*William A. Gamson*

Those of us who are obsessed by the Israeli–Palestinian conflict will find much to fascinate in this rich, subtle, and textured account of the contentious cycle of the Intifada that began in 1987. But here I will try to make the case for why this book is of major importance for those who are not so obsessed by this particular conflict but are interested in theories of contentious politics and their applicability to many conflicts in other parts of the world.

During the first twenty years of the Israeli occupation following the 1967 war, Palestinians in the occupied territories became increasingly integrated economically into Israeli society without, of course, attendant political rights. This produced a situation in which – for the purposes of analyzing their strategies of contention – they could fruitfully be regarded as internal challengers. Some avenues of influence were open but, for the most part, government social control strategies were designed to prevent contentious collective action. Much of contemporary social movement theory attempts to explain the dynamics of contention involved in such challenges. Indeed, the Civil Rights movement in the Southern United States – the paradigmatic social movement for this body of theory – fits the description.

In *Dynamics of Contention* (2001), three major contributors to this theory – Doug McAdam, Sidney Tarrow, and Charles Tilly – attempt an ambitious synthesis of the state of the field. They integrate more recent work on cultural approaches with an earlier emphasis on resources and structure. In making sense of cycles of protest, they argue that the mechanisms and processes are not invariant but are contingent on the particular historical circumstances. The question they pose for researchers is what mechanisms and processes produce different types of contention.

Alimi, in this book, takes on the agenda of *Dynamics of Contention* and carries it through in all its complexity. While many of the specifics of the Israeli–Palestinian conflict are unique, they can often be seen as special cases of conditions which are more or less approximated in other situations. I don't want to spoil the story that lies ahead but I will illustrate with parts of the analysis that seem particularly rich in implications for other conflicts.

As one can see much more clearly with hindsight, the 1987 cycle of the Palestinian Intifada was characterized by a carefully calibrated degree of contention. Compared to the violence of the second cycle that began in 2000 – with its lethal violence deliberately aimed at Israeli civilians – the stone throwing and tire burning of the earlier cycle seems quite contained.

Alimi's explanation is many-faceted, but consider the following. In conflicts with great power discrepancies, the weaker party is likely to pay a great deal more attention to the internal politics of its stronger adversary than the reverse. This was especially true during the years before 1987, when many Palestinians on-the-ground – that is, living in the territories – became highly informed observers of Israeli internal politics. Alimi quotes a Palestinian journalist who told him, "Palestinians put a lot of effort in gaining information of what was going on in Israel. It became almost a 'natural' interest of the occupied to know its occupier . . . an interest that evolved into a need."

They especially followed the development of a significant Israeli peace camp following the 1982 invasion of Lebanon. This close monitoring produced a growing Palestinian awareness of the sharpening division in Israeli society over the future of the territories. As is typical in such situations, the growing familiarity was not mutual; most Israelis had little reason to pay attention to internal Palestinian developments.

In the enormous literature on political opportunity, perhaps the most frequently mentioned variable is a division among the authorities being challenged. In the case of the Civil Rights movement in the U.S., the division between Federal officials and those in states with Jim Crow laws were widened by carefully chosen actions that enhanced these divisions – often by provoking overreactions by opponents. The use of non-violent contentious actions was particularly effective in this regard. But only if the counter action produced media coverage of police beating peaceful protesters and using dogs against them.

Something of a similar sort seemed to be going on among Palestinians living in the territories. There was a clear recognition of how the strategy and tactics of contention could lessen or sharpen the developing division in Israeli society. In more theoretical language, political opportunities facilitated some forms of contention and these, in turn, influenced the opportunities in a recursive relationship. As a grassroots activist told Alimi, "We realized that if we use deadly weapons, we will fail to cause a divide inside your society. We wanted to keep the momentum of fights and conflicts in Israel and not cause you to reunite by using guns. . . . This was our way to strengthen those groups inside Israel that rejected the occupation."

Alimi adds to this picture an awareness and sophistication on the part of the indigenous Palestinian leadership about the role of the mass media and the dramaturgy of collective action. There was a clear understanding of how media images of youths with sling shots confronting tanks would play, not only among third parties in the international arena, but among Israeli citizens who didn't fancy David becoming Goliath. The contained contentious strategy, accompanied by disturbing images of Israeli responses, became a potent weapon for sharpening the debate in Israel about what the occupation was doing to Israeli society and values.

Alimi shows in rich detail the social construction of opportunity and the strategic use of the media in the process. Faced with a military occupation which could censor or shut down Palestinian publications, the Palestinians used the vigorous freedom of expression within Israeli society to get around the constraint. When a Palestinian newspaper translated something already published in Hebrew in *Ha'aretz*, there could be little complaint by the monitors. Quoting a critic of the occupation from the Israeli press, one could say things that would never be allowed if they originated in the Palestinian press. And, in the process, readers could witness for themselves that Israeli society was sharply divided about the future of the occupied territories.

An important part of Alimi's story is the relative ascendance during the period from 1982 to 1987 of indigenous leadership. Living with the experience of the occupation on a daily basis produced a more pragmatic and less abstract and ideological orientation, compared to that of the PLO leadership abroad in Tunisia and elsewhere. This helped to ground the chosen strategy of contention in the concrete realities of the military occupation, including both opportunities and constraints. Palestinians in the territories developed a more nuanced understanding of Israeli society and politics than the filtered version of the official leaders.

Alimi did not systematically study the second, deadlier cycle of contention that began in 2000. But he doesn't use this as an excuse to avoid the inevitable question: What happened to the contained contention of the first cycle? Here, his analysis is multi-factored and inevitably more speculative. The insight that deadly violence would unite Israeli society and undermine the Israeli peace camp certainly proved accurate. Shifting internal politics and leadership in both communities is part of the difference, as the reader will discover in reading Alimi's account.

Alimi also has the courage to address another inevitable question: Given the current situation, is peace possible? The solutions he offers reflect the insights produced by his analysis as well as broader theories of conflict resolution. Overall, this is grounded theory at its best, an analysis of a concrete case that is historically embedded and uses the best insights of theories of contentious politics to illuminate the complex interaction between the construction and maintenance of political opportunity and the strategy and tactics of collective action.

### Reference

D. McAdam, S. Tarrow, and C. Tilly (2001) *Dynamics of Contention*, New York: Cambridge University Press.

# Preface

From the end of World War I and the beginning of the British Mandate, the nature of the conflict between Palestinians and Israelis went through several transformations. Each change in the nature of the conflict affected the ways it was conducted. Indeed, one might suggest that the modern history of the Israeli–Palestinian conflict has witnessed three distinct political settings or structures, while at the time of writing this book the fourth structure is still taking shape.

Thus, from 1920 to 1948 the structure of the conflict can be characterized as two ethnic communities developing their national sentiments under the foreign rule of the British Mandatory system through a mutual infliction of damage. From 1948 to 1967, due to the establishment of the Israeli State and the 1948 War, the structure of the conflict was between Israel and the adjacent Arab States who acted on behalf of the Palestinians and managed the conflict primarily through conventional wars. The 1967 War brought with it yet another transformation of the conflict; as a result of the Israeli taking over of the Golan Heights, the West Bank, the Gaza Strip, and the Sinai Desert, over one million Palestinians were put under Israeli military rule as occupied people. This third political setting of the protracted conflict and the shifts in its mode of conduct is the primary subject matter of this book.

The Palestinian Intifada of 1987–92 marked the end of the third political setting of the conflict, with it afterwards gearing forward a painstaking shaping of yet a fourth structure. The form and content of the present in-the-making political setting are a matter of contention both between and within each of our time-old conflictants.

Being an Israeli who attempts to learn about the ways in which the Palestinians in the occupied territories became familiarized with Israeli society and how such familiarity affected their strategy of resistive politics has unquestionably been a mental burden. As I was moving along and discussing my ideas with whoever bothered to listen, I was often accused of two things. On the one hand, I was accused of doing service for those Israelis who argue that Palestinians should never be trusted and that they have no genuine interest in peace with Israel. On the other hand, I was often accused of doing service for the Palestinians, showing how domestic Israeli divisions over continuing the occupation would be used by Palestinians to escalate their attacks on Israel. This book is my own way of answering these accusations which, no matter how overly simplistic, are unfortunately held by far too many on both sides to the conflict. If I were to be blame for something, it would be for not writing this book.

But this book is much more than coping with accusations. As an Israeli who has suffered a terrible personal loss I have had all the reasons in the world to be swept away by the prevalent conception of Palestinians so pervasively grounded among Israelis. This book, then, is also the result of my decision to make the pursuit of peaceful compromise central to my life and scholarly work rather than seeking vengeance. I know many Palestinians are doing the same; I hope this book will convince many others not to be tempted by the abyss of zealotry and vengeance.

Eitan Y. Alimi
Kefar Saba, Israel

# Acknowledgments

The book you hold is the result of several years of research during which I was a graduate student first at the Hebrew University and then at Boston College. During this period I have been fortunate to receive the support and encouragement of many friends and colleagues to whom I am deeply indebted. I thank all of those who walked with me in what at times seemed like an endless journey, physically as well as mentally.

It was the exceptional support of several friends and colleagues that enabled me to complete the journey with greater ease. As you read this book and in case you have come across their work, you will easily identify the fingerprints of Bill Gamson, Char Ryan, Gadi Wolfsfeld, and Samuel Peleg who have deeply influenced my work and become the best colleagues one could hope for. All four have been wonderful friends and advisors and a constant source of encouragement and guidance from the outset. And, whether because always finding time for my questions and thoughts, commenting on previous versions of this manuscript, sharing me with their thoughts or providing useful suggestions as to how to refine my arguments, I am deeply indebted to Diane Vaughan, Robert Kunovich, Eve Spangler, Kevin Carragee, Matt Williams, Ido Nevo, and many others. As this book started to take shape, I was also fortunate to get the generous support of Chuck Tilly, Sid Tarrow, and David Meyer who provided me with valuable insights as to how to improve my arguments and raised important issues for me to address, thus making the analysis presented herein more convincing and user friendly. Other collaborators to whom my thanks go are Daniella Tougeman for helping me express my thoughts in English whenever my often untamed mind got stuck in Hebrew, Gal Engelhart, Sharon Ashkenazi, and Dimitry Epstein for their assistance with conducting the research, and Morag Segal and Wasfi Kailani for helping me to cope with the subtleties of Arabic. The full and sole responsibility for what follows, no matter how involved the others have been, rests on me.

I would like to thank the Boston College School of Arts and Sciences for providing me with a generous grant, which enabled me to carry on and complete the research. I am especially grateful for the support and encouragement I received from members of the Media Research and Action Project of the Sociology Department at Boston College. The stimulating discussions and the constructive criticism of my work in progress during two years of active participation have become a real personal and academic asset. My thanks also go to Routledge, especially to Joe Whiting and Nadia Seemungal, for their faith in my work and their patient and thoughtful guidance, and to Gary Smith of Wearset Publishing Services who most professionally helped transforming a rough manuscript into a reader friendly book. I have quoted a few passages and illustrations in the book which already saw light in: *Terrorism and Political Violence* 15/3 (2003), *Studies in Conflict and Terrorism* 29/3 (2006) and *Mobilization* 11/1 (2006). I thank Taylor and Francis Group Inc. (www.taylorandfrancis.com), and Mobilization editors (www.mobilization.sdsu.edu) for granting me the permission to use these materials.

Finally, I would like to thank my family, who were supportive and encouraging throughout and showed exceptional tolerance in coping with me from my first days in academia. It is to my mother, my brothers, and in-laws that I am deeply indebted and grateful. But above all my thanks go to Nirit, my wife, a friend, and my biggest critic, and to our two adorable daughters, Romi and Omri. It is to them that my endless love and appreciation go. Their love and support gave me the strength to complete this project.

# Abbreviations

| | |
|---|---|
| AIC | Alternative Information Center |
| ANM | The Arab National Movement |
| DCO | Israeli–Palestinian Defense Coordination Offices |
| DFLP | Democratic Front for the Liberation of Palestine |
| FACTS | The Palestinian Committee for Factual Information |
| GFTU | General Federation of Trade Unions |
| Hamas | The Islamic Resistance Movement |
| IDF | Israel Defense Force |
| IIC | The Israeli Information Center |
| JMCC | Jerusalem Media and Communication Center |
| MAFDAL | Israeli National Religious Party |
| NGC | The National Guidance Committee |
| NIF | National and Islamic Forces |
| PA | Palestinian Authority |
| PCP/JCP | Palestinian Communist Party/Jordanian Communist Party |
| PFLP | Popular Front for the Liberation of Palestine |
| PHRIC | Palestinian Human Rights Information Center |
| PLO | Palestine Liberation Organization |
| PNC | The Palestinian National Council |
| PNF | Palestinian National Front |
| RAKAH | Israeli Communist Party |
| Shabak | Israeli General Secret Service |
| Shabiba | Fatah's Youth Movement |
| Tanzim | Fatah oriented grassroots organization |
| UNCU | United National Command/Leadership of the Uprising |
| UNRWA | The United Nation Relief and Works Agency |
| UPWC | Union of Palestinian Women's Committees |
| WCSW | Women Committees for Social Work |
| WUB | Workers Unity Bloc |
| WWC | Women's Work Committee |

# Introduction

Throughout the twenty years of Israeli military occupation beginning in June 1967, Palestinians in the West Bank and Gaza Strip initiated countless attempts at resistance. Most of these attempts lasted no more than a week and motivated insignificant commitment and participation by the Palestinian population. We are now aware that by 1987, and for approximately the next six years, the Palestinians within the West Bank and Gaza Strip (hereinafter: the occupied territories) succeeded in mounting a widely popular and intensive revolt, demonstrating a well-established and coordinated organizational infrastructure, unprecedented commitment, and calculated use of collective action repertoires. Despite their clear resource inferiority, the Palestinians in the occupied territories ultimately compelled Israel to recognize their genuine collective needs and national aspirations.

Consider the following excerpts documented by students of the Israeli–Palestinian conflict: "In November 1981, a cycle of protest in the Gaza Strip took place. The initiators were [Palestinians] doctors, lawyers, and other professionals who struck in protest of new financial restrictions imposed by the Israeli authorities and were joined by merchants and the Gaza municipality" (Lesch 1990: 4). The Israeli reaction to the events was resolute and harsh; within a matter of hours, order was restored. A few months later, in March 1982, the eviction of several West Bank mayors caused "violent, widespread confrontations ... this time in East Jerusalem, resulting in the death of six Palestinians and one Israeli soldier. The fierce demonstrations lasted for a week and were countered by severe punitive measures by Israeli military forces" (Ma'oz 1984: 203). Six years later, another wave of confrontation consolidated, this time differing in its type of action, actors, scope, and results:

> On May 31, 1987 a large Israeli military force pushed its way into Balata [refugee camp], the largest refugee camp in the West Bank, for the purpose of demonstrating Israeli sovereignty after several days of disturbances in the camp, arresting suspects ... a curfew was imposed on the camp and the soldiers searched each and every house. The military search was interrupted as women started to riot, quickly enjoined by the men who were previously lined up, forcing the military to pull back from the camp ... [six months

later] ... in mid November 1987 an unprecedented wave of violence took place in Jibalyya refugee camp in the Gaza Strip. For the first time the mass of people tried to break through the military fence using stones and sticks and waving PLO flags.

(Shalev 1990: 40)

Several weeks after the Jibalyya incident, additional incidents such as mounting barricades, stone throwing and tire burning occurred. In retrospect, these incidents were a part of a gradually intensifying contention between Palestinian grassroots activists and Israeli soldiers that coalesced into a wide-ranging national insurgency against Israeli military rule – the Intifada (Arabic for "shaking off"). In October 1991, following approximately six years of ferocious contention, and for the first time in the history of the Israeli–Palestinian conflict, the two parties met together at a peace conference held in Madrid to discuss possible resolution to the conflict.

## The Intifada – why bother?

How can we account for such an unprecedented shift in the magnitude of contention? The conventional wisdom in the study of conflict and national insurgencies is that every national minority, facing systematic oppression and lack of possibility to fulfill its human needs, eventually rebels. Compelling as it is, this line of argument does not take us far in understanding the nature and dynamics of conflict, the rise of contentious politics, and the possibilities for their resolution. Why does a minority succeed in mounting such massive contention during one specific historical period and not another? What influences its strategy? Why is it that one form of contention succeeds in achieving political goals where others fail?

Any attempt at understanding the shift in the magnitude of contention as manifested in the Intifada should begin by probing its structural context. In contrast to previous cycles of contention during the deep-rooted Israeli–Palestinian conflict, the Palestinian Intifada may be distinguished by its structural context: the fact that the Palestinians were a national minority under Israeli military occupation as opposed to other past structures of the Israeli–Palestinian conflict (e.g., two national movements struggling under British mandate, 1920–48). The forceful inclusion of Palestinians in the occupied territories as part of the Israeli state led to a major shift in the structure of the conflict and its consequent dynamics. Practically speaking, Israel has turned itself into the Palestinians' direct target of discontent, by constantly depriving them from the ability to fulfill their human needs.

Simultaneously, the fact of occupation affected the sociopolitical realities on both sides of the conflict. The post 1967 Israeli polity ran into a deep internal conflict over the territories' future status that gradually developed into a power deflation situation – a profound sociopolitical cleavage that undermined the cornerstones of the regime's framework and its basis of authority, which manifested itself by the rise in political violence, distrust in the system and unprecedented violation of the rule of law. The Palestinian minority within the occupied territories gradually underwent a developmental growth in national identity and self-reliance.

These two processes grew apace simultaneously with the Intifada, expressing the height of the Palestinians' discontent, only to encounter an occupier wavering as to the proper countermeasures. The Palestinians' capacity to "take the heat" of the Israeli countermeasures brings two intertwined questions to the fore. First, what were the causes behind the Palestinians' competence in promoting such a challenge? Second, in what ways was the Intifada translated into political achievements?

Israel's sweeping victory in June 1967 over the joint front of Arab States, and the ensuing unilateral annexation of the Golan Heights (1981) and East Jerusalem (1980), restructured the Israeli–Arab conflict in general and the Israeli–Palestinian conflict specifically. The results of the war expanded Israel's rule over the Golan Heights, the Sinai Peninsula, the Gaza Strip, East Jerusalem, and the West Bank. *De facto*, Palestinians became integral to the Israeli State's apparatus, yet, at the same time, separate from the Israeli "polity," to use Tilly's (1978) concept, thus constituting a distinct "polity" governed by military rule.

In practical terms, Israeli sociologist Moshe Lissak (1990) argues, "the expansion of Israel's sovereignty created a situation whereby Israel had to maintain two regimes ... the one democratic relying on consensus and negotiation while the other rests on force, fear, and manipulation" (p. 33). This new phase in the conflict, in contrast to the phase between 1948 and 1967, established an intimate relationship between the two conflictants. Such increased proximity led to increased familiarity of the occupied Palestinians with Israeli society. This familiarity, however, was not mutual, as, mostly, Israeli security forces maintained contact with Palestinians in the occupied territories. Nevertheless, the Palestinians in the occupied territories became an integral part of Israeli society.

Recognizing the violent potential of the situation, on the one hand, Israel acted, to moderate the situation through the preservation of existing mediating mechanisms such as municipalities, and by enabling the development of a higher educational system and media institutions. On the other hand, and primarily as a result of the Yom Kippur War (the October 1973 war), the Israeli sociopolitical system experienced a growing process of ideological cleavage over the occupied territories' future status that slowly began to reinforce the pre-existing ethnic and religious cleavages (Horowitz and Lissak 1990). Throughout the 1970s and 1980s, Israeli democracy experienced an acute series of crises that threatened its stability, legitimacy, and cohesion.

Statistical evidence on the levels of confrontations within the occupied territories reveals a striking correlation between Israel's domestic crises and the sharp increase in the level of confrontations. While circumstantial in itself, bearing in mind the Palestinians' willingness to rebel and their growing familiarity with the Israeli polity, such statistics might have a subjective dimension: a

Palestinian attentiveness to these crises which, in turn, could have had influenced their perception regarding conditions ripe for increased contention.

This book will demonstrate that such shared perceptions did indeed exist. We will see that an intersection between a pre-existent *willingness* and *readiness* axes (representing the Palestinian shared discontent and sense of injustice, together with commitment and solidarity) and an *opportunity* axis – demonstrating deepening domestic Israeli divisions over continuation of the occupation – triggered the inception of the Intifada. Specifically, this book is about how a growing Palestinian shared perception of ripe conditions – Israel's system-wide crisis – was translated into contentious tactics that generated a sustained, intensive, and widespread challenge. Concomitantly, Palestinians' use of such tactics successfully, yet not without difficulties, promoted the possibility of a peaceful resolution of the conflict among the majority of the Israeli public and the international community.

## The Intifada – existing explanations

What do we know about the Intifada? Of the numerous works dealing with the Palestinian uprising, four clusters of explanations can be discerned. A first cluster of explanations views the Palestinian uprising as a repercussion of the broader Arab–Israeli conflict. Reflecting an inter-state approach to the analysis of conflict dynamics, it focuses on regional and territorial developments. The roots of the uprising lie in the Palestinians' disappointment with the management of the conflict by the Arab States, especially after the Arab defeat in the June 1967 war, and the subsequent development of a distinct Palestinian nationalist identity in the occupied territories (Abu-Amr 1988; Khalidi 1988). The Arab States' consistent refusal to recognize the role and the importance of the PLO, as was the case in the Arab summit of November 1987, is seen as a central and proximate cause of the Intifada.

In contrast, a second cluster of explanations centers on the internal Israeli context and analyzes the social and economic conditions experienced by the Palestinians under the occupation. As such, it traces the causes of the 1987 uprising to the mounting grievances and frustrations among the Palestinians within the local arena. The death of four Palestinians, hit by an Israeli truck near the Erez military checkpoint in Gaza, on 8 December 1987, is identified as the spark that led to the outburst of the Palestinian uprising (Gilbar 1992; Lesch 1990; Shif and Yaari 1990).

A more recent cluster of explanations to the Intifada focuses on the trends of mobilization within the occupied territories. The initiative of local activists to organize the Palestinian population in professional and communal networks, primarily after the expulsion of the PLO from Lebanon in 1982 by Israel, and the ways in which local activists adapted their mode of resistance to Israeli counterinsurgency tactics are stressed as major determinants of the Palestinian ability to mount and sustain such a widespread challenge (Beitler 1995, 2004; Frisch 1992, 1996; Hiltermann 1991; Robinson 1997; Sahliyeh 1988).

A last, but no less important, cluster of explanations deals with the Intifada per se: its dynamics, tactics, and effects on both sides. Through the analysis of the uprising's effects on Israeli soldiers, the role the mass media played during the confrontation, and the tactics used by insurgents, this cluster contributes significantly to our understanding of this extraordinary phenomenon (Ezrahi 1997; Kaufman 1990; Wolfsfeld 1997). The ability of Palestinian activists to successfully frame their struggle and gain the sympathy of the international community is attributed to carefully planned tactics and the ability of rival parties within the movement to collaborate.

## The Intifada – a synthesis

This book draws on each cluster of explanation just presented. In fact, it is impossible to develop the argument regarding the effect of the system-wide domestic Israeli divisions on Palestinians' shared perception of opportunity to increase contention without insights from each cluster. Still, the truth remains that the protagonists of the Intifada were neither the PLO in exile nor Arab States; that Palestinian willingness to rebel was always present, at least since the 1967 occupation; and that Palestinian readiness to rebel, while shifting over time (among Nationalist, Islamist and Communist groups) and place (between the PLO in exile and local forces), was equally present – yet no one cluster is capable of accounting for the causes behind the Palestinians' competence in promoting such a challenge in this particular time context and not another (Alimi 2003). Attempts to cope with the possibility of a Palestinian shared perception of ripe circumstances to trigger contention – a perspective of inquiry that also has the potential to flesh out the rationale behind the specific tactics employed during the Intifada – are slight and inadequate. However, more should be said regarding each cluster's weaknesses, otherwise risk being justly accused of over-simplification.

While acknowledging the importance of regional political developments and the complex relationship between Arab States and the PLO in the Intifada's inception and dynamics, this book nonetheless focuses on the local structural context within which the Palestinians were situated. The Intifada is a unique cycle of contention in a specific stage of the deep-rooted Israeli–Palestinian conflict: the subordination of over one million Palestinian people by Israel as a result of the Israeli victory in June 1967 and the subsequent occupation of the West Bank, Gaza Strip, and East Jerusalem. Since our case study embodies the dynamics of contention between a state, as a political realization of a national movement, and an ethnic minority systematically prevented from fulfilling its human needs, it seems more adequate to use the inter-communal level of analysis (Azar 1986). As such, dynamics and developments within the local arena are seen as a key factor for the consolidation of sustained contention, but with the proviso that other developments can have, and indeed had, significant effects. After all, the Palestinians were under a state of occupation where the mere ability to leave the territories was dictated by Israeli military rule. Specifically sustained contention was required in order to let other factors and forces have any bearing upon the dynamics and trajectories of the uprising.

This book also acknowledges the importance of objective and subjective hardship, experienced by the Palestinians under military occupation, the mounting shared grievances and frustrations, in their willingness the rebel. Yet, the inclination to present the uprising as a sudden, spontaneous outburst of rage is misleading. Such a portrayal disregards the resource mobilization trends that took place during the 1980s in the occupied territories. Indeed, Palestinian discontent was already extremely intense during the early 1980s, in the context of Israel's invasion into Lebanon in summer 1982. Yet, a sustained, widespread, and intensive challenge as manifested in the Intifada did not consolidate.

An analysis of mobilization trends and endeavors within the local arena and of the ways local activists took the initiative in forming an infrastructure for contention will play a central role in this book. However, attributing the same opportunities for political activity to a national minority under occupation as those enjoyed by political actors in a liberal democratic context is inaccurate and misleading. Not only were Palestinian activists systematically prevented from participating in Israel's political system; in fact, Israeli military rule regulated even the basic right of freedom of speech and movement within the territories. In other words, it is crucial to explore how the changes and developments that took place in Israel, their effects on Israel's mode of occupation, and the Palestinians' reading and attribution of meaning to those changes influenced not only the Palestinians' ability to form a mobilizing infrastructure and trends of mobilization, but also their decision to trigger contention.

Last, but not least, a considerable portion of this book will be devoted to the analysis of the Intifada per se: the dynamics and trajectories of the 1987–92 cycle of contention. Understanding the Intifada action phase, however, without taking into consideration the precipitating developments and processes, the linkage between strategy and tactics, is impossible. It is impossible, for instance, to explain the organizational infrastructure, and the unprecedented level of participation that characterized the uprising without relating to the conditions that enabled it in the first place. In like manner, we cannot comprehend the rationale behind the decision to limit the use of deadly weapons without trying to figure out the development of the strategy from which this tactic emanated.

## The Intifada as collective action

The thrust of this book is an analysis of the Palestinian "first" Intifada as an exceptional manifestation of collective action: a voluminous episode of contentious politics for shaking off the Israeli military occupation of the West Bank and Gaza Strip, established in June 1967, initiated by a Palestinian national-social movement, which consolidated within the occupied territories during the 1970s and 1980s. This conceptualization warrants clarification.

I perceive collective action as comprising of [1] the agent of action (a social movement), [2] that engages in contentious politics as the means of action, [3] targeted always, but not exclusively, against the state (the target of action), and [4] embedded within structure of conflict, that is, the context of action. It is crucial to make, and maintain, such an analytical separation in order to capture the dynamics of collective action. Why?

Students of collective action, in the wake of the turbulent 1960s, were aiming at sharply disjointing themselves from the *Collective Behavior* approach in order to emphasize the deliberative nature of protest and re-conceiving the role and characteristics of the agent of collective action. Instead of viewing protests, demonstrations, or revolutions as mere emotional reaction by a "madding crowd" to societal breakdowns, the new paradigm known as the *Resource Mobilization* approach viewed such actions/events as politics by other means, rather than as social deviance. Putting aside value judgments, politics of contention is about people collectively making claims on other people, claims which, if realized, would affect those others' interest (McAdam, Tarrow, Tilly 1996). Thus, the making of claims can be manifested by peaceful picketing, to strike wave or mounting barricades, passing through brutal attacks, revolutions and even terrorism. Whether the collective claim-making is violent or nonviolent has less to do with ideological creed or innate aggressive human propensities and more with the dynamic interaction between those who act in the name of social order and those who act in the name of social justice during a contentious episode.

Interestingly, however, definitions of collective action tended to blur the lines between the phenomenon and the actor, between collective action and social movement. For example, while starting his conceptualization of collective action with a clear distinction between social movement and events of collective action, Tilly (1978) nevertheless ended up by regarding the former as another type of event. Social movement became an event, a form of contention in his suggested repertoire of contention.

Additional shortcoming concerned the lack of sufficient integration of sources and dynamics of conflict as the structural framework for collective action in forms of contention. By integrating structural factors into the analysis of collective action, Tilly circumvented the exaggerated focus on the agent of collective action, as manifested in the writings of McCarthy and Zald (1977), for instance, two of the main proponents of the *Resource Mobilization* approach. An analysis of changes of and dynamics in the structure of conflict,[1] was deferred to others for analysis.

Political scientist Sidney Tarrow rightly pointed out, and built upon, this lacuna in his groundbreaking *Power in Movement* (1998) by showing how social movements can use their internal powers to influence political conditions. In so doing, Tarrow significantly added to our understanding of the dynamics of social movements. But Tarrow's own definition to social movement continued to under-represent agency. For Tarrow, social movement is "Collective challenges, based on common purposes and social solidarities, in sustained interaction with elites, opponents, and authorities" (1998: 4). Social movement, then, is understandable, again, more in relation to its action and less as a collective actor, hence the ongoing under-representation of its internal characteristics and dynamics. Attentiveness to internal dynamics within a movement would highlight, for example, issues of power and contention among various actors within the movement.

Finally, a fairly ongoing underdeveloped theme concerns issues of power, oppression, and inequality, dealing with them only when challenged. By treating issues of oppression and inequality only when challenged we overlook the historical specificity of social movement: processes and factors in a historically situated structure and dynamics of conflict that affect the development of social movement as a political actor in the first place, let alone its ability to initiate contention of such a magnitude as manifested in the Intifada.

I perceive social movement as the agent of collective action: a collective actor comprising of people, perceptions, social locations, and actions in pursuit of common interest. A social movement as a collective actor constitutes of various actors (individuals and/or organizations) who interact informally with one another through informal networks; the extent to which these actors collaborate and the types of interaction among them, necessitate and depend on solidarity, and political consciousness. The possibility that solidarity, shared perceptions, and political consciousness would crystallize depends on the overall conflict situation and political conditions the collective actor is embedded in, the presence of a mutual target of discontent, and the actual engagement in politics of contention; through contention the collective actor attempts to express what is considered unjust and wrong, and aims to restructure the oppressing sociopolitical setting.

In light of the above conceptualization of collective action, the Palestinian social movement constituted of several interacting, competing groups that manage to mobilize the vast majority of the Palestinians within the occupied territories into grassroots organizational infrastructures. Through contention with a mutual Israeli target of discontent, the Palestinian field of actors starts to develop networks of communication and initiates joint social, cultural, and political activities. Interacting with Israeli authorities and other Israeli opponents and allies,[2] and familiarizing themselves with domestic Israeli sociopolitical developments and events (i.e., divisions over continuing the occupation), these groups gradually reprioritize their goals and aspirations, rearticulate their collective identity, and reshape their action strategies. Finally, Palestinian politics of contention is mainly manifested by disruptive, limited-violence forms of action as a way for influencing the Israeli public, and as a central means of broadening the scope of the conflict outside the arena of contention.

## Methods and approaches

Systematic research on the dynamics of collective action requires detailed information about events and data on changes in the structural context – the socioeconomic and political environment – as well as data on shared perceptions. The introduction of the perceptual dimension is critical for any serious attempt to capture the dynamics of collective action; it is only through analyzing shared perceptions that we can comprehend the effects structural changes might have on social movement formation, the molding of movement members' commitment, and patterns in the pace and tone of contention.

Evidence of events was obtained from archival materials collected by Israeli institutions such as the Israel Defense Force Spokesperson, and Palestinian research/information centers such as the Palestinian Human Rights Information Center. These sources compile statistics in such areas as protest incidents in the occupied territories and numbers of Palestinian detainees.

These and other sources were used to obtain data on structural changes as well. Here, census materials and national surveys conducted by the Israeli Central Bureau of Statistics, the Jerusalem Media and Communication Center, and Al-Haq research center ("Law in the Service of Man") were useful, as they publish annual yearbooks and other reports.

Data on collective perception is crucial for any attempt to link structural changes and contention. As recently acknowledged by sociologist Doug McAdam (2001), so long as processes of framing, that is interpretation, attribution, and social construction of opportunity, are absent, models of contention will fail to link political changes and contention.

West Bank newspapers were the primary source for Palestinian perceptions regarding Israeli domestic events that reflected the deepening divisions over continuing the occupation. Upon their establishment during the early 1970s, Palestinian newspapers became an important asset in the development and propagation of national awareness and identity (Najjar 1994; Shinar 1987; Shinar and Rubinstein 1987), acting as political resources for the widespread mobilization of Palestinians; Palestinian print media institutions became an important convener of internal Palestinian discourse within the occupied territories and a tool for liberation, coordinating the Palestinian debates and competing for the hearts and minds of less active Palestinians.[3] The fact that each chosen newspaper (representing the voice of moderate, radical and militant political groups) reflected the ideology of a specific political organization enabled me not only to capture each political organization's political agenda, but also trends within the Palestinian public discourse (Gamson and Modigliani 1989).

Eight Israeli events, labeled *crisis-event*, were chosen because they stimulated public discourse about the future status of the occupied territories. Each of the eight events was a public manifestation and reflection of an issue-culture with sociopolitical impacts on the Israeli political system in specific and Israeli society as a whole. Such manifestations were assigned cultural significance and were part of an ongoing public discourse that revolved around a specific issue: the future status of the occupied territories.

Investigation of Palestinian framing of political opportunity was guided by four questions:

1 To what extent are Palestinians in the occupied territories interested in and attentive to domestic Israeli politics?

2    What is the depth and scope of the Palestinians' familiarity with domestic Israeli politics?
3    In what ways have Palestinians framed such domestic Israeli politics?
4    What meaning did Palestinians construct to their contention with Israeli forces?

There were two stages to the research, combining two sources of data. First, several preliminary in-depth interviews with Palestinian grassroots activists and Israeli journalists and officials, and second, content analysis of Palestinian print news media published during the 1970s and 1980s. The goal of the interviews was exploratory: to obtain information about the extent to which Palestinians in the occupied territories were interested in learning about Israeli society, the level of their familiarity with Israeli society, and how their knowledge was gathered and circulated. The content analysis of news articles allowed me to look more systematically at the amount and nature of coverage of domestic Israeli events and developments, and of confrontations with Israeli forces, while examining changes among various newspapers over time.

The rationale for this sequential design rested on the need to gain a preliminary understanding regarding each of the above aspects, for the purpose of building and validating a measuring instrument – a coding sheet for conducting the content analysis – the primary method used (Creswell 2003). The interviews were conducted between 1999 and 2001, resulting in data upon which the questions comprising the coding sheet were constructed, while the actual coding took place during the first half of 2003. The integration of the findings and results occurred during the interpretation phase of the research, in which the findings from the in-depth interviews were re-evaluated and compared with the results of the content analysis.

The use of interview data to buttress the analysis of the news articles content proved useful. For example, an in-depth interview's strength is its ability to provide the researcher with the potential to measure his/her precise research question. In-depth interviews also provide us with a contextual perspective by enabling us to get first-hand accounts as they come from the people themselves in the actual setting of the case at hand. And yet, the truth remains that in-depth interviews are low on reliability; it is impossible to replicate or reconstruct the dynamics and interaction that take place during such forms of conversation. Processes of interpretation go far beyond sheer talk and protocol; the researcher tries to immerse him/herself through the gestures, body language, facial expressions, and the likes.

This is especially true when ethnocentrism dominates, as is the case of an Israeli talking to a Palestinian. The collective experience of Palestinians as an occupied people under Israeli military rule, and myself as Israeli, have certainly increased the impact of at-the-time events and developments on the interviews. I tried to handle the problem of the events and developments' effects on the interviewees' accounts by using variants of a given question throughout the interview. As it turned out, the interviewees used recent events to make their points. Such was the case when one interviewee used a statement made by an Israeli political party leader about how "all Arabs are snakes and as such should not be trusted" in order to demonstrate how little the Israelis know about Palestinians and how stereotyped our views are. In situations like these, I tried to use such points in a constructive manner. I asked the interviewee to elaborate on what she meant, and, in the context of this specific issue, I asked whether Palestinians differed from Israelis in their attitudes to and opinions of Israel and Israelis.

This is where content analysis was considered useful in coping with both problems. Content analysis is far more reliable than in-depth interviews, and this is advantageous for the purposes of generalization. In addition, by analyzing news media coverage on events that occurred during the same period that the in-depth interviews focused on, I was in a position to get a complementary view, and consequently, able to compare and assess the findings against the interview data.

## What's next?

This book has six chapters. Chapter 1 is devoted to introducing the key concepts used in this book and to developing the theoretical framework and the model of collective action dynamics, which establishes a synthesis of structural and cultural dynamics of contention, a bridging between two traditions in the study of collective action: *framing processes* and *political processes*. Insights from classical and more contemporary sociopolitical writings such as those of Simmel, Marx, and Weber, and Social Constructionist and Neo-Marxist thinkers such as Goffman and Gramsci are drawn upon to establish the interrelatedness between processes of social construction and political processes, what will be conceptualized as *constructing political opportunity*.

Chapters 2, 3, 4, and 5 are devoted to the analysis of the Intifada's causes and dynamics. In Chapter 2, I cope with the *why* question of the Intifada. Here, I attend to the multi-faceted oppression experienced by the Palestinians in the occupied territories and their shared grievances and discontent. At the same time, I explore the process through which their hardship has been politicized through interaction with Israeli domination. The aspects and dimensions of Palestinian experience under Israeli occupation that have shaped Palestinian political consciousness are termed as the *willingness* to act contentiously.

The thrust of Chapter 3 is the *how* question of the Intifada, where I analyze not only modes of Israeli repressive (e.g., a harsher deportation policy) or facilitative (permitting a higher educational system) measures, but also Palestinian mobilization through the development of various organizations and ideologies. I examine how contention with the Israeli military authorities affected the internal relationships among the numerous Palestinian organizations. The creation of the members' commitment movement, through the development of organizational infrastructure made up of leadership, resource flow, communicational networks, but also ideology, is viewed as the *readiness* to act contentiously.

Chapter 4 copes with the *when* question of the Intifada. I analyze how changes in the social and political conditions faced by Palestinians affected patterns of contention in the occupied territories. The ways in which Palestinian activists gave meaning to such changes, and the effects of these meanings on their action strategies are considered crucial. The possible effects of such changes in political conditions on the shared perceptions of the Palestinians in the occupied territories regarding the ripe conditions to rebel are seen as the *opportunity* to act contentiously.

Chapter 5 concentrates on the Intifada's action phase. In this chapter, I demonstrate how these action strategies affected the specific tactics Palestinian activists attempted to practice in order to translate their struggle into political gains. The Palestinian activists' intention to capitalize on that strategy faced numerous challenges. Some of these challenges were rooted in extant tensions *among* various groups and actors within the Palestinian movement (e.g., the secular-oriented versus the Islamic-oriented groups); others were rooted in the contentious dynamics *between* the Palestinian activists and Israel, primarily the Israeli army and the Jewish Settlers in the occupied territories; and still others were rooted in unexpected *external* developments and events (e.g., the disintegration of the Soviet Union and the Gulf War) that deeply affected the trajectories of the Intifada. All these challenges, separately and jointly, had important impacts on the Intifada, in terms of both its dynamics and its trajectories.

The last chapter provides a summary of the basic argument of the book, introduces the conclusions, evaluates these conclusions in light of the model used and offers several implications for the study of collective action. Based on the conclusions of the book, a subsection suggests several observations concerning the future of the Palestinian–Israeli conflict. Finally, a postscript offers a provisional analysis of the sources and first stages of the current cycle of protest – the "new" or "second" Intifada – based on the conclusions of the book. While no pretense is made at providing a thorough analysis of the second Intifada, aspects of the dynamics in the territories throughout the 1990s are discussed in terms of precipitating the reemergence of Palestinian contentious politics.

# 1 Constructing political opportunity

Framing is a key element in political processes of contention, a cognitive process of interpretation and social construction. It is only through exploring the ways social movement activists frame and reframe their sociopolitical environment that we can argue convincingly that a particular change in the political conditions acted as an incentive for contentious politics. Hence the study of framing allows for a deeper and more dynamic analysis of contention. Specifically, the attentiveness to framing/reframing processes increases our understanding with regard to:

1  The relationship between various groups within a movement and the overall internal dynamics of the movement;
2  The role of cognition;
3  The historical specificity of the conditions upon which contention develops and triggers;
4  How movements cope with their various opponents' attempts at repression; and
5  The link between strategy and tactics.

This chapter is devoted to reviewing the frameworks provided by collective action research for the questions why and how framing processes and political processes are interrelated and to establishing the integrative framework that will be used in the study of the Intifada.

This chapter is divided into three parts. The first two parts are devoted to insights into the dynamics of conflict and collective action grounded in the classical and contemporary sociopolitical writings of Marx, Simmel, and Weber, and Social Constructionist and Neo-Marxist thinkers such as Goffman and Gramsci. Based on those insights, the third part of this chapter will be devoted to a synthesis of framing processes-oriented theories and political process-oriented theories on the study of collective action, and to the development of a dynamic model of collective action, based on such a synthesis.

## Marx, Simmel, and Weber

The sociological tradition provides us with useful insights regarding the emergence and dynamics of collective action. I shall briefly introduce some of those insights as they are rooted in the writings of Marx, Simmel, Durkheim and Weber.

### *Karl Marx (1818–83)*

Marx may not have taken the political conditions for collective action as the crux of his writings, although he provides the basic structural context of conflict, namely, the material conditions of oppression, which set up conflicts that are played out, in every available political and cultural setting, between those who have control over the means of production and those who have not. While Marx showed the origins of class conflicts, he lacked a theory of mobilization. His frequent overemphasis of structural analysis, later to be named as the "mechanistic" interpretation of Marx (Ritzer 1988), prevented him from seeing that the link between grievance and collective action is problematic. Yet, Marx did raise questions about, first, the opportunities for resistance generated by intra-elite conflicts, splits, schisms and, second, framing efforts that promote solidarity and political consciousness within the challenging group.

The "superstructure" facing the potential challenger is a formidable, interlocking set of the political, juridical, and cultural realms. Yet such an interlocking system is not immune to contention. The "superstructure" can be threatened; a crack in the formidable "superstructure" can be opened. It may occur because one apparatus outweighs the other (say the legislative over the economic) or because differences of opinions and values among the ruling elite unfold. In his *German Ideology* (1845–6) Marx introduces what was later conceptualized as *relative autonomy*, a feature of the "superstructure" that might lead to political opportunity for challengers. On this feature, Marx writes the following:

> The division of labor . . . manifests itself also in the ruling class as the division of mental and material labor . . . Within this class this cleavage can even develop into a certain opposition and hostility between the two parts, which, however, in the case of practical collision . . . there also vanishes the semblance that the ruling ideas were not the ideas of the ideas of the ruling class and had a power distinct from the power of that class.
>
> (Tucker 1978: 173)

A fracture in the ruling class's facade reveals to the subordinated class – the proletariat – the false foundations upon which their subordination rests. Marx does not systematically theorize the beginning of contentious politics, yet in his later writing, especially in the *Eighteenth Brumiare of Louis Napoleon*, he introduces a revealing if ad hoc insight into the reframing process. He sees such a process as central to the molding of readiness to act contentiously,

And just when they seem engaged in revolutionizing themselves and things, in creating something entirely new ... they anxiously conjure up the spirit of the past to their service and borrow from them names, battle slogans and costumes in order to present the new scene of world history in this time-honoured disguise and this borrowed language.

(Tucker 1978: 595, 614)

Contention, then, entails reframing, in order to cope with the risks it involves. Reframing involves the use of language as a vocation for construction of meaning and, simultaneously, motivating action. While we are not in a position to know whether Marx had the idea of crisis in the ruling class in mind when he wrote this passage in 1851 (although the proximity is revealing), the conditions for the triggering of framing process are of importance.

### Georg Simmel (1858–1918)

Simmel's treatment of conflict dynamics provides additional insights into the opportunities for contention. For our purpose, the most straightforward insight from Simmel deals with the lack of a group's inner cohesion as a signal for its antagonist to act. Conflict, Simmel tells us, is essentially a form of communication between conflictants.

Through contention, the two parties gather information about each other. When one party to the conflict identifies weakness in its antagonist, such as lack of inner cohesion, the likelihood of contention increases: "In view of the incomparable utility of unified organization for purposes of fight, one would suppose every party to be extremely interested in the opposed party's lack of such unity" (1955: 90). Thus, conflict enhances mutual interest among the conflictants, who want to know each other's strength, and through contention the parties acquire such knowledge.

### Max Weber (1864–1920)

The writings of Max Weber are useful for our purpose in that they provide valuable insights into framing efforts by a group. Weber's central contribution is to examine the way groups of individuals provide meaning and meaningful symbols for their joint action. It is the process of interpretation that allows individuals to provide themselves and others meaning and, consequently, motives for action. For Weber, groups commit themselves to collective definitions of the world and of themselves. Such definitions incorporate goals and standards of behavior. His notion of social action and social relationship is evident in the following citation:

We shall speak of "action" insofar as the acting individual attaches a subjective meaning to his behavior ... [and] ... Action is "social" insofar as its subjective meaning takes account of the behavior of others and is thereby

oriented in its course ... [as such] ... The term "social relationship" ...
denotes the behavior of a plurality of actors insofar as, in its meaningful
content, the action of each takes account of that of the others and is oriented
in these terms.

(1978: 4, 26)

A less developed aspect in Weber is his notion of mobilization. Weber
explicitly stresses the need for resources a group must mobilize in order to initiate action. This includes a well-defined antagonist, shared location, commitment
and leadership.[1] Taking these two contributions within the framework of
Weber's work on religious movements and the role of the charismatic leader,
leadership becomes crucial in coping with organizational challenges such as
maintaining the group members' political consciousness and commitment.

In conclusion, all three social thinkers contribute to our attempt at bridging
political processes with framing processes. The ways such a bridging was
further developed in two more recent traditions constitute the second part of our
theoretical discussion.

### Social Constructionism and Neo-Marxism

Social Constructionism and Neo-Marxism sprang from the classical sociopolitical legacy only to modify and expand their intellectual predecessors. Additional
insights from both traditions can be lumped together to provide a revealing link
between political processes and framing processes.

Perhaps the most significant contribution of the two traditions can be traced
in their treatment of *agency* and *structure* as indissolubly linked. Canadian sociologist Erving Goffman, for example, provided us with the idea of structured
lenses for the organization of experience: Frame. A frame, according to
Goffman, provides the individual and/or the group with ready-to-hand answer
for the question "what is it that's going on here?" Nonetheless, in Goffman, as in
other Social Constructionist scholars, it is the interplay between *structure* and
*agency* that is of importance, since, while experiences are framed we can frame
our experiences.

From a different angle, several Neo-Marxist thinkers contributed to the development of what they considered as the underdeveloped *agency* aspect in Marx's
writings. Such aspects include ideas such as *hegemony*, and *active reader*. These
concepts, and others, were promoted for unpacking the traditional mechanistic
interpretation of Marx with its overemphasis on economic determinism and the
idea of the "superstructure" as a mere reflection of the "base." In the main,
despite various sub-approaches within Neo-Marxism, the traditional deterministic interpretation to Marx was unquestionably modified, opening the way to a
more humanistic, agency-laden approach.

A central figure was the Italian thinker Antonio Gramsci who, attempting to
operationalize Marx, developed the idea of "historical passages" from one
historical block to another, where each bloc is characterized by a specific type of

hegemonic relations. Such passages rest on inherent cracks in any hegemonic mode, and that by essence any historical bloc "is an ambiguous, contradictory and multiform concept..." (1971: 423). While Gramsci introduced the idea of hegemony in the context of a political party's attempt to produce consensus among its adherents, the concept of hegemony should not be confined solely to this tactic. The fact is no total hegemony or "dominio" exists[2] and the operation of hegemony never entirely excludes the existence of opposition and the possibility of true consciousness. Rather, we should perceive hegemony as "the relations of domination and subordination in their forms as practical consciousness, as in effect a saturation of the whole process of living" (Williams 1977: 110). Thus we should be careful never to think of hegemony as an abstract totality.

Yet, as much *agency* as such theorizing emphasizes in comparison to Marx, it lacks (1) the mechanism through which people organize their experience, and (2) explicit treatment of event/noise, which has the potential for stimulating questioning of commonsense. Whereas Neo-Marxist theorizing provides us with the structural elements so poorly developed in the social constructionist school, it fails to specify the source for, and process during which built-in contradictions and uneven developments between structures come to be socially recognized. Specifically, Neo-Marxism falls short in delineating the connection between talk, consciousness, and action. This is where the Constructionist notion of event/noise as a key factor in the process of tension and strain in commonsense comes to the rescue.

Mills in his *Situated Actions and Vocabularies of Motives* (1963) illuminated the link between talk and motives by situating the emergence of motives. For Mills, talk and language are vocation; words can lead to action or inaction, to resistance or submission. He writes:

> Motives are words ... they do not denote any elements "in" individuals. They stand for anticipated situational consequences of questioned conduct. Intention or purpose ... *is* awareness of anticipated consequence; motives are names for consequential situations, and surrogates for actions leading to them ... [as such] ... A motive tends to be one which is to the actor and to the other members of a situation an unquestioned answer to questions concerning social and lingual conduct.
>
> (p. 443)

If that is so, the question remains as to what triggers the shift from accepted frames to the process of reframing. Acknowledging there is no state of affairs in which the dominant motive entirely forecloses debunking, Mills went further to guide our attention to *question* as speech form. He considered the *question* to be the sign of crisis that typically involves the emergence of alternative frames. Sticking to his guns, Mills reminded us that "question is distinguished in that it usually elicits another verbal action, not a motor response. The question is an element in conversation..." (1963: 440).

Conversing about politics is an integral component of framing and/or reframing, of reinvigorating your worldviews and beliefs or questioning them. Still, what has the potential for constituting a crisis, what leads to questioning, is conflict/noise/strain. This theme was already rooted in the Pragmatist School. The source of reframing is the encounter with new experience that destabilizes opinions and beliefs. Thus, according to William James,

> The individual has a stock of old opinions, but he meets a new experience that puts them to a strain ... the result is an inward trouble to which his mind till then had been a stranger, and from which he seeks to escape by modifying his previous mass of opinions.
>
> (cf. Adler and Adler 1980: 23)

However, while for some people an event is perceived as threat, for others the same event can lead to illumination, an opportunity.

Modifying a set of beliefs or opinions is not the same as transforming it; most people would tend to stick to their long-held beliefs. After all, changing or questioning your beliefs may lead to social marginalization. Whether an individual follows one path or another is strongly contingent upon his interaction with others. Collectivization and the sharing of potential challenging beliefs in a public way are crucial for reframing.

Events can act as catalysts for a changing ratio between perceived opportunities and threats. For a discontented challenger who searches for signs of weakness in its antagonists, a particular event may act as a trigger, as incentive. In that case, it is reasonable to expect a process of reframing. When cracks in the assumptions about existing power relations unfold, the process of reframing is imperative for diffusion of new ideas. If events stimulate a contest between dominant and challenging frames, it becomes clear that *reframing implies opportunity, and opportunity implies reframing*.

As we will see, research on collective action has long been influenced by the tension between *positivist/structuralist* and *humanist/culturalist* paradigms, as reflected by the tension between the culturally oriented Framing Processes approach and the structurally oriented Political Process Model. In what follows, I will show how the above-developed interrelatedness between reframing and opportunity can be useful for synthesizing the two contending paradigm-driven approaches. It is to the synthesis of framing processes and shifts in the structure of political opportunities (the key concept of the Political Process Model), and to the development of a dynamic model of collective action, based on such a synthesis, that the discussion now turns.

## A paradigmatic synthesis

The basic tenet of the Political Process Model is that changes in the structural context in which social movements operate are major factors in the dynamics of contentious politics. Whereas contentious politics *begins* when ordinary people collectively make claims on other people, claims which if realized would affect those others' interests, contentious politics is *triggered* when changing opportunities and constraints create incentives for social actors who lack resources on their own (Tarrow 1998). Changes, then, in the political conditions (i.e., the structure of political opportunities [POS]) can explain (1) the shift from a short-term, sporadic mode of action to a wide-scope, sustained contention, and (2) the rise of contentious politics in a certain historical period and not in others.

This line of reasoning became a very influential perspective in the field. Nonetheless, and in a dialectical fashion, a growing number of works flagged the importance of cultural dynamics during which social movements' activists perceive, construct, interpret, and assess such structural changes *as* incentives. A useful and representative place to begin our synthesis is with the development of the Resource Mobilization approach. It is representative because many students of collective action consider the Political Process Model a variant of this approach.[3]

### Resource mobilization – rational actor model for social justice

By definition, a social movement is a dynamic sociopolitical phenomenon both internally (i.e., among its groups and actors) and externally (i.e., between the movement and its opponents and/or allies). Yet, its dynamism has been reified through, among others, the gradual neglect of cognition and structural conditions. The relative neglect of dynamics in social movement theory has mostly been the product of the Resource Mobilization approach, specifically the model outlined in John McCarthy and Mayer Zald's "Resource Mobilization and Social Movement" (1977).

It is well known that students of collective action, in the wake of the turbulent 1960s, were aiming at sharply disassociating themselves from the Collective Behavior tradition in order to emphasize the deliberative nature of protest and in order to reconceive the role and characteristics of social movements. Instead of viewing protests, demonstrations, or revolutions as psychological reactions to societal breakdowns (Park 1967; Smelser 1962; Kornhouser 1959), such actions/events were seen as "politics by other means" and not as social deviance. Social movement was seen as a purposive, coordinated action by individuals who attempt to accumulate power and maximize influence in the pursuit of their common interests.

The Resource Mobilization approach probed the variety of resources that must be mobilized for a movement to survive. It deals with the tactics of a social movement's growth, decline and change, hence responding to the need of activists to establish their tactical choices on firm grounds. The focus on *how* social movements operate stresses, for example, supply and demand logic for the flow of resources, and cost-benefit calculations to explain participation in social movement activity (McCarthy and Zald 1977: 1216). Following this theory, one would expect an aggrieved group of individuals to organize through mobilization of resources and support in order to pursuit their goals through collective action if, and only if, the benefit from engagement in action outweighs the cost.

The severance of the Resource Mobilization approach from its intellectual predecessor (i.e., Collective Behavior) was so complete that questions of grievance and social justice were pushed out of the equation, together with underestimating the influence of political conditions on collective action. Instead of focusing on the dynamics between power and discontent (Gamson 1968), the rational logic of McCarthy and Zald and their focus on Social Movement Organization (SMO) as the prime unit of analysis led to bracketing of (1) the political dimensions seen as limiting rather than encouraging contention, and (2) a total neglect of cognition.

Sociologist William Gamson was the first to pinpoint the two closely related processes implied by the concept *mobilization*. By distinguishing between *creation* and *activation* of commitment (between increasing the loyalty of a constituency to an organization, and efforts to move those who already possess some degree of commitment), Gamson paved the way for circumventing one of Resource Mobilization's major pitfalls, and allows us to better understand the link between commitment and contention (1990).

Drawing on Goffman's work, Gamson developed the concept of micro-mobilization, "The study of how face-to-face encounters affect long-term efforts to bring about social change through the mobilization of resources for collective action" (1985: 607). Whether it is on the individual or SMO levels of analysis, Goffman's legacy regarding "encounters" and "frames" helps us in understanding the emergence of alternative definitions to a situation. It is through encounters with countermovements, media, and authorities, that questioning of the commonsense may lead to a political consciousness, one that supports mobilization for collective action.

Power struggles are, by definition, struggles over definition of a situation (Schattschneider 1975). Such a struggle can be engendered by events that break the hegemony of the legitimating frame. Would-be challengers may use such a context to engage in re-framing, "they need to adopt an alternative *mobilizing* frame as a context for what is happening – a redefinition that questions compliance" (Gamson 1985: 616). In that case, given the distinction between frames and framing, we would expect a social movement organization to challenge existing frames through engaging in the construction of alternative definition of events in order to activate its constituency for contention.

The duality in the concept of frame (i.e., the interplay between structure and agency as it unfolds in the concept of framing) highlights an additional deficiency in Resource Mobilization theorizing, namely, the bracketing of historical specificity that bounds collective actors' strategy and, concomitantly, their chosen tactics. Contentious politics, just as the generation of frames and the process of framing, does not take place in a vacuum (Williams and Benford 2000). Contention takes place in a specific context. The modern state is the fulcrum of social movement (Tarrow 1998) and frames must strike a responsive chord in those individuals for whom it is intended for it to be effective (Snow and Benford 1988).

## Frame, framing, and the structure of political opportunities

While Resource Mobilization, as promoted by McCarthy and Zald, contributed the concepts of organization and leadership, seen here as preconditions for framing processes, the study of social movements needs to differentiate between the *formation* of a social movement and the *activation* of social movement as contentious politics. It needs to bear in mind that the development of a social movement is a result of ongoing contention between groups, all of whom are constrained by structure and empowered by agency. What follows is an analysis of the reintroduction of *structure* to the study of collective action by proponents of the Political Process Model, and the ways the issue of frame/ing helps in coping with the fairly underdeveloped perceptual aspect in this model.

A major factor influencing the prominence of a specific frame is the nature of the sociopolitical setting in which a social movement operates. The success of the frame promoted by the Italian League during the early 1990s ("regional populism") compared with other political groups, was strongly related to the nature of political opportunities (breakdown of traditional political identities) in Italy (Diani 1996). In like manner, as we will see, the dominance of Palestinian Nationalism as an ideology over other ideologies (e.g., Communism or Islamism) among Palestinians in the occupied territories during the late 1970s and 1980s is rooted in the sociopolitical setting in which the Palestinian people were situated (Lesch 1990; Hiltermann 1991).

Not surprisingly, theoreticians' neglect of the political conditions led to the gradual introduction of exogenous factors in the analysis of a social movement's life cycle. The growing focus on external factors, primarily the political conditions, was aimed at probing two central questions. First, why is it that people lend support to social movements in particular historical periods and not others? Second, how can students of collective action account for the shift from sporadic, short-term contention to sustained, broad-based, and long-term contention?

The answers to such questions took shape as the Political Process Model developed. Drawing insights from earlier works (Gamson 1968, 1990; Eisinger 1973; Oberschall 1973; Tilly 1978; Piven and Cloward 1979), McAdam's *Political Process and the Development of Black Insurgency* (1982) further developed the dynamics between power/structure and discontent/agency. Using Eisinger's concept the Structure of Political Opportunities (1973), McAdam showed how changes in political context interacted with other factors, such as the mobilization of resources, previously existing organisations, and the recognition of grievances and injustice, to better understand the rise, heyday, and abatement of the Civil Rights movement. He writes:

The point is that any *event* or broad social process that serves to undermine the calculations and assumptions on which the political establishment is structured occasions a shift in political opportunities ... the political process is based on the idea that social processes such as industrialization promote insurgency only indirectly through a restructuring of existing power relations.

(1999: 41)

Political scientist Sidney Tarrow (1989, 1998) further showed the importance behind distinguishing between stable and volatile structures of political opportunities, where the latter can be further divided into long-term and short-term opportunities. The *stable* dimension includes such factors as the strength of state institutions, strength of social cleavages, political cultures of belief systems which are embedded within political institutions and culture and change only slowly if at all. The *volatile* dimension consists of opportunities such as splits among elites, increasing access to the political system, elections or legitimacy, and public discourse. These types of opportunities structures shift with events or policies; they are more permeable to political actors' participation and influence. The more volatile structure of political opportunities can be long-term or short-term in nature. Long-term opportunities affect the rise of contentious politics in structuring the forms and nature of movements and the mode according to which they express their political demands. Short-term opportunities, however, trigger contention by signaling to challengers that the time is ripe to act contentiously. In other words, changes in the structure of political opportunities can affect a social movement's mode and form of mobilization for politics of contention.

Additional expansion of the model by Tarrow deals with how opportunity's structure can be molded to social movement's goals. In doing so, Tarrow further developed Tilly's argument (1978) regarding the connection between opportunities and choices of tactics made by social movements, showing how specific tactical *powers* of movement can cope with the fickleness of opportunities. By choosing specific frames, modes of contention, and the way leadership core is linked to activists and potential constituencies, social movements can influence the depth and breath of contention, thereby increasing the impact of the challenge.

Social movement activists should be viewed not as atoms of the madding crowd, but rather as agents engaged in conscious planning and strategizing. They consciously make decisions about the proper modes of action, just as they look for ways to intensify their constituency's zeal and tenacity through "collective action frames" (Snow and Benford 1988). Collective action frames are the result of the challengers' reframing process, the redefined situation is linked to a mechanism for maintaining and broadening support and mobilization. Collective action frames are sets of collective beliefs that serve to create a state of mind in which participation in contention appears meaningful.

The process through which opportunities could be molded to movement goals is an impressive contribution. Absent, however, is the role of social movement in identifying and propagating perception of opportunities. Jointly and separately, Meyer and Minkoff (1997) and Meyer (2004) systematically analyzed the impact of "issue/actor-specific" opportunities, thereby substantiating Tarrow's distinction between long-term and short-term opportunities. Using data on civil rights protests, the authors showed that whereas "general" (equivalent to Tarrow's long-term opportunity) opportunities do not have a significant effect on the probability of protest, issue-specific (short-term/signals) opportunities do have a significant influence on the likelihood of protest. Concluding his work,

Meyer concluded that much needs to be learned regarding how collective actors share perceptions, debate, reach common understandings, act and reflect on their actions as a collective force. The problem, for Meyer, lies in the, "presumption underneath a political opportunity approach ... that the development of movements reflects, responds to, and sometimes alters the realities of politics and policy although most work gives short shrift as to how" (2004:139).

A closely related, still pending question is whether an issue-specific opportunity can be said to be sufficiently concrete from the vantage point of challengers. A systematic explanation of the possible impact of opportunity entails an analysis that is open to falsification, simply because such impact is an indeterminate process. Otherwise, we are trapped in tautology; wherever there is opportunity, look for the movement (Meyer 1990). Whether a social movement perceives political changes as an opportunity to act is, in essence, a matter of social construction (Kurzman 1996, 2004a, 2004b).

In like manner, the simple visibility of opportunity is not enough, especially when dealing with a challenger facing a fixed "blocked opportunities" situation (Merton 1968) coupled with geographical remoteness, as was the case with Palestinians in the occupied territories. In that case, it is not only that mechanisms by which possible changes in the structure of political opportunities are being constructed and propagated become crucial. In fact, attentiveness must be kept to the examination of the relevant aspects of POS from the vantage point of the challenger. It is precisely in such circumstances that Snow and Benford's (1988) analytical distinction between the diagnostic/prognostic tasks and the motivational task of framing gains additional importance (see below).

One attempt to cope with the tangibility of opportunity is Della-Porta's "policing of protest" (1995). The direct, tense, often violent interaction with police forces during contentious gatherings concretizes the intangible social cleavages or shifting alignment between elites. Still, such a solution renders the role of activists in providing their preferred meaning to events somewhat marginal. It disregards the process through which political actors propagate and amplify specific interpretations for the purpose of activating commitment and enhancing mobilization. As such, policing of protest can acquire meaning *only* within an already existing reframing with regard to conditions ripe for contention.

In fact, protest policing also fails at capturing the internal dynamics – indigenous perspective, to use Morris's approach (1984) – a movement goes through, which have considerable impact on the movement's ability to initiate a challenge. Finally, the policing of protest fails to consider incidents where the frames promoted do not necessarily correspond to what actually occurs. As Ryan (1991) insightfully argues, frames are vulnerable less to facts, but, rather, to communication which, in turn, governs events, " 'Truth' doesn't stand alone; rather, people engage in a selection process, actively making sense out of a confusing flood of experience" (p. 53).

Entering framing processes into the equation of structure-agency casts light on the specific *powers* a social movement introduces into contentious politics.

Returning to Tarrow's *powers* in movement, one would be in a position to understand better the logic behind a specific preferred mode of action, and the forms of mobilizing structure the movement constructs. Framing process helps us, then, to better understand the link between strategy and tactics, i.e., what is the process behind the end-product manifested as specific collective action frames and/or modes of contention. The specific nature of a political opportunities structure may lead to an advantageous frame (Diani 1996), yet the eventual prominence of a given frame can be a matter of debate and, at times, be a source of contention among different groups within the same movement.

Thus, the specific *power* a movement uses depends also, to a large extent, on internal processes within a movement. Within a movement, there usually is a spectrum of various ideologies, political visions, and preferred modes of action. Some groups can hinder the others' preferred mode of action. The process through which existing SMOs engage in attempts to mobilize resources for collective action should not be seen solely as a logical, taken-for-granted process.

Framing can be seen as such a process under reference. In an attempt to clarify ambiguity in the concept of frame, Benford (1997) insightfully distinguished between frame and framing. This distinction is central for our purpose as it clarifies the overly limited and sometimes misplaced use of collective action frame. Benford writes,

> *frame* refers to an interpretive schemata that simplifies and condenses the "world out there" by selectively punctuating and encoding objects, situations, events ... before collective action is likely to occur, a critical mass of people must socially construct a sense of injustice ... the *injustice frame* is the seedling for the development of a *collective action frame. Framing* refers to this signifying work ... the process associated with assigning meaning to or interpreting relevant events and conditions in ways intended to mobilize potential adherents.
>
> (1997: 4156)

In that case, through the social construction of a shared diagnosis (what is at issue), prognosis (what should be done about it), and motivation (calls for action), framing or reframing processes are the link between commitment mobilization and action mobilization. Framing, Benford further argues, is "...particularly fundamental to the issue of grievance construction and interpretation, attribution of blames/causality ... strategic interaction, and the selection of movement tactics and targets" (p. 410). Several years later, Jasper (2004) returns to this notion of strategic choices as helpful in acknowledging collective actors' reflexivity. This is not a short, deterministic process and surely far from being emotion-free. For an evolving social movement that is in a developed stage of mobilization engaged in strategic interaction, changes in the structure of political opportunities can engender a shift from framing to reframing, of a shared interpretation of conditions as an opportunity to activate mobilization. This is especially likely in response to transformative events and other occurrences.

## Constructing political opportunity

The process of social construction does not rest on the assumption that there is a real, objective world out there; social actors engage in the process of constructing meaning and collective interpretations to their surroundings. The concept of *framing political opportunity* as promoted by Gamson and Meyer (1996) is a useful synthesis of the *agency–structure* interplay. It is an elegant extension of preexisting agreement regarding framing tasks. If frames contain diagnoses, why should the structure of political opportunities be immune? The activation of commitment, then, rests on framing and reasoning processes, constructing the way movement members should think about an issue, and what should be done about it (Gamson and Modigliani 1989; Snow and Benford 1988). Recalling Snow and Benford's distinction, such activation entails "a call to arms or rationale for engaging in ameliorative or corrective action" (1988: 199).

The focus on the interrelatedness of framing processes and political processes holds the promise for illuminating not only how collective actors define the issue at hand, but also what they construct as the appropriate mode of action; whether they face opportunity and of what type, and whether they should act, and how, are all central aspects, which necessitate systematic analysis. As such, it is not only that changes in the structure of political opportunities are likely to bring about a reframing process by social movement activists in an attempt to enhance mobilization, or that social movement framing of political opportunity may influence its strategy of collective action, but also that the social movement strategy of contention is likely to affect the nature of its tactical powers designated for seizing and expanding the cycle of contention.

Gradually, proponents of the Political Process Model have been acknowledging the promise of bringing back in the role of shared perceptions and cognition. Pointing to a central lacuna in social movement research in the second edition to his *Political Process* (1999: xi), McAdam argued that it is highly important to combine structuralist and culturalist perspectives. That,

> the sharp – if reified – distinction between objective conditions and their subjective interpretation ... have generally been absent from later political process formulations ... It is not the structural changes that set people in motion, but rather the shared understandings and conceptions of "we-ness" they develop to make sense of the trends.

Identifying his perspective as a mixture of Marxian and Weberian, McAdam nonetheless settled for survey results in order to measure the existence of what he called "cognitive liberation," namely, movement activists' attribution of meaning to shifts in the structure of political opportunities as favorable for contention. Among other methodological limitations, survey results fall short in providing us with the process during which such a shared perception is being constructed. In fact, we are forced to attribute the existence of collective, shared perceptions on the basis of an aggregated set of individual responses. They also fail to capture the dynamics among movement actors as they may agree or disagree on the actuality of "cognitive cues" and the nature of such cues. What is needed is an analysis of framing processes from "inside the head" of a social movement, to use Ryan, Anastario and Jeffreys's metaphor (2005).

Framing, as argued above, involves power issues both internal and external to the movement. The readiness to take the risks of contention entails a mixture of both cold-headed calculation and, even more important, "hot cognition" (Gamson 1992). If a division of labor between SMOs and other actors within a movement is the result, it crystallizes social movement activists' and adherents' sense of injustice, a notion of "we" against "them" and a feeling of righteousness, thereby increasing commitment and mobilization on the way to contention.

Framing is a group activity, a historically embedded process where frames, ideologies and power join in political discourse, and is adaptive to constantly changing sociopolitical circumstances (Ryan 2005). In this case, we are looking at collective actors who (1) share definitions of political opportunity, (2) discuss actual context, (3) discuss strengths and weakness of their group in relation to context, and (4) debate strategy and tactics in light of the perceived political opportunity and the actual context within which they are situated. Through highlighting social wrongs, making diagnostic and prognostic causal attributions, and articulating and linking a set of events in a meaningful fashion, framing processes act as a major determinant in movement engagement in contention.

### A new, yet unfinished agenda

Recently, following a similar path, two comprehensive works aimed at reformulating the study of social movements in an attempt to amplify the dynamics of contention: *Dynamics of Contention* by McAdam, Tarrow, and Tilly (2001), and *Silence and Voice in the Study of Contentious Politics* by Aminzade *et al.* (2001). The two works recognized, among other things, the importance of perceptions to the Political Process Model. Thus, as an example, McAdam, Tarrow, and Tilly pinpointed "attribution of opportunity/threat" as one mechanism of contention among others (e.g., competition, coalition formation, certification, etc.). They write,

> Rather than look upon "opportunities and threats" as objective structural factors, we see them as subject to attribution. No opportunity, however objectively open, will invite mobilization unless it is a) visible to potential challengers and b) perceived as an opportunity . . . the same holds for threats . . . Attribution of opportunity or threat is an activating mechanism responsible in part for the mobilization of previously inert population.
>
> (p. 43)

Such an acknowledgment is a considerable stepping forward from the original outlining of the Political Process Model. It is a step in the direction suggested by many students of collective action, who systematically called for the integration of cognition and collective perception (Benford and Snow 1986,

1988, 2000; Gamson 1982, 1988, 1992; Gamson and Meyer 1996; Goodwin and Jasper 1999, 2004; Goodwin, Jasper, and Polletta 2000; Kurzman 1996, 2004a, 2004b; Polletta 1998, 1999). Yet, in their attempt to delineate an overarching research agenda of contentious politics that would fit different types of contention (i.e., from strike waves to revolutions), McAdam, Tarrow, and Tilly's research agenda has several weak points of which three are relevant in the context of this book. While some of their suggested mechanisms will be used in analyzing the Intifada, it is important to specify how I plan to do so.

First, there is a difference between threat and/or opportunity as "subjected to attribution" and the social construction of events and political changes *as* opportunity and/or threat. The crucial difference is that attribution is a possible end product of social construction processes: an indeterminate, debatable, and even contentious process of activation of commitment. Attribution may be a relatively smooth process for one individual. It is an entirely different thing when it comes to a collective actor comprised of various groups and organizations, let alone when these groups have conflicting ideologies and action strategies. While the notion of attribution of opportunity/threat, in itself, opens up the way for the integration of agency into the study of contention, such opening is too narrow, marginalizing agency, thereby failing to distinguish between the *agent* of collective action: social movement, and the *means* of collective action: contentious politics.

Neglecting the process of social construction would lead to a *post factum*, suggestive analysis. For example, using the case of postwar Kenya for illustrating the role of opportunity/threat attribution, McAdam, Tarrow, and Tilly write, "Kenyan nationalists viewed these events [trends toward decolonization] as evidence that an unprecedented opportunity for independence lay at hand" (2001: 96). While this may be so, the questions remain as to how Kenyan nationalists came about their shared definition, was this process peaceful, was such definition consistent with the specific opportunities structure, and did such a shared definition influence the mode of contention taken by the nationalists?

In that case, the mode of analysis of opportunity and threat dialectic, as perceived by social movement activists and adherents promoted in this book, has the potential to preserve the fruitful separation between structure and agency, thereby furthering a dynamic analysis of contentious politics. In analyzing the collective meaning constructed by social movement activists to changes in the structure of political opportunity and the effects of changes in the structure of political opportunity on social movement activists' framing processes we can be better positioned to decide what sorts of opportunity may actually be germane to what sort of mobilizing effort. Otherwise, as Flacks (2004) and Gamson and Meyer (1996) warn, the concept of political opportunity would be of little use.

Second, the preservation of the distinction between the actor and the phenomenon under study, but also the structural context within which contentious politics may consolidate, is of importance. Failing to do so leads to nominalism, that is, instead of linking issues of power, inequalities, and injustice with their origins, the approach assumes that injustice is ubiquitous and, as such, deals with injustice only when it is challenged. Such an approach cannot be used to explain the varying history of resistance. In cases such as the Palestinian Intifada, the mere ability to challenge Israel in such magnitude must not be taken for granted and act as the starting point of analysis. Once the role of the agent and the historical context are used to guide the analysis, it is possible to speak of the relative weight of a given mechanism and the ways other mechanisms are influenced and shaped accordingly.

Last, but not least, it is of importance to note the possible effect of political opportunities on a social movement's tactics (or *powers* to use Tarrow's concept) during the cycle of contention. What mediate between long-term changes and cycles of contention are events. Events and/or changes in the structure of political opportunities matter; they can lead activists of social movement to engage in reframing processes, which, in turn, can shape their strategy and ensuing tactics.

McAdam and Sewell (2001) raised a similar point in their attempt to develop the notion of temporality in the study of contention. They argue that models of contention are incomplete as long as the processes of social construction and interpretation of events are absent. For the authors, framing process as developed by Snow and his colleagues is insufficient since it fails to capture the earlier processes of collective interpretation that lead the conflictual definition of the situation that Snow and his colleagues speak of.

Thus, events for McAdam and Sewell are central to such "noise" as they apparently serve the function of cracks in the taken for granted. However, this account depicts the effects of events from the outside. It is only through "getting into the head of the collective actor" that it has the potential to ground the ostensible influence of events on perceptions and the ways perceptions and reframing, in turn, make contention feasible.

In concluding, the process of *constructing political opportunity* requires a systematic analysis in order to go beyond correlative and suggestive explanations. Changes in the structure of political opportunities may act as an incentive, but a collective actor does not react automatically; opportunity is being perceived only in relation to threat, and both are driven not only by facts on the ground, but also by the communicative processes by which these facts are discussed. The social construction of opportunity is an indeterminate process, one that is contingent upon historical specificity and the actors' sense of opportunity/threat, as they dialectically fluctuate in accordance with other actors in a multi-actor field (e.g., authorities, countermovement, allies, competitors, etc.). The analysis of these dynamics necessitates not a *post factum* analysis, but a prospective one, in the making. Only through such an analysis, can we grasp how relative the opportunity is, how the dialectic of opportunity and threat affects social movements' mobilization and the internal dynamics within a movement, and how the constructed shared perception of opportunity/threat shapes contentious politics.

The model attempts to establish a dynamic analysis of collective action by integrating three interrelated vectors of analysis: The *why* question (dealing with

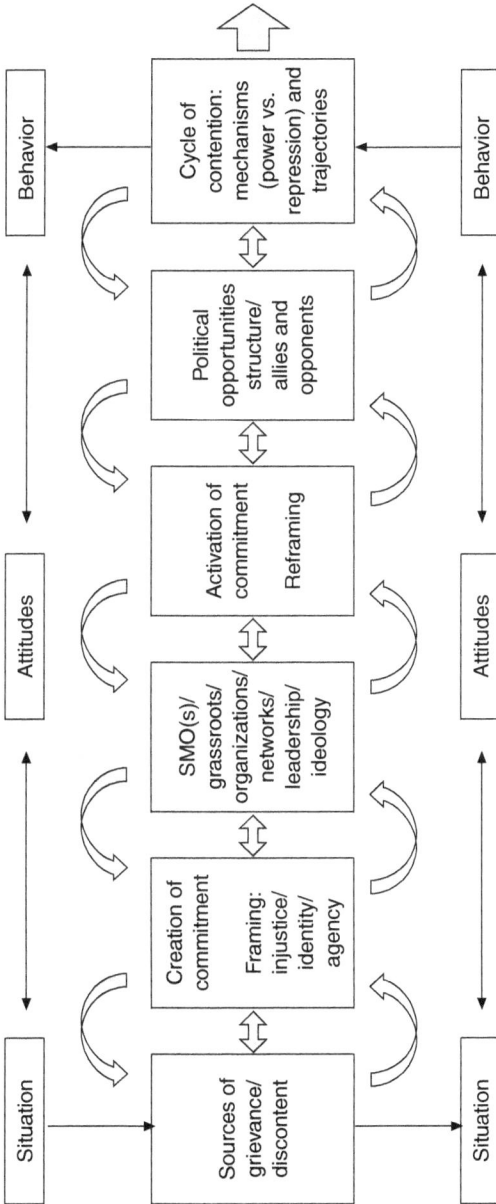

*Figure 1.1* Dynamics of collective action.

the *willingness* of individuals to rebel); the *how* question (dealing with the process by which individuals' *readiness* to act contentiously was molded); and the *when* question (dealing with the influence of changed sociopolitical conditions on a discontented group's construction of shared perception regarding an *opportunity* to act), as all three concatenate to form a cycle of contention: the Intifada.

The indeterminate, dynamic process of social movement crystallization and struggle for change unfolds within the overall structure of conflict. Each vector highlights the interplay between two levels of analysis: social and political circumstances (*structure*), and strategies and tactics for action (*agency*). Each component in the process stresses the various phases through which a collective actor develops and consolidates as a movement. The double arrows denote the indeterminate nature of the process where the progression from one component to another is contingent upon other factors not shown in the model, such as the countermoves of authorities and outside supporters. The curve-shaped arrows above and below the various components stress the effect each of the components has on the entire process together with the mutual effect between each two consecutive components.

Thus, for example, the powers used by a movement (the last component) during a cycle of contention can influence the nature of the political opportunity structure and the role played by authorities, opponents, and third parties. Equally as well, they can influence the relationship among actors within the movement, and the content of the framing of discontent. Yet, no matter how competent, judicious, and resourceful movement leaders and activists may be in attempting to promote their political agenda, the truth remains that the trajectories of contention are unpredictable. Whether because processes and developments within the movement, between the movement and authorities or externalities over which both have no control, even the most meticulously crafted contention develops a life of its own. Thus, the single-headed arrow at the end of the process represents the open-ended nature of cycles of contention. While the cycle may bring about a change in the structure of the conflict and/or a possible resolution of the conflict, which, in turn, address the movement sources of grievance, other less optimistic scenarios are equally probable.

## What's next?

The next part of the book is divided to three chapters, dealing with each vector in turn. In discussing the *why* question of the Intifada, we will analyze the multifaceted oppression experienced by Palestinians in the occupied territories and their shared grievances and discontent. At the same time, we will explore the politicization of their hardship as a result of the interaction with Israeli domination, through the development of various differing, conflicting political agendas outside and inside the occupied territories, and how the interaction with Israel affected the relationships between the multiple Palestinian "voices." This dimension of the Palestinian experience under Israeli occupation, which shaped

Palestinian political consciousness, constitutes the *willingness* to act contentiously.

We will then proceed to analyze the *how* question of the Intifada, examining Israeli measures that were both repressive (e.g., a harsh deportation policy) and facilitative (e.g., permitting higher education), alongside Palestinian mobilization through the development of various organizations and ideologies. Here too, contention with the Israeli military authorities affected the internal relationships within and between the numerous Palestinian organizations. The molding of commitment within these organizations through the development of organizational infrastructures – leadership, branches, resource flow, communications and ideology – translated into a *readiness* to act contentiously.

The analysis of the third vector, the *when* question of the Intifada, illuminates how changes in the social and political conditions of the Palestinians affected patterns of contention in the occupied territories. Of crucial importance is the Palestinian activists' perception of the significance of these changes, and the effects of these interpretations on strategies for action. The influence of changed political circumstances of the shared perceptions of the Palestinians in the occupied territories regarding conditions ripe for rebellion translated into the *opportunity* to act contentiously.

It is to the analysis of the development of Palestinian *willingness* to act contentiously within the particular structure of the Israeli–Palestinian conflict shaped in June 1967 that we now turn.

# 2  The *why* question of the Intifada

Political opportunity becomes tangible only in relation to threat; the notion of opportunity and the shared perception of the existence of opportunity gains meaning only in relation to the willingness to act, and can be activated only when based on an existing readiness to act. It is, therefore, essential to analyze the *why* and the *how* questions of the Palestinian Intifada before demonstrating the Palestinian construction of a shared perception regarding a developing political opportunity to act contentiously inside the Israeli polity.

This chapter will analyze the origins of the Intifada: the aspects and dimensions of the shared Palestinian experience under Israeli occupation that shaped the Palestinian *willingness* to engage in contentious politics in order to shake off Israeli occupation. In order to demonstrate the development of a Palestinian's state of mind, one that supports participation in politics of contention, this chapter focuses on various dimensions of Palestinian grievances and discontent, and the ensuing development of various action-oriented approaches out of which the *willingness* to rebel evolved.

## The structuring of Palestinian discontent

In analyzing the origins of Palestinian discontent, it is important to distinguish between the period before the Israeli occupation in June 1967, and the period between June 1967 and 1987. This book focuses on the latter period, a unique phase of the Israeli–Palestinian conflict that engendered the politicization of the Palestinian discontent by restructuring the relationship between the two conflictants in such a way that turned Israel into the fulcrum of the would-be Palestinian national-social movement. However, it is of importance not to de-contextualize the period between 1967–87 since, as will be shown, the origins of Palestinian discontent and national aspirations are rooted in earlier developments and dynamics of the conflict.

The analysis below will be structured according to three deeply interwoven dimensions of grievance and discontent: the political dimension dealing with tension between order and justice, the socio-psychological dimension dealing with tension between estrangement and unity, and the economic dimension dealing with tension between equality and inequality (Tinder 1995).

*Order and justice*

In a dialectical manner, the origins of Palestinian discontent are historically embedded in the establishment of the Israeli State. The Israeli War of Independence in 1948 was, simultaneously, the origin of the Palestinian refugee problem as tens of thousands of Palestinians either fled from their homes to the West Bank and neighboring Arab States in fear of Israeli vengeance, or were forced out of their homes by Israeli forces. From the Palestinian perspective, the results of the 1948 war became to be known as *al-Naqba* – the Palestinian national catastrophe. The refugee problem was worsened as a result of the June 1967 war, in which many other Palestinians, residing within the Israeli State, were encouraged to relocate in the West Bank or, alternatively, to Egypt.[1] As we will see, while the objective and subjective infrastructure of grievance and discontent can be said to have been experienced by the vast majority of the Palestinian population in the occupied territories, it was, nonetheless, more intense and complex for the people displaced in 1967.

The period 1967–87 represents a distinct phase in the protracted Israeli–Palestinian conflict. After approximately twenty years of conflict between Israel and the Arab States (1948–67), acting on behalf of Palestinian aspirations, Israel occupied the West Bank and Gaza, thereby extending its domination over most of Mandatory Palestine. This included East Jerusalem, where Israeli law had already been implemented by 1967, and which was formally and unilaterally annexed by Israel in July 1980.

The results of the Six-Day War (labeled by Palestinians and Arabs alike as the June War), had far-reaching consequences: Israel's victory shifted back the conflict's dynamics from an inter-state dynamic to an inter-communal one (Benvenisti 1992), the type of dynamic that characterizes intractable conflicts. This time, Israel became not only the rival national movement, as was the case under the British Mandate, but also the ruling state. The occupation meant not only the expansion of Israel's rule over new lands that more than doubled its territory, but also the incorporation of over a million Palestinian residents under military occupation.[2]

This phase of the conflict restructured Palestinian grievances by situating them in direct conflict with their age-old antagonist, as an occupied national minority. As such, the clashing interests began to revolve around Israel's interest in the preservation of order and stability in the occupied territories, and Palestinians' quest for justice through the fulfillment of human needs and national aspirations.

The implementation of Israel's concern for order and stability, at the expense of Palestinian concerns, is further illustrated by the following factors. First, the very essence of the occupation, the source of order in the territories, was conducted via martial law. While Israel initially took steps to maintain the social and political fabrics of Palestinian society through, among others, collaborating with public representatives (Ma'oz 1984), while also exercising repressive measures, this policy gradually underwent a significant shift. Towards the late

1970s, Israel's military government became much more dominant over the Palestinian population by imposing and maintaining order through force and violence. According to a brief by Al-Haq, a Palestinian research center on the violation of Palestinian human rights, "The occupied territories are currently ruled by a myriad of martial laws (1191 in the West Bank and approximately 900 in Gaza) as well as unserialized regulations, which have amended and transformed the pre-existing Jordanian law beyond recognition" (1988).

The post-1967 Israeli regime, according to Israeli sociologist Moshe Lissak (1990), reflected a system of dual rule where hierarchical stratification was based on ethnic affiliation. This regime encompassed most of mandatory Palestine, yet was divided into two polities. The first polity rested on power, rule of law, and legitimacy, while the second polity rested on force and coercion, military decrees, and deterrence. Figure 2.1 illustrates the duality of the Israeli ruling system.

The figure illustrates the scope of the Israeli regime after the June 1967 war. Triangle A denotes the Israeli polity. The authority of the regime relies on citizens' compliance with the law and their acceptance of the "rules of the game," which in turn provides power to the authorities. Triangle B, the segregated Palestinian polity within Israel, delineates a different model. The essence of the military rule is force. Military decrees, fear, brutal violence, and manipulation – the opposite ingredients of polity A – maintain order in the territories.

Such a system imposed its interests on an occupied people, lacking civic or political rights, deprived of most human rights, and whose only duty was to submit to martial law and regulations, or risk facing repressive measures such as deportation from the occupied territories. The deportation of Palestinians from the occupied territories was one of Israel's administrative measures for punishment and control of Palestinians considered to be a security threat. For example, in the six years between 1967 and 1973, roughly two thousand Palestinians were deported from the occupied territories (Hiltermann 1988). Other administrative measures included administrative detention, town arrest, and the demolition and sealing of houses.

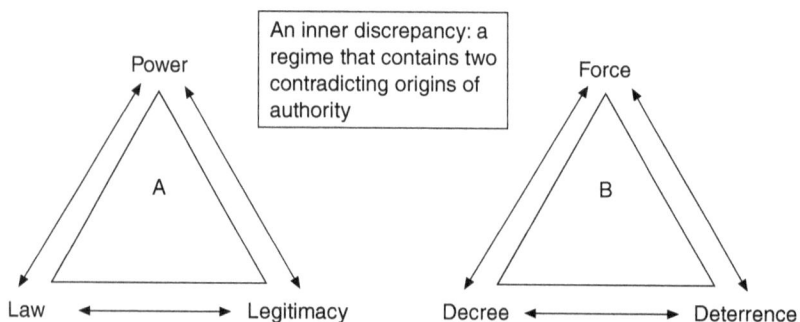

*Figure 2.1* Israel's dual regime system post-1967.

The rationale for the introduction of such punitive administrative measures was Israel's interest in control over the Palestinian population, enabling the military authorities to impose severe punitive measures on residents of the occupied territories without charge or trial. By extending the use of the British Mandate Defense (emergency) Regulations of 1945[3] within the occupied territories, Israel provided the West Bank and Gaza Area Military Commanders with the authority to assert power based on their judgment of Israel's security interests (Hofnung 1991).

Palestinians in the occupied territories had, in principle, the right to appeal. For example, Palestinians were entitled to petition the Israeli High Court of Justice. Yet, as elaborated by Al-Haq (1988), the scope of petition was highly restricted, amounting in no sense to a full appeal, while the chance of success in such proceedings was very limited unless based on a technicality. The reasons for this are numerous: evidence closure for security reasons; the fact that it is the subject's onus to prove the excessiveness of the order; the military composition of the review committees, and the lack of examination of the substance of the allegation, were and are only a few reasons for the futility of such proceedings from the viewpoint of Palestinians. To this, one may add the traditional primacy of Israeli national security considerations among the different government branches, including the judiciary, which provided the rationale and justifications for numerous Israeli decision rules in issues of settlement, deportation and detention of Palestinians, and, among other issues, maintaining Israel's domination over the territories.

In the political dimension, the Palestinians in the occupied territories faced oppression on two levels. First, the Israeli political arena was completely closed to any form of individual or collective Palestinian participation. Palestinians interested in exerting political influence on the Israeli political system faced a "blocked opportunity" situation. The only open channel for Palestinian political actors or organizations, when interested in promoting any kind of initiative, was through informal contact, and usually strictly confidential. Such was the case with informal contacts between Sirtawi, a member of the Fatah, and Israeli Peace organizations and activists during the late 1970s. Sirtawi was later assassinated by the members of Black June, a fanatical group formed by dissenters of the Popular Front for the Liberation of Palestine, in April 1983. Throughout the 1970s and 1980s, contacts with PLO parties and organizations were illegal in Israel and any attempt at such was considered treason.

Second, political life in the occupied territories was systematically scrutinized and circumscribed. For example, after 1976 (when PLO candidates won a majority of seats in the municipal elections in the West Bank), no municipal elections were held. In fact, Israel allowed for no political activity, and any group or public figure that spoke out in a manner that was construed as "political" was subjected to administrative measures. This left open only non-institutional forms of political activity, such as demonstrations and rallies. Israeli military authorities tolerated a certain level of such activity as long as it was considered a form of restrained or restricted radicalism (Mishal with Aharoni

1989). Another form of political activity, still informal in nature and lacking in executive powers, was the National Guidance Committee (NGC), formed in 1978 primarily for objecting to the Camp David Accords and expressing an initial attempt to represent the entire Palestinian population in the occupied territories. The military authorities eventually acted against the NGC in 1982, guided by the harsh Israeli policy implemented by then Minister of Defense, Ariel Sharon.

The structured oppression of Palestinians in the occupied territories has had other facets, less sophisticated and more brutal. A report based on research conducted by the International Center for Peace in the Middle East (1983) presented three aspects of Israeli oppression: attacks by Jewish Settlers, casualties inflicted by military forces, and a policy against educational institutions. This research, covering the time period 1979–83, revealed, for instance, that thirty-six Palestinians were killed by military forces, most of them shot during demonstrations held between May 1979 and July 1983. During the same time period, approximately seventy incidents of illegal activities were carried out by Settlers against Palestinian residents and Palestinian properties including: deaths, injuries, destruction of crops, the burning of cars and shops, appropriation of houses and property, threats and intimidation of public figures, and the like.[4]

### *Estrangement and unity*

While many of the Palestinians in the occupied territories had been experiencing feelings of estrangement as a result of the establishment of the Israeli State and the consequent expulsion of numerous Palestinians from their homes, such a cognitive and affective state was further broadened and deepened as a result of the occupation and growing numbers of refugees and/or displaced people. Where, after 1948, Palestinian refugees were uprooted from their homes inside what became Israeli towns and cities (Tel-Aviv and Lod for example) the occupation of 1967 forced Palestinians out of their homes and/or resulted in the destruction of homes that were located in the soon-to-be-occupied territories. As such, within the time framework of this book, the territories' population was expanded by two major waves of refugees who joined Palestinians residing there prior to 1948.

The first wave of refugees into the West Bank and Gaza Strip came as a result of Israel's 1948 war victory, leading to a wave of approximately 375,000 Palestinians fearing Israeli vengeance for their part in the war (Kimmerling and Migdal 1999), and nearly 390,000 Palestinians located in neighboring Arab countries (Ghanem 2001). The second wave of refugees (more accurately, displaced people according to UN resolution 237), the one most relevant to our purpose, originated in June 1967, as a result of Israel's victory, with the consequence of the Palestinians' mass migration to Syria, Lebanon, Jordan, etc., and the rest of the population's relocation in refugee camps within the territories to which they escaped during the war.

From sociological and psychological perspectives, the resulting social structure in the territories was that of a profound, multi-layered, alienation between various social strata: between the 1948 refugees and the older generation, and between these two social groups and the 1967 refugees. In fact, during the first half of the 1970s one can characterize the social dynamics among Palestinians in the occupied territories as one of hierarchical social stratification, mutual distrust, antagonism, and alienation. Senses of indignation and frustration received expressions in mutual hatred and inner struggles.

Additionally, in spite of the Israeli policy of *de facto* integration in regard to Palestinians in the occupied territories, the latter experienced social and economic conditions of de-development and systematic denial of basic human rights (see below). These conditions became increasingly frustrating, objectively and subjectively, given the presence of Israel's affluent society across the "green line" and, even more frustrating, the growing presence of the population of Jewish Settlers in the territories. The acute, daily contrast with the conditions under which Jewish Settlers were living and the growing number of settlements all over the territories intensified these feelings, as the fear of extinction came to be seen as a viable reality among many Palestinians (Al-Haq 1988; Hass 1996).

One of the central aspects of Israeli policy that established such a fear of extinction among the Palestinians was the 1967 appropriation of water resources and their declaration as public property. According to a report by the Israeli information and research center B'Tselem, this decision immediately translated into numerous restrictions which prevented the Palestinians from using the water in a manner sufficient to accommodate their daily needs.[5]

An expression of such feelings of estrangement in the face of remoteness from their land and homes can be found in the writings of Palestinian poets. The symbolic metaphor used to express longing for Palestine is often the olive tree. The olive tree has two representations: the motherland and the connectedness between the land and the tree. Ashrawi (1978: 91) provides the following excerpt from a poem by a young West Bank poet, Mahmud Abas, illustrating this point:

> The sun reproaches us / It came, as usual / Asking us to be patient / To remain like olive branches – deep in the ground / Lightning, thunder, prayer / hurricane, storms; And floods break the branches / But the roots of the olive / Return and stretch in the depth of the ground.

As we will see in later chapters, the symbolic use of the olive tree was extended to represent the notion of steadfastness denoting the idea of a Palestinian perseverance in coping with their situation as occupied people.

Palestinian estrangement was also relational and was nurtured by the incremental Israeli appropriation of what was seen as the Palestinians' rightful land, and by the sheer fact of occupation under foreign rule. Still, it is important to distinguish between two layers, unequal in depth and severity, of estrangement among Palestinians residing in the occupied territories. For the veteran Palestinians, who had been living in the West Bank and Gaza Strip prior to 1967, the occupation generated a sense of impotence in the face of loss of control over

their lives. Among the 1967 displaced people, the situation was far more complicated and severe.

The 1976 displaced Palestinians were uprooted from their homes, land, and
their primary familial ties. This state of uprootedness and disconnectedness
generated a craving, a genuine need for belonging to a solid ground where the
burden of uncertainty could be lessened. The Palestinian refugee was placed in a
state of homelessness and disorientation, experiencing a deep crisis of identity.
On this, Israeli scholar Harkabi, who studied the Israeli–Arab/Palestinian conflict, writes the following:

> It seems reasonable to argue that the conditions experienced by the refugees
> inside the Palestinian society ... were far from being satisfactory, and that
> among them one can find a deep sense of alienation. It is precisely because
> of their primary local identification, which overclouded other types of iden-
> tification, that their presence in places where they were not born or lived led
> to feelings of alienation even among their Palestinian brethren.
>
> (1997: 251)

The 1967 displaced Palestinians, then, experienced estrangement not only
towards their occupier, but, more importantly, towards their own people. Relo-
cated and concentrated inside refugee camps built by Israel throughout the occupied territories, and represented by UNRWA (UN Relief and Works Agency)
rather than by the municipalities as was the case with the veteran Palestinian
residents, the refugees faced humiliation and disrespect from the veteran Palestinian residents of the territories (Lesch 1991). Thus, it was not only their mere
presence in refugee camps that acted as a fertile infrastructure out of which feelings of estrangement and uncertainty accrued, but the simultaneous severance
from their homes, inside of what they saw as their homeland, coupled with disrespect from their brethren. In the face of such profound degradation, having no
confidence in their identity, lacking any framework for identification, and alienated from their own people, the psychological state of estrangement experienced
by the Palestinian refugees becomes harshly clear.

### Equality and inequality

Given their place under foreign occupation, and the psychological state of
estrangement and alienation, Palestinians in the occupied territories experienced
a third dimension of grievance: the tension between equality and liberty as they
were embedded in social, economic, and political dimensions.

By definition, as an occupied national minority Palestinians in the occupied
territories lacked any form of liberty both as individuals and as a collective. The
basic rights exerted and preserved within any democracy, such as the freedom
for association, freedom of expression, and freedom of movement, were
severely restricted and circumscribed by Israel's military regime. Within the
framework of military rule, Locke's notion of right of property (writ large) was

nullified, as Palestinians had no right over their own body or other assets. Any kind of possession or property was contingent upon the interests of Israel's military regime.

Several examples are in order. Palestinians were not allowed to freely form trade unions and, in fact, most requests to form trade unions were rejected or, in effect, ignored. The mere ability to move and travel throughout the West Bank and Gaza Strip was occasionally prohibited and identity cards, which Palestinians were required to carry, were often confiscated as a safety measure. As part of the administrative measures, Palestinians suspected of resistance activity were placed, for instance, under administrative detention, which, as elaborated above, was imposed without charge or trial. The detention order was valid for a period of up to six months, yet it was renewed continuously and indefinitely for additional six-month periods contingent upon the judgment of the Israeli area commander.

Additionally, Palestinians in the occupied territories were not free to travel outside the territories or to return, without permission from the military authorities. Also, in order for a given newspaper to operate, an operating license had to be granted by the military authorities, and editors were obliged to submit all the materials they intended to publish to a Military Censor in West Jerusalem. Moreover, according to Al-Haq (1988), the retention of any written materials was not allowed unless a permit was obtained for each particular publication from the military authorities.

Measured against the ideal of equality, Palestinian existence under Israeli rule as a *de facto* integral segment of Israeli society stood in sharp contrast to the Jewish population and other groups such as the "Israeli Palestinians." The deprivation of Palestinians as individuals and as a collective encircled the entirety of their existence, where the living conditions enjoyed by other groups within Israeli society acted as a reference point against which their state of living was measured. The Palestinians' aspiration for equality was fully expressed by their demand for self-determination within the framework of their own state – the essential condition for liberty.

On the face of it, one can argue that Palestinians actually enjoyed better conditions of living under Israel's rule than under Jordan's, and that their situation was far better compared to other Palestinian refugees residing in the surrounding Arab States; that throughout the twenty years of occupation many Palestinians actually experienced an increase in their overall quality of life. For many Israelis, such a line of reasoning, promoted and supported by the Israeli government, was used to cope with the cognitive dissonance they had been experiencing as a result of the occupation.

In fact, Israel published numerous reports in order to demonstrate that the quality of life of the Palestinian population was being addressed, and that the Israeli rule was, in fact, an "enlightened" one. As an illustration, consider Figure 2.2, based on a report published by the Israel Information Center (IIC) in 1986. The figures are relevant to the West Bank only, yet data on the Gaza Strip shows a similar pattern.

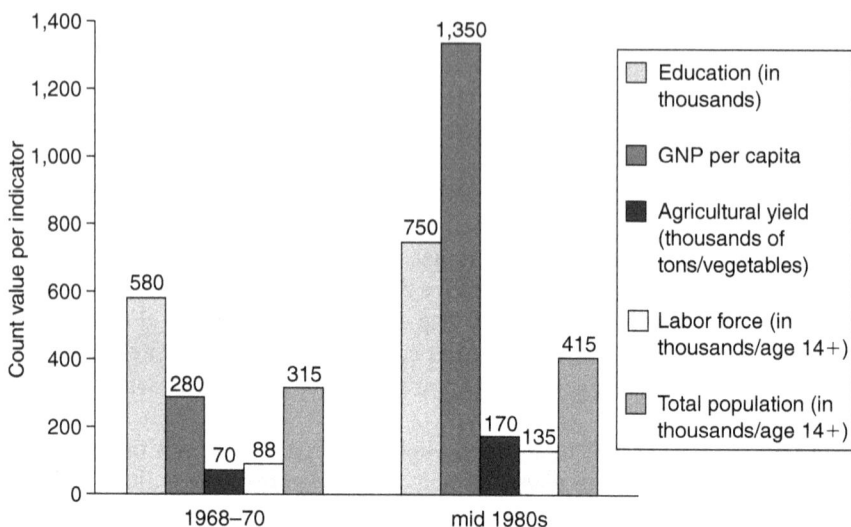

*Figure 2.2* Palestinian quality of life under occupation.

In trying to promote Palestinian compliance with its rule and lessen its own inner conflict that stemmed from the occupation, Israel acted, albeit in a very limited manner, to improve the living conditions of Palestinians in the occupied territories. Yet, while statistics show an impressive increase in per capita GNP, agricultural production, labor force, and educational participation during the mid-1980s, when compared with the period 1968–70, the figures must not be taken as absolute or out of context.

First, the figures are based on the averages, which, as is always the case, are influenced by extreme, individual cases. Such extreme cases may have had a considerable impact on the overall pattern shown. Second, no matter how substantial the difference between the two periods was, such a rise is always relative and relational; when compared with the standard of living in Israel and the Jewish settlements, no matter how impressive the improvement was, the "enlightened" occupation was, first and foremost, an occupation.

Third, other statistics on repressive measures and the expansion of Jewish settlements provide a wider context according to which the Palestinian hardship under occupation is revealed. For example, no matter how high the rise in labor force participation was, such a rise could not have coped with the fact that the overall population in the occupied territories almost tripled between 1967 and 1987: from 559,900 in the West Bank and Gaza Strip in 1967 to 1,433,700 in 1987. During most of the twenty years of occupation, thousands of Palestinians were forced to migrate from the occupied territories in order to look for jobs to support their families.[6]

Moreover, punitive measures such as Israel's deportation policy or the demolition of Palestinians' homes as punishment for their alleged participation in illegal activities provide a very different picture. Despite the lack of precise data during 1967–78, in which case I used the mean values, Figure 2.3 provides an additional aspect of the oppressive environment in which the Palestinians lived.[7]

Manifestations of such systematic oppression are numerous. For example, Palestinians in the occupied territories faced harsh restrictions, including, but not limited to, the restriction on economic entrepreneurship through limitations on occupational possibilities and individual initiatives, the restriction on the scope and variety of academic and educational syllabi and curricula, censorship on the content of information, and over all cultural activities.

Other manifestations, which further demonstrate the superficiality of the data presented in Figure 2.2 above, were more sophisticated. One of the major Israeli decision rules in regard to the territories was the opening of the Israeli market to Palestinian labor shortly after the June 1967 War. Since the early 1970s, Israel began to absorb large numbers of Palestinian workers for Israeli construction, various services, agriculture, and the industrial sector (Tamari 1988). The primary proponent of this policy was Moshe Dayan, Israel's Defense Minister at the time. Despite ideological opposition within the Israeli cabinet, voices that were calling for a strictly Jewish market that would promote the ideal of a productive Jewish people (Horowitz and Lissak 1990), the dynamics of the post-1967 Israeli economy set the tone for Dayan's agenda.

The boom–bust economic cycle after the war created an unprecedented demand for labor. This demand led to additional, related decisions, which slowly resulted in a merger of the two markets, a merger that was characterized by the absolute dependency of the Palestinian market on the Israelis. As an example, Israel decided to introduce its currency into the territories in addition to the Jordanian currency, and to replace Jordanian banks with Israeli banks.

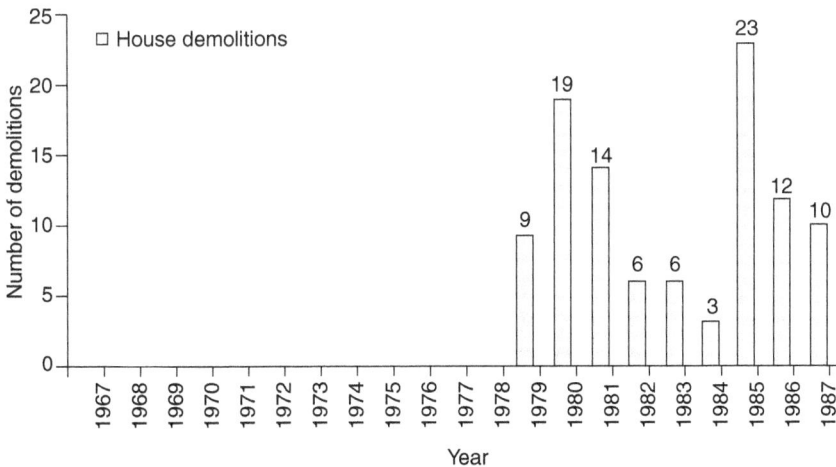

*Figure 2.3* Demolition of Palestinian homes between 1967 and 1987.

The fact of the matter is that while the territories' population became consumers of Israeli commodities, the Israeli market was not limited to Palestinian production. True, the Open Bridges Policy, a policy that was aimed at allowing Palestinian exports to the neighboring Arab States, lessened such a dependency. However, the weight of the Israeli market was far greater than that of the additional markets open to Palestinian producers.

Palestinian scholar Salim Tamari (1988) argues that nearly 90 percent of all goods imported to the territories came from Israel, more than 11 percent of Israel's total exports. Additionally, Tamari further elaborates, the Palestinian market was tariff-free, a fact that made it highly non-competitive. Israel did not allow Arab commodities to move into the Israeli sector, yet thwarted the development of the local industrial manufacturing sector for the Palestinians themselves.

Israeli journalist Amira Hass (1996) supports Tamari's argument by emphasizing the unidirectional flow of goods and commerce. According to the author, taxes were imposed on foreign merchandise and raw materials that entered the territories via Israeli harbors, just as in Israel. Yet, the taxes on those same imported commodities purchased in the territories were not used for reinvestment in the Palestinian market or for improving living conditions, but were, rather, diverted to the Israeli State Treasury.

An additional aspect of the economic integration of Palestinian society into Israel was physical infrastructure. During the early 1970s, Israel seriously invested in restructuring the transport and communication networks, re-linking the West Bank and Gaza Strip to Israel. The idea was to facilitate the connection between the settlements and Israel, coupled with providing Settlers with the possibility to move freely without the need to pass through Palestinian towns and villages (Tamari ibid.). It was also aimed at facilitating the movement of military forces into the territories whenever such a need arose. Additional infrastructures were water and electric grids. By connecting towns and other concentrations of Palestinian population with Israeli governmental companies (e.g., "Mekorot," the water company or "Hevrat Hashmal," the electric company), Israel deepened the Palestinians' dependency on Israeli services and utilities.

Together with the mechanisms of markets and infrastructure, the proletarianization process of the Palestinian worker (Tamari ibid.), a direct result of Dayan's policy, laid the foundations for Palestinian society's *de facto* integration with Israel. Already in the 1970s, the Israeli army issued a decree according to which all Palestinian residents had the right to enter Israel. The new job opportunities that opened up for Palestinians led to an immediate improvement among many of them who, prior to that decision, were unemployed, receiving support from UNRWA, depending on seasonal jobs, or living on money sent from family members working in neighboring Arab States.

Israel aimed, equally, at the fulfillment of additional interests, other than economic ones. Israel's primary interest in regard to the territories was political. Thus, while for many Palestinians the opening up of the Israeli market had some benefits, the dependency of the Palestinian market on Israel was strictly maintained through various methods. In addition to those mentioned above, Israel did its best to prevent substantial economic and industrial development in the territories. This consisted in low budget allocations, heavy taxation, and a system of rigorous bureaucratic regulations that left scant opportunities for Palestinian investment. In addition, Israel systematically exploited natural resources in the territories, such as water and land (Hass 1996).

A useful indication, albeit partial and biased, of Palestinian dependency on Israel would be the overall scope of Palestinian workers employed in Israel. In spite of the fact that the figures came from an Israeli employment agency, one can still get a good idea of the extent of this dependency. In 1967, 5,000 Palestinians from the Gaza Strip applied for jobs in Israel, whereas the numbers increased significantly to 23,000 in 1987. Of those applications, only 2,600 were granted in 1967 and 14,000 in 1987. According to other sources however, the number of Palestinian workers in Israel was much higher, demonstrating the gap between the formal and informal estimates. According to the 1995 UNRWA report, by 1987 the rate of Palestinian workers in Israel had reached 40,000 in the Gaza Strip alone, and 80,000 in other locations.

Thus, the analysis of fiscal indicators such as GNP may lead one to argue that despite all the above, the 1970s witnessed a relative economic improvement for Palestinians in the occupied territories. Still, drawing inferences from such fiscal indicators can be misleading. When one takes into consideration other indicators (e.g., social inequalities), and analyzes the economic dimension within the context of other dimensions, one receives a very different picture. In fact, Benvenisti maintains, Palestinian society experienced deepening social disparities, where, despite relative improvement in the life conditions of many, the majority of Palestinians remained under horrendous living conditions. The economic reality in the territories, Benvenisti continues, "should be defined as an exceptional mixture of individualistic growth and collective stagnation, it is a separated sector, subservient to the Israeli economy" (1989: 7).

Indeed, within the territories and among Palestinians, sharp gaps developed between the refugees and the veteran residents in terms of residential conditions, sources and levels of income, education, and other public services. A major factor responsible for the perpetuation of such a stratified social structure was that Palestinian refugees were under the care of international, humanitarian organizations such as UNRWA, and not under the responsibility of the municipal system of the veteran residents. Second, such stratification also fit the interests of the veteran Palestinian residents, who feared further deterioration in their traditional authority. On this point, Lesch (1990: 6) argues the following: "That order [the traditional social order] seemed legitimate and natural to the elite. They opposed Israeli rule because it was alien and constricted their authority. But they also opposed the mobilization of poor sectors and refugees, since that might undermine their own bases of power."

Third, the objective and subjective inequalities were deepened in the face of the growing presence and expansion of Jewish settlements. The presence of Jewish settlements with better living conditions, access to roads that cut through

Palestinian land, the size of the land allocated to them, and the amount of resources they received, further intensified the level of frustration and depriva-tion of Palestinians in general and Palestinian refugees in particular (Siniora 1988). Data on the expansion of Jewish settlements within the West Bank, Gaza Strip, and East Jerusalem, is presented in Figure 2.4.

Figure 2.4 demonstrates that Israel's policy of settling the occupied territories with Jewish population cannot be said to be the initiative of a specific adminis-tration. While it is clear that the Likud Administration, elected in 1977, pro-moted the establishment of more settlements in comparison to the Labor Administration (1967–77), the latter was the one that essentially initiated the process and/or allowed for the establishment of numerous settlements. It is also clear, however, that after 1983 a steady decrease of new settlements is evident, returning to the pace characterized by the Labor Administration. It is important to note that the relative decrease follows the apex of the Lebanon War, and the administration of the Israeli Unity Government (1984–8). We will return to this point when dealing with the *when* question of the Intifada.

## The rise of the rebellious man

For those who experience interlocking oppression, repression frustration, and deprivation, the shift towards political activism should not be seen as inevitable. For people to say no, it takes more than shared deprivation and rage. People rebel only on the basis of a political consciousness that makes meaning of such a gap and extrapolates it from the private sphere to the public one. Such political consciousness shifts the deprived and aggrieved from a state of mind that promotes naturalism (i.e., man as object of historical changes), towards volun-tarism (i.e., man as subject of historical change). In order for a person to rebel,

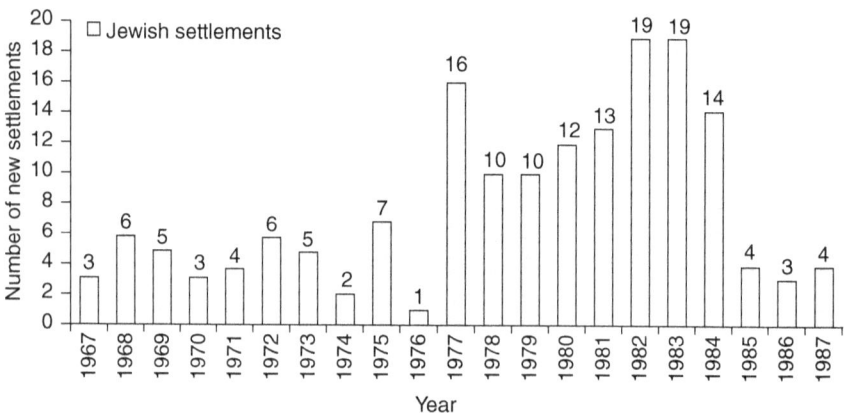

*Figure 2.4* Number of Jewish settlements per year (source: PALGRIC, Survey of Israeli Settlements in the West Bank and Gaza Strip, 1995).

then, it takes, primarily, political consciousness, the type that supports participation in politics of contention (Gamson 1992).

Nationalism is one such political consciousness. Palestinian nationalism began to develop prior to the occupation and outside what was later to become the occupied territories. It is possible to identify three stages in the development of Palestinian nationalism, seen also as three catalysts in this process.

The first stage in the development of Palestinian nationalism is rooted in deep Palestinian disappointment with the Arab States' management of the Palestinian question, in both regional and international arenas. According to Harkabi (1997), many of the younger generation born after 1948 were highly involved in Pan-Arabic organizations.[8] The growing feeling that the Palestinian question had become the Arab States' tool for gaining and exercising influence in the politics of the region, led disabused activists to call for the formation of a Palestinian organization. Additionally, the common belief that the Palestinians' "return" to the land of Palestine would grow out of a joint Arab State front against Israel was shattered by the results of the Six-Day War in June 1967.

The second stage in the development of Palestinian nationalism was the realization of such calls: the formation of the Organization for the Liberation of Palestine (PLO) in May 1964. The formation of the PLO was led by the prevalent conception regarding the need for a genuine Palestinian organization, coupled with the growing recognition that Arab politics, dominated by narrow interests, bitter rivalries, and nationalistic rather than Pan-Arabic orientations, would be fickle for the promotion of the Palestinian question.

Still, the actual formation of the PLO was the product of the awareness of Arab State leaders of such Palestinian restiveness. Encouraging the formation of the PLO was a preemptive act aimed at containing possible unrest by Palestinians in their own societies, for example in Egypt or Jordan. The formation of the PLO was formally proclaimed during the covenant of the first congress in May 1964, at the initiative of Ahmad Shuqairy who was nominated by the Arab States as "Palestine's Representative."

However, the artificial PLO was soon to turn on its creators; the formal, declared purpose of the PLO, as proclaimed by Shuqairy, was to take an active role in the liberation of Palestine and the self-definition of the Palestinian people. Such an agenda went far beyond the intentions of Arab leaders, who wanted Shuqairy to use the PLO as an international mechanism to propagate their diplomatic front against the Zionist Entity.

Ironically, what had been considered too radical for Arab leaders was too moderate for young Palestinian activists, who saw Shuqairy as an opportunist and not as a genuine liberator (Harkabi 1997). Highly influenced by the success of the Cuban and Algerian revolutions, Palestinian activists became aware of the potential of guerrilla warfare for the liberation of Palestine by using the people's own resources. The *Fida'yyin* organizations[9] were a result of the Palestinians' adoption of the Cuban and Algerian revolutions. In their guerrilla activity against Israeli targets inside and outside Israel, the *Fida'yyin* represented a major political challenge to the PLO. Yet it was not before the failure of June

1967 and Shuqairy's subsequent resignation that *Fida'yyin* forces took control of the PLO and Yasir Arafat became the PLO's chairperson in December 1967.

Arafat's ascendancy to power as the chairperson of the PLO expressed a major shift in Palestinian nationalism. Largely, the PLO turned into an autonomous organization with diminishing dependency on Arab States, demonstrating a decade-old conception of liberating Palestine through an armed struggle. Such a conception had already materialized during the late 1950s with the formation of the Fatah and the Arab National Movement (ANM) which had initiated guerrilla attacks against Israeli targets. According to Hiltermann (1990), the activity of these organizations gained increasing popularity among many Palestinians as they revived the Palestinian cause and gave voice to Palestinian aspirations and goals.

The formation of the PLO was not the end of the *Fida'yyin* organizations; some of them refused to collaborate with the PLO even after it was taken over by the Fatah leader, Arafat. Nonetheless, the PLO formulated Palestinian nationalism in a systematic fashion. It was the PLO, under Shuqairy, that created the organizational infrastructure within the occupied territories by organizing trade unions, women's groups, student cells, and health committees. In doing so, the PLO combined diplomatic activity with organizational initiatives, a combination that strengthened many Palestinians' national sentiment and their desire to return to Palestine.

The third stage in the development of Palestinian nationalism was unquestionably the June 1967 War and the occupation of the territories by Israel, which also resulted in the encapsulation of the majority of the Palestinian people into Israeli polity. The sweeping Israeli victory against a joint Arab front in a matter of six days led to the bankruptcy of the approach to liberating Palestine through a joint Arab military venture. It took an imposition of foreign rule to force many of the Palestinians in the occupied territories to understand that a solution to their problem would be the result of their own efforts (Beitler 2004; Bishara 1993).

It was the PLO's capacity to embody this emerging consensus for self-reliance that led to its growth in influence. Through its sheer presence as an authentic Palestinian organization and its national ideology, drawing heavily on the national revolutions in Cuba, Vietnam, and South America, the vision of national liberation through guerilla warfare resonated with many Palestinians in the occupied territories. The PLO's relative success in the battle of Karame against Israeli forces in 1968 further contributed to the ascendancy of the PLO as a genuine and promising Palestinian representative. The ability of PLO forces and Jordanian residents to cause serious casualties to Israeli forces vindicated the domination of the Fatah inside the PLO and the approach of liberating Palestine through an armed struggle (Taraki 1990).

However, despite, or perhaps because of its successes, the PLO was forced to act from outside the territories, locating in Jordan, in Lebanon, and in Tunisia. As we will see in following chapters, while it acted as a central source for guiding, funding, and arming resistive operations, the forced remoteness of the PLO from the occupied territories and its status as a representative of the *entire*

Palestinian people brought about a complicated and tense symbiotic relationship between the Fatah-led PLO and its constituency within the occupied territories.

It is important to note also that the Intifada was not the initiative of the PLO, but rather, primarily the result of grassroots national activists in the occupied territories. The fact that the PLO did not see the Intifada coming and underestimated, just as Israel did, its momentum and power, was in many ways indicative of the built-in tension between the developing unique needs of the Palestinians in the occupied territories and the all-Palestinian representation of the PLO. While it is of importance not to underestimate the role of the PLO in the development of the national Palestinian movement within the occupied territories and its role in the Intifada (two themes that will be developed in subsequent chapters), it is nonetheless important to examine the rise of Palestinian action-oriented political consciousness as it evolved from within the occupied territories.

### *Constructing a territories-based Palestinian* we-ness

The development of nationalistic sentiments *within* the occupied territories originated, primarily and dialectically, out of the forced inclusion of Palestinians into Israeli polity. The unprecedented proximity between Palestinians and Israelis was established as a result of the occupation, and the *de facto* Israeli policy of incorporating the territories into Israeli society brought about a sharp contrast between the two societies that acted as a major factor in the development and refinement of the Palestinians' shared awareness of their situation and national sentiments.

The emphasis of the distinct Palestinian tradition (see below) was, according to Taraki (1990), the by-product of the developing trend of increasing Palestinian political–national consciousness within the territories. Manifestations of such a process began to appear within the occupied territories during the mid-1970s in a twofold manner. First, the willingness of the PLO and the Jordanian Communist Party to join hands and form the Palestinian National Front (PNF) was a result of the PLO's slow-paced recognition that it could not overlook such nationalistic trends in the local arena; trends that took the form of community-based grassroots committees aimed at lending support and assistance to Palestinians in need. We will return to these organizational developments which took form as grassroots committees for voluntary action, and elaborate on the PNF and the Communist Party in the next chapter.

Second, in parallel to the formation of community-based committees stood the revival of the Palestinians' cultural heritage. Such a development was expressed through the establishment of theaters and discussion-groups in which cultural issues, uniquely Palestinian, were raised and discussed. In like manner, daily newspapers founded during the early 1970s, such as *a-Sha'ab* and *al-Fajr*, started to publish literary works by Palestinian novelists and poets, becoming a central arena upon which Palestinian voices were heard.

Other examples were the beginning of the documentation and preservation of cultural works. The Society for the Renewal of the Palestinian Family founded a journal named *Heritage and Society* in 1974, where works by Palestinian artists and intellectuals were published (Taraki 1990). Additionally, students from the Bir-Zeit University organized a literary event in 1976 called Palestinian Week, during which panels were held and lectures were given on Palestinian literature. While other similar events became a permanent feature in the daily lives of Palestinians in the occupied territories, according to Siniora (1988), this specific event was widely attended and indicative of a growing sense of collectivity. The fact of the matter was that because of and despite Israel's restrictions on publications and its harsh military censorship, the number of small neighborhood forums for poetry readings and other cultural activities was on the rise.

## A diversified Palestinian collective actor

The analysis of the various types of political consciousness that existed in the occupied territories during the 1970s and 1980s is important in that it can highlight the processes through which individuals collectively define their situation and it can provide links between their defined sources of grievance and rage, and their formulation of appropriate ways of managing their situation. It is through the formation of such a state of mind that the willingness to engage in politics of contention crystallizes.

The formation of a Palestinian collective of actor(s) within the occupied territories should not be seen as monolithic. It is important, however, that any analysis of existing types of political consciousness from within the territories must be made through the adaptation of an indigenous perspective. It is only through such an internal perspective that we can circumvent the pitfall of wrongly attributing extremist characteristics to sociopolitical approaches and worldviews. For example, if we are to put on the lenses of the Israeli authorities, we may label any act or behavior that went against the imposed norms and procedures as an act of extremism, thereby failing to distinguish other possible worldviews that are far from being extreme.

What follows is an attempt to map the various types of political consciousness that existed in the West Bank and Gaza Strip during the 1970s and 1980s, and to present the sociopolitical forces with which these types of political consciousness were mostly identified. This mapping will serve us throughout the book, and while presenting the various groups and organizations in succinct form, we will have more to say on each and the relationship between them in following chapters.

It is possible to differentiate between three types of action-oriented political consciousness within the occupied territories which developed during the 1970s. The first Palestinian voice was the "moderates." The "moderates" were those who tended to come to terms with Israeli rule and maximize their situation under the given circumstances. Here, I am referring to the older generation and the veteran residents of the territories who, for the most part, experienced the occupation of the territories in June 1967. The "moderates" are usually those who are part of the traditional elite, and those who hold administrative roles in the municipalities, the police force, merchants, and other liberal professions.

According to Sahliyeh (1988), who studied the Palestinian leadership in the West Bank, the group that fit most with such categorization was the pro-Jordanian elite. This group, to which we can add pro-PLO public figures after 1982, was practically immune from the repressive measures exerted under Ariel Sharon as Defense Minister. Not only did they strictly avoid going against Israeli policy, but they also kept acting along the lines of the norms imposed by the military authorities.

Within this framework, the "moderates" attempted to initiate or support a political solution to the occupation, solutions that would preserve their own basis of power and, at the same time, mesh with both Israeli and Jordanian interests. Such was the case with the idea of Jordanian Confederation or Federation, depending on the different variant that was raised, according to which Jordan would, *de jure*, become the Palestinian State. A second group that fit this categorization was the Communist Party within the occupied territories, which, during most of the 1970s avoided adopting political demands and goals and focused mostly on social activities for which contacts with left-wing, socialist Israeli parties were cultivated (Kaminer 1996).

It is possible to classify the second Palestinian voice as the "radicals." Palestinian "radicals" were those who sought to transform the situation within which Palestinians found themselves as a result of the occupation, by addressing the roots (i.e., "radix") of the problem. For Palestinian radicals, comprised mostly of young refugees, students, and the leftist factions within the PLO, clinging to the notion that fighting the Zionist Entity is important, but acting to prevent the annexation of the territories by Israel and ending the occupation, is the primary and most pressing goal. Compared to the "fanatics" or "extremists" (discussed below), the "radicals" made a clear distinction between the Grand Scheme (i.e., the ideal vision) and political pragmatism, thereby taking into consideration the costs and benefits of any action from the vantage point of the Palestinians in the occupied territories along the way for a possible resolution (Harkabi 1986).

An additional sociopolitical power that fits this label was the right-wing faction inside the PLO – the Fatah. Following the events of Black September during 1970–1 (the result of King Hussein's decision to eliminate the growing influence of Palestinian guerrilla forces in Jordan), the Fatah adapted a "phases plan," which involved peaceful, non-violent, means such as diplomacy, together with its traditional approach of armed struggle. As we will see in the next chapter, the Fatah's decision to adopt political pragmatism, whether tactical or not, led to deep tensions and animosities inside the PLO's institution regarding the strategy for combating Israel, and the extent to which the local arena (i.e., the occupied territories) should be strengthened (Sahliyeh 1988).

The third Palestinian voice that can be classified among the various types of collective actors that existed in the occupied territories is the "extremists." In speaking about Palestinian extremism, I am referring to a worldview that tends to adopt the most extreme goals and most extreme means for the promotion of such goals. The "extremists" disparage the "moderates" and repudiate the means and goals of the "radicals"; the "extremists," just as the "radicals," strived to cope with the Palestinian situation by dealing with the roots of the problem, yet they were willing to use the most drastic means in order to achieve these goals. For the "extremists" (e.g., militant factions inside the PLO or the Hamas), the use of terror and self-sacrifice, in its extreme form of martyrdom, were justified and seen as imperative in the fight against Israel.

An important variant in the "extremists" are the "fanatics." It is important to make such a distinction for avoiding a monolithic, simplistic perception of extremism, a perception that is based more on moral criteria and value judgment than on realistic discernment. The "fanatics" (e.g., the Islamic Jihad) rejected any possibility for compromise, even in terms of tactical considerations, given the existence of a Jewish State; they were motivated less by cost/benefit calculations and, as such, the cost the Palestinians in the occupied territories would have to endure was seen as a legitimate sacrifice for their actions. At times, the notions of the sort of an "ends to justify the means," and "no compromise," went as far as "anyone who disagrees with our stance is an enemy and deserves to be treated as such."

"Fanatics" in the occupied territories negated any form of negotiation with Israel, or other forms of diplomatic initiative for the resolution of the Palestinian situation (Khalidi 1988; Nassar and Heacock 1990). The scenario for change is, then, uncompromising and absolute, as can be seen in the following calls made by the Islamic Jihad on November 1983: "Oh masses of our Muslim people, they [Israelis] want none of us on this land so let's fight them. We have no other choice but to fight. We have nothing but jihad ... and crying will not do. Fight them back with everything you have" (Meyda/1, 1983).

Table 2.1 summarizes the three major "voices" in Palestinian society according to three framing questions that will serve us later when analyzing the ways in which these voices gave meaning to events and developments in Israel.

The above-suggested categorization should not be seen as mutually exclusive and unchanging. Changes within categories and shifts among the different action-oriented political worldviews took place during the twenty years of Israeli occupation, as well as during and after the Intifada. As an example, "radical" groups have shifted towards extremism, and vice versa. Such was the case with the Populist Front for the Liberation of Palestine (PFLP) that withdrew from the PLO because of the latter's decision to adopt a less militant means of fighting Israel during the twelfth conference of the Palestinian National Council (PNC) in 1974. Later on, the PFLP supported a two-state solution at the nineteenth PNC meeting in Algiers in November 1988. Once again, during the Intifada, we will see that the PFLP reverted to extremism.

Among the "extremists" and the "fanatics," it is important to further distinguish between a Muslim "revolutionary" orientation (e.g., the Islamic Jihad), and a Muslim "millenarian" orientation (e.g., the Muslim Brotherhood).[10] While the former called for liberating Palestine through elimination of the Israeli sociopolitical order and forming an Islamic State, the Brotherhood saw Israel

Table 2.1 Existing Palestinian voices

| | "Moderates" | "Radicals" | "Extremists/Fanatics" |
|---|---|---|---|
| *What is the issue?* | The issue is whether the Israeli authorities will let us continue with our traditional ways of life. | The issue is whether Israel will end the occupation and let Palestinians fulfill their rights and aspirations. | The issue is whether the Zionist Entity will be destroyed; whether the holy land will be freed from the Jews. |
| *How to think about the issue?* | The Israeli domination is not necessarily the worst possible, so long as we can preserve our basis of power and maximize our interests. | The Israeli occupation is the prime cause of Palestinian hardship; as such, no solution that ignores Palestinians' human needs and aspirations is acceptable. | The Zionist Entity is the prime cause of Palestinian hardship; the Israelis want to eliminate the Palestinian people, Israeli presence in Palestine is the source of all evil. |
| *What should be done about it?* | It is important to try to establish working relationships with Israel and strictly keep acting along the lines of the norms imposed by the military authorities. | Fighting the Zionist Entity is important, but acting to prevent the annexation of the territories by Israel and ending the occupation is the primary and most pressing goal. | No recognition of the Zionist Entity; Islam is the solution; we have no other choice but to fight the Israelis. We have nothing but Jihad, fight them back with everything you've got. |

only as a secondary concern. The origin of the Palestinian problem was not the Israeli occupation but the Palestinians' turning away from Islam as a way of life. The strength of Israel has been the by-product of Arab weakness, a weakness to be overcome when Islam will reign again among Palestinians and throughout the Arab world, hence focusing on preparatory religious educational groundwork. Still, we will once again see that, even within the Muslim Brotherhood, changes took place and a more activist, politics-oriented group developed during the Intifada – Hamas – that was less millenary in nature and later began to adopt a pragmatic approach (Mishal and Sela 1999; Robinson 2004).

Understandably, the ongoing occupation led "moderate" groups to shift towards radicalism. Such was the case with the Communist Party in the territories, which divorced from its Jordanian base and adopted a more activist approach during the first half of the 1980s (Hiltermann 1991). An expression of this is found in an article published in *al-Taliya*, the news organ of the party, in April 1984:

> The facts and the crying discrimination [against Palestinian workers in Israel] are known to our workers as they live them on a daily basis. There is no solution other than freeing them from such policy, when they will be living in their own state and the [Israeli] nationalist discrimination in the work place will be gone.
>
> (Meyda/5, 1984)

The various formulations of Palestinian grievance and the different approaches in regard to possible solutions have shaped the *willingness* of Palestinians in the occupied territories to act. Such formulations provided the Palestinians with a sense of belonging, belief in their capabilities, hope for change, and possibilities of change. The result was the proliferation of varying organizations, with different ideologies, that aimed at mobilizing the Palestinians living in the occupied territories. As we will see in the following chapter, the "radical" approach gained popularity and support from most Palestinians living under occupation. The reasons for this popularity are to be found in the methods for mobilization and organization, ideological resonance, and forms of leadership adapted and promoted by the "radicals." The pulling power and political leverage of the "radicals' approach" was also the result of developments and changes that took place inside Israeli society.

# 3    The *how* question of the Intifada

The *willingness* of Palestinians in the occupied territories to rebel, analyzed in the preceding chapter, sets the preliminary cognitive and affective preconditions for resistive action. The *willingness* to act contentiously is a necessary yet insufficient process for the development of a collective actor: a Palestinian national-social movement. It is essential, then, to analyze the process through which the Palestinians' *readiness* to act was molded: the *how* question of the Intifada.

The molding of *readiness* to act contentiously necessitates the development of organizational infrastructures, including leadership, networks, resources, communication apparatus and ideology; the latter is created through a framing process that links individuals' understanding to the social movement's interpretive orientations (Snow *et al.* 1986).

Indeed, whether individuals are willing to say "no" or remain submissive, says little about their *readiness* to engage in contentious politics. Individuals may suffer hardship, but the possible shift from personal resentment of hardship to one's *willingness* to act, to actually engaging in, and sustaining, contentious politics is contingent, to a considerable extent, upon the rise of a resourceful collective actor with a mobilized constituency ready to shake off the yoke of its oppressor. It is only on the basis of such sustained commitment that a mobilization *to* action, namely efforts to move those who already possess some degree of commitment to take action (Gamson 1990), may be fruitful.

The analysis of the *how* of the Intifada will be divided into four parts. First, we will analyze the development of several Palestinian organizations outside the occupied territories and their respective attempts to mobilize Palestinians within the occupied territories. Second, we will examine the relationships among these organizations, and between them and Israel within the context of their attempts to create commitment among their respective constituencies and mobilize them to action. We will then (third) move to analyze the developing shift in gravity in the process of Palestinian mobilization, that is, the gradual increase in the role played by activists *within* the occupied territories in further strengthening commitment and expanding organizing efforts.

The ascendancy of local organizations was manifested in two ways: in growing autonomy regarding mobilization (both *creation* and *activation* of commitment), and regarding relationships with each other.

The fourth section will be devoted to the analysis of a process through which the various internally-based organizations clustered around a particular master-frame: "National Liberation." We will see that while maintaining their core ideologies, grassroots activists in the occupied territories converged on prioritizing the action frame of "End to Occupation."

## An externally-based mobilization

Several observations on the developing Palestinian movement are in order. First, the *creation* of Palestinian commitment in the occupied territories should be analyzed in two arenas: outside the occupied territories, that is, the source of organizing is rooted and located *outside* the West Bank and Gaza Strip (henceforth: externally-based organization), and *within* the occupied territories, that is, the source of organizing is rooted and located in the West Bank and Gaza Strip (henceforth: internally-based organization). To understand how Palestinians mobilized within the occupied territories we must attend to mobilization processes initiated by externally-based as well as internally-based organizations.

Second, the Palestinian movement should be characterized as consisting of numerous organizations with different ideologies and preferred modes of action. Some of these organizations were formed prior to the Israeli occupation while others emerged during the period under study (1967–87). Yet, the proliferation of new, and the growth of extant organizations were largely the result of organizing efforts designed to fight the occupation.

Third, most newborn organizations that sprang up post-June 1967 operated within the local arena, namely, the occupied territories. Some of these organizations, according to both Shalev (1990) and Hiltermann (1991), were a local branch of the externally-based organizations (e.g., the Shabiba – the youth movement of the Fatah faction of the PLO). Local activists had founded originally and independently other new organizations such as trade unions or professional unions. Despite differing orientations to one of the various ideologies promoted by the externally-based organizations, this type of organizing was far more independent in setting its own agenda when compared with the local branches of the externally-based organizations. As it turned out, however, the latter gradually became autonomous due to several changes and developments inside and outside the contentious arena.

This fact, however, should not lead us to expect a total rift between the two foci of Palestinian mobilization. While tension and differences of opinions existed between the two by reason of developments and events that took place during the timeframe of this book (on which I shall elaborate below), it would be wrong to underestimate the role of the externally-based organizations in the Intifada's inception, and the inextricable link between the two arenas (Nassar and Heacock 1990).

Fourth, whereas the externally-based organizations were characterized by a hierarchically rigorous structure, the local organizations tended to be more flexible, less formal, and decentralized in nature (Taraki 1990). Such a structural difference between the two organizational levels was further translated into differences in type of members and action orientations. Thus, whereas the externally-based organizations comprised mostly of elite members, usually trained individuals in their twenties, the grassroots internally-based organizations were usually staffed by members from all walks of life, where age of membership, for instance, tended to be much broader. As to differences in action orientations, the internally-based organizations tended to "paint" their political agenda with a socialist tone and to focus more on daily service and assistance to the population. In contrast, the externally-based organizations were much more straightforward in their political, militant orientation. Not surprisingly, Israel considered most as illegal in the occupied territories, hence forcing them to operate underground.

A major factor responsible for these differences was the oppressive environment within which the internally-based organizations operated. The restrictions imposed by Israel on political activities in the occupied territories, together with the daily misery of life, had a considerable impact on the Palestinians' mode of organization, forcing them to adapt their activity to the available space of action and the ongoing threat they experienced.

Still, the fact of the matter was that the internally-based organizations were the initiators of the 1987 Intifada. These organizations consciously adapted their mode of action to their given available resources, and formed a mobilizing infrastructure that set the preliminary conditions for sustaining an Intifada (Nassar and Heacock 1990).

What follows is an analysis of the various Palestinian organizations in both external and local arenas. The analysis will focus on each organization's characteristics, types of leadership, preferred mode of action, forms of mobilization, and sources of funding. The categories according to which the analysis will be structured are Nationalism, Islam, and Communism. I find this categorization to be exhaustive, despite several variants, which will be taken into account, of the entirety of the ideologies that existed in the occupied territories.

### *An externally-based nationalism*

The Organization for the Liberation of Palestine (PLO) has been the central carrier of Palestinian nationalism. Despite numerous internal crises, splits, secessions, and military defeats, the PLO under the leadership of Arafat continued to be considered by most Palestinian people as the genuine representative of the Palestinian people. This is so especially as of 1974 following the decision reached by Arab States in the 1974 Arab Summit in Rabat recognize the PLO as the sole legitimate representative of this Palestinian community. This Arab resolution was followed by the UN Resolution of November 1974 to acknowledge the PLO as the representative of the Palestinian people, and the right of the Palestinians to self-determination and statehood.

By early 1969, largely as a result of the humiliating Arab defeat by Israeli forces, and the military achievements against Israeli forces in Karame (March 1968) by Fatah forces, the latter (formed independently of the PLO, already in 1958) became the most influential organization inside the PLO with its leader Yasir Arafat acting as the chairman. Attempts by Arafat predecessors to stress unity and a more activist approach within the PLO following the humiliating defeat of 1967, were too little and too late for Palestinian guerrilla groups. At the National Council, held in February 1969, Arafat was elected chairperson of the PLO Executive Committee (Rubenberg 1983).

It would be more accurate to characterize the PLO as an institution rather than an organization, as it consisted of several organizations, such as the Fatah and the Democratic Front for the Liberation of Palestine (DFLP). The PLO was organized as a hierarchically structured institution with a chairperson, a legislative body, military forces, and numerous organizations with differing ideological emphases and modes of action. While each organization maintained a certain measure of autonomy, all were subjected to the decisions arrived at by the Palestinian National Council (PNC).

Traditionally, the PLO has been an elite-type organization, the initiative of the Palestinian pioneers who thought of themselves as the vanguard. This was so primarily during the first stage of the struggle against the Zionist Entity, a struggle that would be transformed in time, so it was hoped, into popular struggle. Membership or affiliation with the PLO was not based on social status or ideological commitment, but on the actual willingness to take up arms in the name of the national cause. As such, the link between members of the PLO and its supporters was not institutionalized through formal membership procedures of acceptance. Rather, it was on the battleground that such a link materialized. Accordingly, organizational rigor was seen as insignificant; it was not bureaucracy that set the decisions in regard to strategy and tactics, but ideology. The mobilization of the mass, when required, will not come about without a doctrine. It was upon such a doctrine only – the Palestinian right for self-determination and the struggle for fulfilling this right – that power could be acquired. Organization formation was the result of warfare and not the other way around, as it was the passion of the battle that would lead to the rise of a charismatic leader (Harkabi 1997: 289).

This approach was expressed also in the rise of leadership. A liberation movement, so it was seen, should not be the result of an elected leader in the technical, procedural sense. Election should not be the substitute for revolutionary democracy. Palestinians needed to be organized in numerous clandestine, compact groups which, through guerrilla warfare, would slowly expand and produce a revolutionary leadership. In the interim, given the lack of a fixed base, together with the geographical dispersion of the Palestinian people, it was necessary to form a coordinating body (i.e., executive committee) that would coordinate the activities of the myriad groups and would convene at the will of the revolutionary leadership.

Ideologically, the PLO called for an independent Palestinian action aimed at fixing the wrongs of the 1948 and 1967 Wars, the historical injustice that had been preventing Palestinians from defining themselves and implementing their national and historical rights on their land. Accomplishing those rights would enable the Palestinian people to establish a secular, republican state and to gain equal status among Arab States. The way to accomplish these goals would be through an armed struggle based mostly on guerrilla warfare.

The armed struggle approach, originally promoted by the PLO, faced an acute crisis as a result of the Black September events of 1970–1. The painful crackdown by Jordanian forces forced the PLO to both look for other territorial base and accommodate its approach. The accommodated approach became to be known as the "phases approach," which meant a distinction between the "grand design" and "policy" coupled with the introduction of diplomatic activity aimed at mobilizing international pressure on Israel (Harkabi 1986). Thus, as of the early 1970s, specifically during the twelfth session of the PNC in Cairo 1974, the traditional PLO slogan "revolutionary armed struggle" received a slightly different meaning: from liberating Palestine for the purpose of establishing a Palestinian democratic secular state to a two-states solution, from the Organization for the Liberation of *P*alestine to the Organization for the Liberation of *p*alestine, denoting, at least in principle, a Palestinian State on parts of Palestine (ibid. 33). This shift in the PLO's policy led to deep tensions and discords within the PLO as a result of which, for example, the Rejectionist Front was formed by George Habash, one of the PLFP leaders.[1]

Still, despite tensions and dissension, the Fatah-led PLO under the leadership of Arafat gained the recognition as the Palestinian representative by both Arab States and the majority of the Palestinians in the occupied territories (Litvak 1991; Ma'oz 1984). Additionally and for institution building ("state building") for the state-to-be, the PLO was successful in achieving the Arab States' funding of 150 million dollars allocated annually for ten years at the Baghdad Arab Summit on 1978. The money, according to Frisch, was transferred to the occupied territories through a joint Jordanian and Palestinian fund. Other sources of funding were a fixed tax levied on all Palestinians and collected by the Arab governments of the states in which they lived, and loans and contributions from Arab governments and friendly nations (Rubenberg 1983; Frisch 1992).

Throughout most of the 1970s, the Fatah-led PLO acted to mobilize Palestinians in the occupied territories through the foundation and support of public institutions and political organizations such as the Palestinian National Front (PNF – see below). However, such a policy was highly limited. In fact, as will be elaborated below, the Fatah-led PLO policy of state building grew out of fear that a competing, occupied territories-based leadership would develop[2] rather than out of a genuine interest in furthering the institutional infrastructure development of the would-be state.

### *An externally-based Islam*

The two central Islamic organizations operating in the occupied territories have been the Muslim Brotherhood and the Islamic Jihad. Both organizations were mostly centered in the Gaza Strip in which the Muslim Brotherhood started to operate already during the 1950s, the time during which the Gaza Strip was under Egyptian rule. According to Paz (1992), the Brotherhood's branch in the Gaza Strip became independent of its Egyptian base in 1967 while its branch in the West Bank, which was smaller and less influential, maintained its relationship with and followed the guidance of, its Jordanian Muslim Brotherhood base.

### The Muslim Brotherhood

The Brothers organized their activities in the form of "societies" (a synonym for association), of which al-Mujamma' al-Islami (the Islamic center) located in Jurat al-Shams Mosque became the most influential Muslim "society" in comparison to other societies founded by the Brothers in the Gaza Strip. The Muslim Brotherhood used the word "society" (i.e., an association) for two closely related reasons. First, to stress their socioeconomic agendas, and second, to alleviate possible Israeli oppression, as the right of association was prohibited throughout most of the period under study.

According to Shalev (1990), the number of this particular Muslim Brotherhood society's activists stood in early 1987 at approximately 1,200. As with the Mujamma' and other branches of the Muslim Brotherhood, the mosques became the center of operation. This was so largely because Islam has always been an integral part of Palestinian life, and the fact that, according to the military regulations, public gatherings inside mosques were permitted.

The "society" was, in fact, a cover name for the first manifestation of Islamic political activity by the Muslim Brotherhood, which, up to early 1987, acted as a religious organization with no declared political agenda. A further step in that direction was the foundation of Hamas, the Islamic Resistance movement (Harakat al-Muqawama al-Islamiyya), in January 1988, during the early phases of the Intifada. With Sheikh Ahmad Yassin, who had just been freed from nine years in Israeli prison, as its leader, Hamas articulated its own covenant in August 1988.

Traditionally and tactically, however, the Muslim Brotherhood avoided any violation of the military regulations in order to promote its prime goal: to indoctrinate and propagate Islam throughout the occupied territories in order to establish an Islamic society in Palestine and Islamic nation in the Arab world. Other bodies that coordinated the activities of the Muslim Brotherhood in the Gaza Strip were the Islamic Association (al-Jam'iyya al-Islamiyya) founded in 1976 and based in the Shatu refugee camp, and the Islamic University established in 1978 with Saudi and Jordanian funding (Hatina 2001) as an academic extension of Egypt's al-Azhar University. In general, Jordan and the Gulf States (primarily Saudi Arabia) financially supported the Brotherhood, a support that enabled the movement to expand its activities in mosques, charitable organizations, schools, student councils, and trade unions.

For the Muslim Brotherhood, the land of Palestine is *the* holy land, which meant any diplomatic solution to the Palestinian question that entailed a compromise over the land stood in contrast to their interpretation of the Islamic creed; there was no solution to the Palestinian problem but Jihad: war against those who disavow Islam. The establishment of an Islamic state in Palestine by means of Jihad, however, was a long term goal, which, for the meantime, required preparatory educational groundwork. Hatina (2001: 19) provides a useful example of such an approach, demonstrating the attitude of the movement to the land of Palestine and to the secular organizations:

> The land, all the land, will be either heretic land or Islamic land. There is no place for Arab, Palestinian or Jewish land ... The land is entirely for Allah, and there is no room for consecrating the land, as consecration is for Allah alone. Nationalism as a tie to the land does not appear except in the sector ruled by intellectual and ideological degeneration.

The origin of the Palestinian problem, then, was not the Israeli occupation but the Palestinians' turning away from Islam as a way of life. The strength of Israel has been the by-product of Arab weakness, a weakness to be overcome when Islam will reign again among Palestinians and throughout the Arab world.

Largely, the Muslim Brotherhood has acted to expand its influence among Palestinians in the occupied territories through a communal involvement in the daily lives of the population. It operated kindergartens, and took a major role in community-based activities, mostly through charitable networks, such as the Islamic Charitable Association. In 1981, the Islamic "society" branch of the Muslim Brotherhood formed the Islamic Juvenile consisting of a hundreds of young women, which was the only organization of Islamic woman in the Strip.

### The Islamic Jihad

The second most influential Islamic organization has been the Islamic Jihad. The occupied territories-based Islamic Jihad has its origins in the Egyptian militant Jihad movement which influenced two of its central leaders Dr. Fathi 'Abd al-Azi al-Shiqaqi and Shaykh 'Abd al-Aziz Awda. It started to operate publicly as of 1981, in Gaza, upon the return of its two leaders from Egypt. The Islamic Jihad labeled itself as such only during the early phases of the Intifada: the Islamic Jihad (Movement in Palestine). Prior to the Intifada, the movement consisted of numerous groups who, despite a common ideological ground (see below), were occasionally contentious with each other (Hatina 2001).

The movement had no fixed or distinct organizational location. While it is possible to argue that by reason of its goals and means for action organizational flexibility was necessary, given the environment in which the movement operated, it seemed that the major reason for this was ideological. The emphasis on organizational flexibility was rooted in the movement's commitment to an idea rather than to an organization. As was expressed in an article that appeared in *al-Tali'a al-Islamiyya*, the movement's central news organ, "The organization is a tool that ratifies the goal. It is not an arena for demonstrating haughtiness and authority, but a zone for promoting responsibility and awareness" (cf. Hatina 2001: 31).

The Islamic Jihad has been calling for the liberation of Palestine through armed jihad; it is a revolutionary movement with an emphasis on Khomeini's ideas and goals, looking to the Iranian Revolution (1979) as its model. Despite the significant difference in the Islamic Jihad's religious interpretation of Islam, namely a Sunni movement as opposed to Iranian Shi'i movement, both movements, as well as other movements with the same ideological ground (e.g., the Hizbolla), prioritize the unification of the Islamic Nation, both Sunnis and Shi'is.

Similar to the Muslim Brotherhood, the Islamic Jihad promoted the vision of a Pan-Arabic Islamic Nation. Yet, unlike the Muslim Brotherhood, the Islamic Jihad saw Israel as the primary concern of the Palestinians rather than their relative neglect of Islam. Islam, then, was a faith of liberation out of which an Islamic State in Palestine would be established. The accomplishment of this vision was through forcing Israel to leave by means of holy war: Jihad (Abu-Amr 1988: 394). The following excerpt from an interview given by Shiqaqi in August 1989, demonstrates the attitude to the other organizations and groups in the occupied territories:

> Those who carried the flag of Islam did not fight for Palestine, and those who fought for Palestine removed Islam from their ideological framework. However, we, as young Muslim Palestinians, have discovered that Palestine is found at the heart of the Qur'an ... we understood that the way of the jihad in Palestine is the way of salvation for ourselves as individuals, as a group and as a nation.
>
> (cf. Hatina 2001: 26)

The Islamic Jihad's center of operation was located in the Sheikh 'Izz al-Din al-Qassam Mosque in Bayt Lahiyya. This mosque and others provided medical and welfare aid to the needy, but acted also as public forums in which radical preaching and indoctrination took place. They also acted as provisory centers for membership recruitment. Yet, as argued by Hatina (2001), the central mode of recruitment was by word to mouth mostly, during Islamic festivals, but also on campus and at schools. Those Islamic festivals (e.g., the Ramadan Fast) were used also as major occasions for fund-raising. The Islamic University, just as with the Muslim Brotherhood, was another center of activities, where, in spite of clear Muslim Brotherhood dominancy, the Islamic Jihad established a student association called the Islamic Society (al-Jama'a al-Islamiyya) and devoted much of its funding to the publishing of periodicals, which dealt with Islamic and Palestinian issues.

### An externally-based Communism

Communist organizing was the oldest and most systematic mobilization of Palestinians in the West Bank. The Palestine Communist Party (PCP) was founded during the British Mandate (1923–47), merging, and labeled accordingly, with the Jordanian Communist Party (JCP) after 1948, the time when the West Bank came to be ruled by Jordan. By 1967, however, the Israeli occupation led to a separation of the two parties, while the West Bank part of the organization reverted to its original name, the PCP, during the mid-1970s.

During the first decade of occupation, the Israeli authorities considered the PCP as an integral body of the JCP. This was so primarily because the PCP adopted the name of the Jordanian Communist Party as a tactical step aimed at coping with Israeli repressive measures. The JCP, while considered illegal in the occupied territories, was the only Palestinian organization that did not call for the destruction of Israel and promoted the idea of a Palestinian State in part of Palestine (Ma'oz 1984). In 1975, however, mostly because of increasing tension with the PLO over the support by, and influence on the Palestinians in the occupied territories, the PCP, with the approval of the JCP, reverted to its original name.

During the late 1970s, the activity of the PCP broadened significantly and focused on establishing trade unions and, as of early 1980s, founding women's organizations. The agenda of the trade unions, during the 1970s, was mostly socioeconomic as, in contrast to the Fatah, fighting social injustice and inequities as a way to implement the Communist vision was far more important than immediate political goals. The working and living conditions of the Palestinian worker were seen as the most pressing problem that Palestinian society faced. Such a situation was the result of class division between refugees and the veteran residents, and the perpetuation of such division was the interest of the elite, coupled with the structured dependency of the Palestinian market on the Israeli economy.

The Communists had been calling for the formation of a classless society on the way to an international socialist society. While the Israeli economic oppression of Palestinian society as a whole made the national issue an integral part of Communist concerns, the national issue was secondary to their priorities. According to Frisch (1992), the Communists realized that, given the contemporary socioeconomic development of the territories, the Nationalists' political agenda would, at best, result in a Neo-Feudal power structure, which would be, in effect, a self-defeating strategy on their part.

Whether it was the Marxist-Leninist variant of the Communists (i.e., the model of the Russian Revolution) or the National-Socialist variant (i.e., the model of Zionist Socialism), the central goal of the Communist Party was drawn from a mixture of both variants: the improvement of the Palestinian laborer's working conditions and securing his rights and well-being both in the occupied territories and inside Israel. The political agenda generated from this prime goal was the establishment of two states in Palestine based on social and economic equality. For that purpose, the PCP maintained frequent contacts with Israeli far-left-wing political parties such as RAKAH (the Israeli Communist Party) in order to improve the labor conditions in the territories and also, later on, in

Israel. Interestingly, prior to 1980, however, Palestinian workers in Israel were considered traitors by both the PCP and the Popular Front for the Liberation of Palestine. A shift in that attitude took place only after the mobilization of these workers by the Democratic Front for the Liberation of Palestine, which immediately led to mobilizing efforts by the PCP and the PFLP. We will have more to say about this issue below.

The fact of the matter was that during 1968–79 trade unions in the occupied territories were, largely, the result of Communist initiatives, which also involved the foundation of what was the first and largest trade union federation: the General Federation of Trade Unions (GFTU). The GFTU was a coordinating body for dozens of unions spread throughout the occupied territories, located in both towns and villages. The Federation was also a collective forum in which the agenda of the organization was articulated.

The most central contribution of the Communists to Palestinian mobilization, in addition to the organization of the workers, was the organizing of West Bank women, a population fairly neglected until the late 1970s. In early 1980s, the PCP founded the Working Palestinian Woman's Association, which operated in Ramallah, Beit-Lehem, East Jerusalem, Nablus, and the Gaza Strip, together with the foundation of the Committee for Medical Assistance. Nonetheless, it is important to note that the first women's organization was established in 1978 by a small group of women from Al-Bire in the West Bank, who were oriented to the ideology of the DFLP. The PCP was indeed the first to organize the women in a systematic manner, yet their status within the organization was relatively marginal.

The PCP's mode of organizing was largely through the formation of voluntary, action-oriented committees, which were dispersed around the greater Jerusalem area and Ramallah. The committees focused on communal activities such as forestation, public cleaning, cropping, and were highly involved in connecting the villages in the area to the West Jerusalem electricity supply (Frisch 1992). An additional focus of activities was the campus where the PCP organized students' movements, (which, however, were far less influential than other students' movements) affiliated with the Islamic movements or the Fatah.

## Repressive structure and warring agents

Each of the three externally-based organizations acted independently in establishing mobilizing infrastructures in the occupied territories. The differences in means and goals, and the simultaneous struggle over the support of the same constituency resulted in ferocious rivalry among the three Palestinian organizations. At times, the contentious relationship reached the level of deadly confrontations, as was the case with PLO activists setting fire to the Communist Union offices in 1980 or assassinating Ismail al-Hatib, a Muslim Brotherhood member, in November 1984.

The Israeli authorities played a role in heightening the violent potential among the organizations, a potential that was inherent within the ideologies contending for influence among the Palestinians of the occupied territories. The framework of constraints and restrictions imposed by the military authorities was, to a large extent, designed as a strategy of divide and conquer. Such a policy further confined the space of action open to the externally-based organizations, intensified the potential of contention among them, and, as a result, led to a relative neglect of the Palestinian situation. Indeed, during the first half of the 1970s, the level and extent of Palestinian political mobilization within the occupied territories was conspicuously slight.

Several reasons for the lack of a more systematic and broader Palestinian mobilization are of relevance. To begin with, while both Muslim Brothers and Communists were deeply involved in the lives of Palestinians in the occupied territories, their endeavors at mobilization were mostly socially oriented. As to the PLO, political mobilization of the masses was scant. In fact, with the exception of the Palestinian National Front, the only mode of political mobilization was through the public activity of the pro-PLO public figures who were members of the elite (see below).

Second, among existing organizations and political bodies such as the municipalities, procedural elections that were designed, in principle, to enable and encourage political mobilization did take place. Yet, in actuality, elections were a "sold-game" as the elected mayor was the product of preliminary arrangements among the various candidates. Further, as was systematically analyzed by Ma'oz (1984), the West Bank mayors were not quick to cooperate with the PLO. For pro-Jordanian mayors, it meant going against their own preferred agenda, and for pro-PLO mayors it meant a threat to their status vis-à-vis the military authorities, while yet others were looking for the promotion of an independent Palestinian entity on the West Bank, as was the case with Sheikh Muhammed 'Ali Ja'bari, the mayor of Hebron.

Third, Israeli repressive measures, together with tension among representatives of the externally-based organizations, acted as a deadly combination when it came to attempts at mass political mobilization. At least until 1981, Israel allowed for what Mishal and Aharoni (1989) call "restricted radicalism." The Israeli willingness to put up with political activism in so far as it did not threaten its interests had its sources in Israel's interest to cooperate with Jordan about a possible solution over the West Bank and the latter's collaboration with the PLO at the time. Ironically, all three parties had a common interest in preventing any manifestations of independent political initiative, such as the National Guidance Committee (NGC), from gaining significant political influence. The Palestinian National Front set an additional prior example. Founded in 1973, the Front was originally a genuine joint initiative by the PLO and the Communists to mobilize the Palestinian mass. However, internal conflicts between the PLO and Communists regarding who would have had more control over the Palestinian National Front's activities in the occupied territories, coupled with Israeli crackdown of the PNF's activities, quickly led to the dissolution of the organization.[3]

Nevertheless, several developments and events that took place during the late

1970s and early 1980s changed this situation. To begin with, Israel shifted its mode of occupation in the territories. Under the Likud Administration (commencing in 1977) a shift from "controlling populations" to "controlling territories" (Frisch 1996) took place. This change in emphasis meant more freedom for Palestinian local politics in those same places Israel did not consider as vital to its security; the rationale was to "let Arabs take care of their affairs by themselves" (Abu Shakrah 1986). Thus, social, medical, economic issues were left for the Palestinians to administer.

Second, the intensifying tension inside the Fatah-led PLO and between the PLO and the Communists over the traditional Fatah policy to prevent the development of leadership cores in the occupied territories led to growing mobilization efforts by the leftist factions (e.g., PFLP, DFLP) inside the PLO.

Third, as of summer 1981, the Israeli policy for the occupied territories went through another shift. Under Sharon's office as Defense Minister, the prime objective was to eliminate the PLO presence in the territories, and, as it turned out, in the region altogether. During his first year of office, Sharon practically abolished the Gaza Municipality, removed from office several of the West Bank mayors who were considered to be PLO supporters, outlawed the National Guidance Committee, introduced tougher restrictions (e.g., closure of universities, strict censorship on media, more curfews on towns, etc.), and established the civil administration. According to Ma'oz (1984), this meant a reorganization of Israeli domination over the occupied territories by replacing the military administration, although not the military government that still had the greater control and responsibility for overall operations, by a civilian management, one that was to consist also of Palestinians.

Accordingly, and as a replacement to the dismissed mayors, Minister of Defense Sharon and Menahem Milson, the first head of the administration, formed the Village Leagues in hope of cultivating an alternative leadership to the pro-PLO mayors from among the supposedly silent two-thirds majority of the West Bankers, the village population. This grand scheme failed either because of PLO intimidation and threats or because the village population was, at the time, far from being silent or moderate. The result of this policy was a sociopolitical vacuum that was filled by local community-based organizations (Mishal with Aharoni 1989).

Fourth, Israel's invasion of Lebanon in summer 1982, and the resulting expulsion of the PLO from the region, forced the PLO to acknowledge the importance of strengthening its hold in the occupied territories. In fact, the Palestinians in the occupied territories became the prime constituency to mobilize from the viewpoint of the PLO in exile. Consequently, the PLO acted to broaden its mode of operation in the territories by founding more local organizations (this time, also socially oriented ones) and expanding mobilization efforts to additional sectors such as the women and the workers. An additional change in that regard was the PLO interest in the renewal of dialogue with Jordan (as from September 1982), aimed at taking part in every political initiative for the occupied territories that might be promoted (Sahliyeh 1988).

The first half of the 1980s, then, witnessed the thickening and broadening of mobilizing initiatives by the externally-based movements, parallel to signs of rapprochement between the old-time rivals Arafat and King Hussein, a rapprochement that influenced similar trends in the territories between pro-PLO and pro-Jordanian public figures. Yet, the attempts by the Fatah-led PLO to keep its hold in the region came at a time when the internally-based organizations and activists had already developed a measure of autonomy in their attempts at mobilization; it was the local arena that started to set the pace and tone of Palestinian mobilization.

Before moving on to the analysis of mobilizing trends in the local arena, two further significant developments are worth mentioning. The first development was the relative tempering the PLO went through as a result of the Lebanon War (i.e., the growing reliance on diplomatic initiatives) and the renewal of the relationship with Jordan.

In an interview given to Egyptian academics in 1985,[4] Arafat provides his own account of the meaning of the collaboration with Jordan, specifically of the Amman agreement signed between the parties earlier that year.

> This agreement is an "action-initiative" and not a political initiative ... aimed at joint action in the Arab and international arenas ... we have agreed on "land for peace," but "land" for the Palestinian people ... a confederation with Jordan only after the constitution of the Palestinian state, an international peace conference with all relevant sides involved and a comprehensive solution to the [Palestinian] problem.

Such a change led to a rift inside the PLO, the expressions of which were dissension by the Rejectionist wing that refused to accept such a change and increasing tension between the mainstream Fatah and the leftists' factions (e.g., the DFLP) that had traditionally been calling for the strengthening of the local arena. Only in 1987 was this rupture healed (Khalidi 1988).

The second development was a deterioration of the public status enjoyed by the "moderates," namely pro-PLO and pro-Jordanian personalities, mayors, and elite members. The major reason for such a development was the lack of appreciation and recognition by the popular, grassroots organizations who saw the "moderates" as an "armed-chair" leadership detached from the reality of the occupation (Litvak 1991). In fact, those grassroots organizations became the dominant sociopolitical power in the occupied territories beginning in 1982–3. Whereas the PLO was preoccupied with promoting solutions to the Palestinian situation through Jordan and the US, local forces pushed in a different direction, rejecting any solution that was perceived as failing to recognize the genuine rights, needs, and aspirations of the Palestinians in the occupied territories (Abu Amr 1988).

It was the internally-based organizations with their different ideologies and political goals that started to join hands and developed a territories-based Palestinian Nationalism (Hiltermann 1991; Kuttab 1988; Lesch 1990). They were responsible not only for organizing the population, but also for the *creation* of unprecedented commitment among the occupied Palestinians.

## An internally-based mobilization

The multitude of organizations founded within the occupied territories during the first half of the 1980s may be categorized as grassroots organizations. This categorization is based not only on the Israeli crackdown that forced Palestinian activists to adapt their mode of mobilization (Beitler 1995, 2004). It was equally the form of organization that was capable of communicating with the vast majority of Palestinians so far neglected by the externally-based organizations. While grassroots organizations were, originally, the initiative of the three exter-nally-based organizations (Nationalists, Islamists, and Communists), dynamics outside the occupied territories (as elaborated above), and, more importantly, within the occupied territories, forced a shift in mobilizing initiatives towards the local activists.

Local activists translated such a shift into growing autonomy. As an example, the first West Bank women's organization, the Women's Work Committee, founded in 1978, went through a deep schism as a result of the PLO tempering, and the ensuing inner tension and dissensions within the latter following its expulsion from Lebanon. Several members of the Women's Work Committee (WWC) rejected the dominance of the DFLP within the organization and decided to form a parallel organization, the Union of Palestinian Women's Com-mittees (UPWC), with their own ideological orientation: the PFLP. The same process reoccurred with other members of the WWC as they founded other women's committees according to their orientation to the various PLO factions (Hiltermann 1991).

Palestinian grassroots organizing introduced a new mode of mobilization. Unlike the former, hierarchical, elite-type organizations located outside the territories, the new style of mobilization indicated a shift from institutional mode of action to decentralized mode dispersed throughout the territories. The new organizations and committees were structured, according to both Taraki (1991) and Abu-Amr (1988), as a "mass democratic framework," that is, totally decen-tralized, with the style of direct democratic decision-making. In addition to that, the leadership was usually made up from lower strata, coming from the villages and the refugee camps. No special skills were required from members and, as such, any member could easily function as a leader. This meant also that when-ever a given leader was put in administrative detention or was deported from the territories numerous other members could easily replace him. Also of import-ance was the fact that these grassroots organizations had no fixed agenda in comparison, for instance, with the Communist trade unions. As a sectoral, community-based organization, a given grassroots organization set its own agenda in an ad hoc fashion, i.e., according to the rising needs of a given sector.

Such a mode of organizing turned the grassroots organizations into collective agents of mobilization. Their characteristics and mode of activity made them practically invisible from the viewpoint of the Israeli authorities. The fact that they were an organic part of their environment with no fixed location and no fixed members made it impossible for Israel to eradicate them as it did with the National Guidance Committee, for example. Of this point, Frisch writes the following:

> The shift of gravity from institutional political activity to hundreds of committees ... reduced the vulnerability of the committees to Israeli crackdown and control. It was not only that the new leadership was less familiar, and that the committees' goals and agendas were more dispersed ... Legally, it was much more difficult for Israel to cope with these committees as they fused political action with public services.
>
> (1992: 57)

Beginning in 1982, the occupied territories witnessed the proliferation of hundreds of organizations and committees founded almost exclusively by local activists. Figure 3.1 illustrates the general pattern and structure of Palestinian mobilization, demonstrating its scope and depth.

A few points of elaboration are in order. First, the flow of the chart from top to bottom is congruent with the chronology according to which the various organizations were founded. Thus, for example, the Fatah founded the youth movement, and the youth movement founded the Union of Women's Committees for Social Work (WCSW). Second, during the Intifada an additional phase of organization took place, during which each committee founded numerous popular committees. We will elaborate on this organizational process in Chapter 5.

Third, as of 1982–3 it is accurate to use the term "sectoral movement" when referring to those organizations and committees that operated in the same sector of the Palestinian population, as they interacted frequently and started to put aside ideological differences. Indeed, during the 1980s a process of convergence among the various organizations and committees was slowly in progress, paving the way for a territories-based nationalism. The alignment of the Communists with the PLO in April 1987 was, in effect, a compliance with a prior alignment that had taken place within the occupied territories. Although a similar process did not occur between the Nationalists and the Islamists, seeds of collaboration developed between the PLO (mostly the Fatah) and the Islamic Jihad, prior to and during the Intifada.

Fourth, according to Litvak (1991), who studied the dynamics among the various levels of organizations, the leadership of the grassroots organizations may be labeled as "organizational leadership." Unlike various public figures and personalities (see below), these local leaders with their own respective organizational affiliation, while focusing on their own respective area leadership, played parallel roles throughout the territories. At times, Litvak argues, the same person acting as the head of a public institution was also the leader of a grassroots committee. As example, Azmi Shu'aibi acted as

**Islamists**

Both Muslim Brotherhood and Islamic Jihad mostly operate in the Gaza Strip. Both are primarily active on campuses, but also among women and children. The Muslim Brotherhood is a-political up until Jan. 1988.

**Nationalists**

**Communists**

Despite the contentious relationship with the PLO, and the struggle over the same constituency, the alignment of April 1987 provides the rationale for viewing the Communists as part of the PLO

An independent initiative for the mobilization of women begins in 1978. The initiators are young women, a portion of whom are students, with clear DFLP ideological orientation. In 1981 a split takes place within the organization, as a result of which other women's organizations are founded with different ideological orientations.

Numerous public institutions are founded with clear nationalist orientation, for the purpose of "state building", such as research institutions, newspapers, professional associations, and charitable associations.

**Palestinian Communist Party/Popular Front/Democratic Front/Fatah**
(Following the Lebanon war, a split takes place inside the PLO as a result of which each faction simultaneously operates within the same population sectors. In 1987, a reunion takes place, parallel to the one inside the occupied territories.)

Collaboration between the Nationalists and the Islamic Jihad starts in 1982, and continues all the way into the Intifada.

**Progressive Block/Union Block/Action Front/Youth Movement**
(PCP)      (DFLP)      (PFLP)      (FATAH)

| PCP | DFLP | PFLP | FATAH |
|---|---|---|---|
| **Women:** Union of Palestine Working Women's Committees **Workers:** Progressive Workers Block **Students:** Progressive Block of Students Association **Youth:** Voluntary Action Committees | **Women:** Working Women's Committees **Workers:** Workers' Union Block **Students:** Students' Union Block | **Women:** Union of Palestinian Women's Committees **Workers:** Progressive Unionist Action Front **Students:** Progressive Front of Students' Action | **Women:** Women's committees for Social Work **Workers:** Workers' Youth Movement **Students:** Shabiba's Student Movement **Youth:** Shabiba's Social Action Committees |

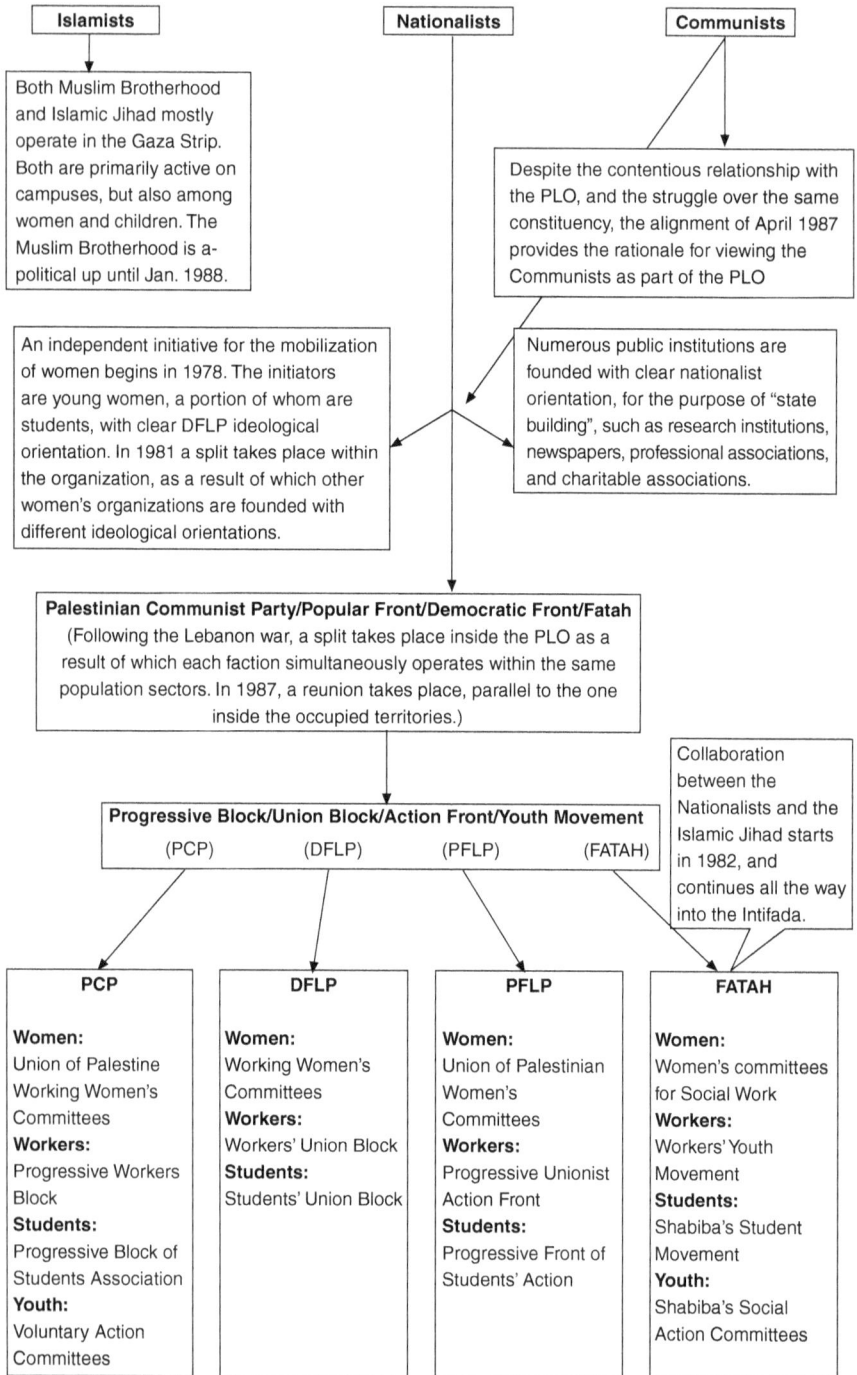

*Figure 3.1* Patterns of Palestinian organization in the occupied territories.

both chair of the Dentists' Association and leader of a DFLP-oriented committee.

Fifth, the Nationalistic Organizations were the dominant sociopolitical force. As of the late 1970s, the Fatah-led PLO changed its policy for the occupied territories by expanding its scope of mobilization into the social and economic dimensions. For example, in 1978 Unity Bloc's women activists, the central local branch of the DFLP, founded the Workers Unity Bloc (WUB), and several women activists of the DFLP founded the Working Women's Committees (WWC).

The growing dominance of the PLO was, according to both Frisch (1992) and Taraki (1990), a major factor responsible for the significant lowering of tension with the Islamic Organizations towards the second half of the 1980s, and the creation of a *modus vivendi* on the eve and during the Intifada. Still, such lowering of tension was in itself a result of the Fatah-led PLO's traditional policy of recognizing the importance of integrating religious elements into its national arch-ideology coupled, as will be elaborated below, with growing convergence of action-frame among local activists. Indeed, such an understanding between the two sociopolitical forces found expression in joint efforts of organization already amidst the War in Lebanon (1982), with the foundation of the Islamic Youth Association in East Jerusalem out of which two social work committees were founded.

Lastly, an additional component not included in Figure 3.1, largely because it is an individually-driven and not collectively-driven mode of organization, comprised of two groups of public figures. Despite the relative deterioration of their public status and influence, they are worth mentioning in brief. The two groups consisted of moderate elite members, mostly those same pro-PLO and pro-Jordanian public figures that enjoyed a relative increase in their public support between 1982 and 1986 (Sahliyeh 1988). This group of public figures may be divided into the Independent Nationalists and the Shakhsiyat (general personalities).

The Independent Nationalists were, in fact, public figures who had no formal affiliation with any of the PLO factions. They became representatives of the public because of the public position they held, such as Bassam Shak'a the pro-Jordanian mayor of Nablus or Hidar Abd al-Shari the chair of the Red Cross in Gaza. The Shakhsiyat were also public figures, but ones who did not hold any formal position. They were well-respected journalists, lawyers, and academics who acted as spokesmen of the population vis-à-vis Israeli and international media. Those people, such as Hanna Siniora and Ziyad Abu-Ziyad, enjoyed a relatively high level of public support as they were formally committed to the PLO. Nonetheless, increasing numbers of Palestinians towards 1986–7 started to view those two groups as "salon leadership," out of touch with the population, and, accordingly, with regard to the Shakhsiyat, refused to recognize their right as PLO spokespersons (Hiltermann 1991; Litvak 1991).

*Mobilizing the mass – the Labor Movement*

Thus far, we have familiarized ourselves with the two arenas of Palestinian mobilization, learning about the spectrum of the externally-based organizations and their attempts at mobilizing the Palestinian population in the occupied territories while simultaneously grappling with each other, and with Israel. The analysis then shifted to introducing the variety of local branches – the internally-based organizations – that, while initially founded by the externally-based organizations, started to act independently, thereby thickening and extending the organizational infrastructure in the occupied territories. Each of the internally-based organizations acted to mobilize the Palestinian population according to four main sectors: the youth, the workers, the women, and the students. Out of each sector emerged a sector-based social movement.

The discussion now shifts to an in-depth analysis of one of those movements: the Labor Movement. The analysis of the Labor Movement is a useful case study as it shows the gradual prioritization of national sentiments by an organization that, initially, had no political agenda of that sort. It is also representative: in spite of minor differences in style of mobilization, the other three movements went through similar processes.[5]

As observed above, first to organize Palestinian workers were the Communists, who centered their activities mostly in the East Jerusalem area as early as 1970–1. This fact, however, was not translated into wide public support, and their overall influence was relatively low. According to Frisch (1992), despite attempts to broaden their scope of operation beyond the East Jerusalem area, the Communists had little influence on sociopolitical dynamics when compared with the PLO.

Several reasons are worth noting. To begin with, the fact that the Communists centered their activities mostly inside the cities and in the East Jerusalem area seriously undermined any attempts to expand their operations. This fact unquestionably undermined their connectedness with other more distant Palestinian cities, villages and camps. Second, traditionally, the Communists prioritized the social and economic struggle over the political struggle. The fact that the West Bank and the Gaza Strip became highly politicized during the late 1970s, seriously weakened their public support. Last, but not least, was the Marxist-Leninist ideology they held and promoted. For many Palestinians in the occupied territories Marxism had scant chance of resonating with their conditions of existence, largely because the PCP refrained from political activism against Israel and maintained institutional ties with Israeli socialist organizations such as the largest Israeli trade union federation, the Histadrut.

The slow penetration of the PLO into the workers' sector brought about an intense struggle between the organizations, what Hiltermann (1991) labeled as "the War of institutions." The PLO's initiation of mobilization among Palestinian workers was an imminent threat to the Communists. Communist cooperation with the PLO during the early 1970s and their joint founding of the Palestinian National Front (PNF) had been possible in so far as the Fatah-led PLO had no intentions of changing its policy towards the occupied territories, namely opposing the strengthening of local political forces. The PNF was no threat in that sense. However, given the lowering of tension with the PLO, the Communists saw the PNF as an opportunity to increase their power in the territories (Daqqaq 1983). As it turned out, the attempt to use the PNF as a springboard for hegemony in the territories, thereby establishing an alternative to the PLO, was a major cause for the PNF disintegration. In addition to the shift in PLO policy concerning the mobilization of the workers, the fierce struggle mostly revolved around the issue of whether to accept or reject the Camp David Accord, and the resulting defection of many Communist activists to the PLO factions in reaction to the latter's rejection of the Accord.

As was the case with the three other sectors (i.e., youth, students, women), the PLO's operation within the workers' sector resulted in internal schism and the subsequent formation of other parallel organizations. When local activists realized, amidst the tension in the external arena, that they were incapable of promoting their preferred agenda, they moved to form parallel organizations. Accordingly, several local activists who favored the agenda of the DFLP founded the Workers Unity Bloc in 1978, an act that was imitated by other activists with different ideological orientations between 1979 and 1980. Communist activists founded the Progressive Workers Block, Fatah activists founded the Workers Youth Movement, and PFLP activists founded the Progressive Union Action Front.

Hiltermann (1991) classified the differences among the various organizations according to four themes:

1   Mobilization strategy according to different ideology (i.e., how much weight should be given to unionist-social goals in proportion to nationalist-political ones);
2   How to cope with Israeli policy in regard to the workers (i.e., what would be the appropriate reaction to closure of union offices or difficulties with registration of new unions);
3   The attitude toward the PLO's policy in regard to the promotion of the Palestinian issue (i.e., positions taken vis-à-vis the Hussein–Arafat agreement of 1985); and
4   The ways to cope with economic problems in Israel and the occupied territories (i.e., how to confront the rise of unemployment and inflation in the territories during the mid-1980s).

In spite of these differences, increasing the workers' commitment to a given union was the central goal promoted by all four organizations within the Labor Movement. In order to do this, the various grassroots Communist activists focused on providing help and assistance for the workers. These activists started to develop supportive networks for workers and their families, to learn about the specific problems workers were facing in their workplace, and to form special bodies aimed at securing workers' rights, such as hiring lawyers who would act to secure those rights under the Israeli labor regulations.

The following excerpt is taken from an interview with Sofian Sultan, the chairperson of an-Najah University employees union, published in an-Najah newsletter, in April 1985. I find it important to quote from the interview at length since it provides valuable insights into the structure of the workers' unions, their relationship, and their functioning in a specific locality. It is indicative also of the clustering of grassroots organizations around the action frame of "national liberation," on which I shall elaborate below.

Q:  How did the most recent elections to the union executive committee come about?

A:  Our union has 300 dues-paying members within the University. It is one chapter, albeit the mother, of the Union of Teachers and Employees of Universities and Private Institutions. Other branches are found at Bethlehem, Bir-zeit and Hebron Universities, as well as the Hebron Polytechnic. Under its constitution, the union must hold yearly elections ... There were then elections within the executive committee, which determined the distribution of posts for the coming year.

Q:  What relations if any do you entertain with sister unions in the occupied territories?

A:  We have some contacts, but unfortunately of a very limited nature [given obstacles raised by Israeli authorities], with the unions of other professional branches. But where the teaching profession is concerned, we maintain strong and ongoing ties. Our union is part of the central committee of the union confederation of educational branches.

Q:  What are currently your most important projects?

A:  We have ... been working on setting up a nursery and kindergarten for the dependents of employees ... we have finished establishing a health insurance fund, whose governing body has just been elected. We are in the process of finishing work on a club for employees ... Last year's establishment of a consumer cooperative for employees was an important step, and we are working to expand it.

Q:  Dr. Sultan, you are Assistant Professor of Biology ... Is this compatible with your union work?

A:  Science cannot be divorced from the society ... Working for the staff union means, most importantly, furthering the national goals of my people. Union work is national work. Without an independent Palestinian state, objectives such as job security, the freedom of academic endeavor, and the achievement of the employees' material, social and psychological well-being will never come to be.

Mobilization was straightforward. Grassroots activists would arrive at a given work place, talk to workers in order to identify who among them was not affiliated with a union, and, when that was the case, offer them services such as medical services, cultural activities, legal counseling in case of labor disputes, and participation in group support discussions that were usually taking place at the union's nearby office. Other grassroots activists would arrive at pick-up places for daily workers. Those places, called "slave markets," were fixed places where Palestinian workers would gather in order to wait for Israeli contractors in hope of getting a temporary job. The idea was to convince the workers of their rights and the benefits they would gain from joining a union, while not obligating ideological orientation as a precondition for membership.

An additional way to increase mobilization was a contest between union branches of a given organization for recruitment of new members. Such was the case with the "socialist contest" initiated by the DFLP-oriented Workers Unity Bloc between 1984 and 1985. The contest was, according to a statement by the central bureau of the Bloc,[6]

> An important event in the life of the Bloc and the trade unionist movement [and it was aimed] at making a qualitative change in the Bloc's size, role and effect ... it was known as "the campaign to recruit 2000 new members to the WUB ranks." The slogans were "No trade union must be left without a workers unity bloc" and "No workers unity bloc must be left without base units."

Yet it seems the factors most influencing a worker's decision whether to join formally or informally a given union or not, and which union, were familial and social ties. The fact that a Palestinian had a family member or an acquaintance affiliated with a given union was central to the decision, even beyond the material benefits that membership could offer. As we will see, the impact of non-material incentives was the more decisive, the stronger national sentiments became.

Tension between the grassroots organizations within the Labor Movement (i.e., comprising of the various local PLO factions and the Communists) was compounded for two reasons. The fact that as of the Baghdad Summit in 1978, the flow of funds from Arab States went directly into the hands of PLO and pro-Jordanian representatives in the territories was one reason (Frisch 1992), as only those who adopted a nationalist orientation, specifically, the Fatah's line, enjoyed ample funding. Unsurprisingly, Fatah's Workers Youth Movement enjoyed the most. A second reason stemmed from tempering of the Fatah-led PLO after the Lebanon War and the increasing inner tension between the latter and the leftist factions that, more than before, argued that a local leadership on the West Bank would serve the Palestinian cause better than the Fatah's plan to cooperate with King Hussein of Jordan.

Consequently, a similar development took place within the local institution that was aimed at coordinating the various organizations' activities and interests: the General Federation of Trade Unions (GFTU). The fact that each worker was free to choose his own ideological orientation led to a spectrum of ideological preferences within one union committee. And, since representation in the General Federation was based on the size of the membership in the various union committees, a situation where an individual union did not receive an adequate representation in the Federation, given its small size, was not infrequent.

Thus, amidst the external tension within the externally-based PLO and its projection on the local workers' Federation, local activists from the different PLO factions facing dominance of a rival faction and consequent misrepresentation of their favored agenda founded their own federation. For example, Fatah's activists founded the GFTU-Workers Youth Movement in 1981, and the GFTU-Workers Unity Bloc was founded by DFLP activists in 1986.

In short, although formal membership (i.e., union dues) of Palestinian workers in unions prior to the Intifada was relatively small (around 20 percent), it seems that informal ties with and general support for, or identification with, one of the various unions were at least three times greater. Such support, however, was not exclusively oriented towards a socialist agenda of the type of the Communist Party. Rather, it was imbued with strong nationalist sentiments. While the conditioning of funding by the PLO on the adoption of a nationalist orientation might have pushed trade unions to adopt, at least as lip service, a nationalist attitude, other factors played a more significant role in the rise of internally-based Palestinian Nationalism; this is the theme of the following section.

## The ascendancy of the local arena

The distancing of the PLO from the occupied territories, the attack on Palestinians in Lebanon, and the role played by Israel in the institutional vacuum as from 1982,[7] acted as a major impetus for the local, grassroots activists to take the initiative. Indeed, since 1982 the internally-based movements had been setting the tone of the contentious dynamics in the occupied territories.

In addition to the Israeli government's inadvertent role in this process, several other factors must be enumerated. First, the recognition among local activists that any form of public, hierarchical organization and leadership would not do by reason of its visibility and fragility vis-à-vis repressive military measures. The ease with which Israel cracked down the National Guidance Committee was an unforgettable, eye-opening lesson. Second, the grassroots activists, as elaborated above, were comprehensive in their mobilizing attempts; in effect, grassroots mobilization encompassed any locality, class, age group, and gender. Third, the Fatah's student movement managed to take over most universities during the campus elections of 1985/6. This achievement demonstrated that the power of the local arena was no longer necessarily contingent upon that of the external arena (Frisch 1992). Fourth, any political initiative undertaken by the pro-PLO and pro-Jordanian representatives in the occupied territories failed. Not only were those initiatives rejected by most of the population as they circumvented the interests of the Palestinians in the occupied territories (Abu Amr 1988), the Israeli introduction of the "iron fist" policy in August 1985 ridiculed any such attempt. Fifth, the collaboration between the Fatah and the Islamic Jihad unquestionably strengthened the competence of the grassroots level. Yet, this collaboration was, in itself, rooted in the growing awareness of the local activists of the damage the ongoing rivalry between the two camps had been inflicting on the Palestinian cause.

The collective experience of the various grassroots activists in the occupied territories contributed to such an understanding. The shared misery and hardship, coupled with the ongoing lack of any solution that would address the authentic needs and aspirations of the Palestinians under occupation, acted as a major factor in the growing autonomy in decision-making and strategizing by the internally-based movements. Such a development was already felt among members of the National Guidance Committee in the face of the PLO and Jordan's attempt to contain the influence of the former. Ibrahim Daqqaq, a member of the NGC, put it in the following way, "People in the occupied territories have a central position because they are the people on the land ... but this also means that outsiders [PLO and Jordan] want to influence their decision-making" (Daqqaq, 49, cf. Hiltermann).

This understanding became prevalent not only among public representatives, but also among the grassroots activists who favored the cultivation of resistance from within the territories. Hass (1996), who spent several years in Gaza and conversed with some of the Intifada's central activists, provides valuable insights into a collective mood that became widespread among the grassroots activists on the eve of the Intifada. The following is an excerpt from a talk she conducted with several members of what later became the united leadership of the uprising:

> All revolutions took place in the place where occupation exists, but in our case revolution is abroad, we came to the conclusion that leadership should be developed here, to found the PLO here ... we were convinced that the old leadership does not really want to fight the occupation and therefore should be pushed aside ... only the people of the West Bank could really make a difference ... we worked pragmatically, no permission asked, we learned from the Israelis to create facts on the ground.
>
> (p. 42)

Those activists came from all PLO factions including the Communists. Their approach, fully crystallized by the time of the Intifada, had started to emerge already during the mid-1980s. The grassroots activists pragmatically adapted themselves to their surroundings and situations by giving up on the armed struggle approach, encouraging coordination between the various organizations and committees, and initiating joint projects. By the time such an approach was adopted by the externally-based organizations and their local representatives, the grassroots "radicals" had already taken over the "Palestinian street."

The collaboration among the grassroots organizations of the various movements and between the movements was flowing. In 1984, for instance, the four main women's organizations decided to form an informal coordinating framework for economic and social activities. Thus, during a hunger strike of political detainees, the women's movement organized sit-ins of women and mothers in front of the Red Cross offices throughout the occupied territories – a joint action that was repeated in 1986. Another joint action took place in early 1987. During

International Women's Day, the women's movement used the symbolism of the event to mount a mass demonstration of their cooperation in East Jerusalem. Further, an example of the collaboration between the women's movement and a professional organization took place during Health Day in July 1987, during which the women's movement collaborated with the Palestinian Health Organization to provide free medical service and counseling for hundreds of people (Lesch 1990).

This trend of "national alliances" developed in all the other movements, and between the Nationalistic and the Islamic camps. In a statement published by the DFLP-oriented Workers Unity Bloc on 5 July 1985, calling for the first general conference, a call for uniting the various trade unions in the occupied territories were put forth together with an illuminating example of the multi-layer commitment of what was called the "trade unionist movement." After calling for Palestinians to be aware of Israel's plan to liquidate the Palestinian existence in Lebanon and of the dangers stemming from the Amman agreement between the Fatah-led PLO and King Hussein, and specifying the achievements of the union, the statement ends in the following way:

> All this in order to consolidate the national struggle against occupation and in order to reunite the PLO and preserve its nationalist line against Imperialism and Reaction [diplomatic initiatives with Jordan] as a condition to extract the historical rights of our people at the forefront of which come the rights to return, self-determination and set up the independent state. Long live the WUB first general conference; Long live our working class; Yes to trade unionist movement unity.

An instructive example of the Islamic Jihad's willingness to collaborate with the Nationalists can be found in the words of 'Abd-al-Aziz Awda, one of the central figures of the movement, during an interview he gave to *al-Fajr*, the Fatah-oriented daily, in August 1987. In this interview, he explains the convergence between the goals of the two movements: "We consider the central cause of the Islamic Movement to be the Palestinian cause. There is an inseparable connection between serving Islam and serving Palestine ... we respect the opinion of the mainstream and all nationalist groups since we believe that dialogue is the only means to reach mutual understanding."

Doubtless, the fact of occupation played a central role in this trend. In addition to the creation of a general atmosphere of rage and indignation, Israel's oppressive and repressive measures actually formed foci that, inadvertently, turned out to be a favorable setting for such a trend to accelerate and deepen. Such was the case with the Israeli prisons. Shalev (1990) argues that the numbers of Palestinians who served time prior to the Intifada reached the height of 25,000. Those prisoners, who were rehabilitated by the grassroots organizations and committees, played a major role in the Intifada, especially as they were highly motivated to fight the occupation.

Yet, Shalev neglects the function of the actual imprisonment from the viewpoint of the prisoners themselves. According to Taraki (1990), for example, Palestinian prisoners actually went through a process of politicization during the time they served. This process did not mean so much the development of political consciousness, as most of them had been imprisoned for actual or alleged political involvement. The Israeli prisons, for Taraki, acted as educational forums. The prisoners learned a great deal about Israeli society, learned additional languages such as Hebrew and English, participated in seminars and group discussions on political issues, and, for some, the prisons also acted as elementary schools for developing reading and writing skills.

An expression of this can be found in a petition sent to the Prisoners' Friend Association of Nazareth, on December 6, 1985 by the "Jenin Palestinian prisoners," who went on hunger strike to protest against the humiliating conditions they were experiencing. In the detailed list of general demands, they devoted a special section to education, where they demanded weeklies, journals, and dailies, notebooks, pens, and drawing materials, together with a table and two chairs for each cell. The petition ends with the call "Long live the prisoners' and oppressed peoples' struggle."

Severed from daily reality, yet also from the ongoing rivalry among the various factions and organizations, Palestinian prisoners became strongly attached to one another, and engaged in planning joint future actions upon their release. These friendships and mutual appreciation and respect were exported outside the prisons as the prisoners were considered symbols of heroism among the Palestinians (Hiltermann 1991; Taraki 1990).

It would be far-fetched, however, to assume Palestinian prisoners came back to a non-politicized setting upon their release from prison. The opposite was true. Signs of regrouping and in-group cohesion, but also of between-group cohesion were already on the rise during the mid-1980s. Abu-Shakrah (1986) argues that Palestinian resistance during the mid-1980s was characterized by mass, bodily presence vis-à-vis Israeli repressive measures, a tactic of resistance that contributed to the regrouping among activists from different organizations. The author uses an incident in January 1986 as indicative of such a trend. When the Israeli Knesset's Interior Committee came to the Temple Mount (Haram al-Sharif) to demonstrate Israel's sovereignty, escorted by the police force, hundreds of Palestinians tightly held hands, used their collective bodily strength to disrupt the visit, and forced the police to back off. Another example was the collective reaction to the arrest of 'Abd-al-Aziz Awda in November 1987. The arrest resulted in mass sit-ins by students from the Islamic university, and the consequent closure of the campus for two weeks. In addition to the sit-ins inside the campus, grassroots activists from every faction and movement, including Muslim Brothers, jointly demonstrated to condemn the arrest.

Israel's repression had strengthened Palestinian collective identity; it operated as a bodily and mental reminder of their shared circumstances in face of their occupier. The Israeli crackdown, Khawaja (1993) suggests, helped Palestinians to overcome social cleavages and rearranged previously factional groupings into a unitary whole, "Identification with those who suffer from repression creates unity and is, therefore, an important factor for such regrouping and the eventual crystallization of collective identity" (p. 66). Collective identity was indeed the product of both oppressive and repressive environments, as the following sub-section will demonstrate. Yet it was, equally, the product of grass-roots activists' initiatives that, while prudently maintaining the link with the externally-based organizations (Nassar and Heacock 1990), gradually developed the organizational infrastructure that would sustain the *willingness* to act contentiously.

### The formation of a territories-based nationalism

Of all three ideologies prevalent in the occupied territories as promoted by the various externally-based Palestinian organizations, nationalism became the most popular ideology among Palestinians under occupation. This is not surprising given the fact that, while tactically the PLO had steered clear of ideological rigidity in order to enable the existence of various factions within one organizational framework, nationalism was developed into an umbrella ideology that consisted of various ideological elements. Nationalism, as an ideology, provided the symbolic framework within which any Palestinian, regardless of his personal ideological commitment (e.g., Marxism or Islam) or concrete personal situation could identify himself.

Additionally, nationalism resonated better with the nature of the Palestinian situation in the West Bank and Gaza Strip. Indeed, Palestinians perceived themselves as part of the Palestinian people, part of the Arab world, part of the Islamic world, and many of them suffered discriminations and hardship, say, as workers. However, Palestinians in the occupied territories were first and foremost an occupied people. They were, to recall Daqqaq's words, the people *on* the land that experienced in body and mind an ongoing hardship. By not rejecting Islam, acknowledging the merits of leftist ideologies, and traditionally promoting the Palestinian distinct identity, PLO Nationalism resonated with most layers of Palestinian identity.

Then, too, measured against the sources of Palestinian grievance, the nationalist vision promised to address better the interlocking oppression Palestinians were experiencing under occupation. Primarily, the Palestinian grievance was one of an occupied national minority that was systematically prevented from defining itself as such. The nationalist vision suggested a diagnosis and a prognosis that consisted of a solution to all three dimensions of Palestinian grievance (see Chapter 2). The idea of self-determination meant a promise for the Palestinians' sense of belonging within their own land, ownership of property, a measure of control over their lives, and the ability to participate in and design their own destiny – all of which rested on an authentic Palestinian identity. Communism or Islam did not address the yearning for such an identity. Both offered transnational identity which could have been attractive had the Palestinians enjoyed a core identity of their own to begin with.

Indicative of the difficulties Communists were experiencing in promoting their ideology, and of their gradual acknowledgment of the importance of the action-frame promoted by the Nationalist Camp, is the following statement made by Adel Ghanem, the Secretary-General of the GFTU. Complementing the words of Sofian Sultan, the chairperson of an-Najah employees' union, Ghanem admits,

> This is a unique occupation. It wants to kick us out, while the British and French [as colonial powers] only sought to exploit. Lenin never imagined that a situation would arise where people would get together from everywhere in the world and throw out another people ... The situation here is worse than in South Africa, because there people are being exploited, but here they are being thrown out.
>
> (cf. Hiltermann 1991: 76)

Indeed, the Nationalist goal was far more tangible and acute than the ones offered by the Communists or the Islamists, as it stood for an action-oriented approach according to which Palestinians had the ability to improve their conditions *here* and *now*, and not when circumstances would be ripe, as was the case with the approach promoted by the Muslim Brotherhood. That is not to say Islam, as promoted by the Brothers, lacked credibility but, rather, that it lacked a prioritization of a Palestinian identity and situation as occupied people. This stood in contrast to the Fatah-led Nationalism that promoted the idea of Palestinian liberation as a prerequisite for any other regional agenda, insisting that a unification of the Arab world would come about only through the liberation of Palestine and not vice versa (Harkabi 1997). As we will see later in the book, Hamas, as an action-oriented, liberation-oriented offshoot of the Muslim Brotherhood, turned out to be a serious threat to the dominance of the Nationalist camp.

In that sense, the Islamic Jihad's approach was similar in that it promoted an action-frame that emphasized a distinct Palestinian identity: Islam was a faith of liberation, thus embedded within the occupied land. Yet the Islamic Jihad's ideology was problematic on two grounds. First, it called for a total, uncompromising transformation of the self – the type of commitment few could hold on to. Second, the mode of action promoted by the Islamic Jihad (i.e., terrorist activity) entailed sacrifice and risks that, again, few were able to bear. The popularity of the Islamic Jihad was high among Palestinians in the occupied territories, yet sympathy was not translated to actual broad affiliation (Frisch 1992).

Palestinian Nationalism, as promoted by the PLO, resonated with most Palestinians' layers of identity; most but not all. It gradually deserted also the exclusiveness of the armed struggle approach, a shift that made the PLO's organization more popular; more but not entirely. It was the appropriation of the PLO's nationalism within the occupied territories by the internally-based organizations that fully developed its potentiality.

The occupation of the West Bank and Gaza Strip, and the ongoing hardship that the Palestinians in the occupied territories were experiencing resulted in several important changes. First, the Israeli occupation practically isolated a major portion of the Palestinian people. Second, the PLO was a leadership in exile, prohibited from setting foot in the territories. Third, the ongoing isolation of Palestinians under occupation, as argued above, formed a unique collective identity born out of the injustice of the military occupation, the intimate contrast between them and the Jewish/Israeli population, and the slowly developed belief in their capabilities to alter their situation.

Being the people on the land, facing ongoing oppression and repression, meant that the collective identity of Palestinians in the occupied territories was embedded in the historical specificity they were experiencing daily. The PLO's nationalism held promise and hope. But, given the ongoing rivalry between the various externally-based organizations, the role Israel played in these contentious relationships,[8] and the ongoing absence of a political solution that would address their unique situation, Nationalism has been appropriated by Palestinians in the occupied territories (Hiltermann 1991), a process conceptualized by Sandler and Frisch (1984) as the "territorialization of the PLO."

Such an appropriation meant (1) a growing awareness of their unique situation and the need for a resolution that would address this uniqueness, (2) acknowledging the importance of forming a united front from all the various factions and organizations, even if only tactically, and (3) a recognition that the Marxist or Leninist ways, the armed struggle approach or the way of terror, would not do. In practical terms, such appropriation meant the collectivizing of the Nationalist action-frame: "an end to the Israeli occupation."

An indication of the growing centrality of this action-frame can be found in the words of Adel Ghanem, demonstrating the centrality of the national cause among the Communists: "We discovered that the danger from the occupation was greater than that from the capitalist ... So we wanted to help the national industries because this way we would also protect the workers. And so we decided to freeze the class struggle" (Hiltermann 1991: 63). The decision to freeze the class struggle took place during the mid-1980s, in the wake of the Lebanon War. Such an awareness as to the centrality of the national cause as the most pressing and joint goal of all Palestinians in the occupied territories was prevalent among Islamist activists as well. In an interview given to *al-Fajr* (October 25, 1987) by the father of Imad al-Saftawi, an Islamic Jihad activist, a stern critique was raised against those Islamic groups for their neglect of the national cause, and the need the prioritize the national cause above all others.

In December 1986, an Israeli military force overran the Islamic University in the Strip, arresting one of the Shabiba leaders. His subsequent detention in January 1987 led to massive demonstrations in his hometown, Han Unis. As Lesch (1990) observes,

> The soldiers and students played cat-and-mouse throughout the next month: students demonstrated against the occupation, soldiers tear-gassed the campus ... protests surged again in late May when the government arrested and deported a second leader of Shabiba. Communist and Islamic Jihad

students supported the protests. Even those connected with the Muslim Brotherhood were swept up in the demonstrations, despite their organization's hostility to Fateh.

(p. 14)

In concluding, grassroots Palestinian activists fully grasped the origins of their discontent and united around the ways to alleviate their grievance. Their shared experience under occupation, and the growing recognition regarding the threat to their existence as a people geared forward a convergence process. Such a clustering was the result of a shared understanding concerning the origins of their grievances and discontent (i.e., a structural oppression exerted by military occupation), the target responsible for their discontent (i.e., the Israeli authorities), and the way to remedy their situation (i.e., ending the occupation).

This chapter has attempted to analyze such processes and to point out the slow crystallization of a Palestinian collective actor in the occupied territories. Together with the preceding chapter, analyzing the inter-locking dimensions of Palestinian grievances, we are in a position to better comprehend the *why* and the *how* of the 1987 Intifada. But *willingness* to act contentiously and *readiness* to actually engage in and sustain contentious politics do not tell us why is it that mobilization to action surges with such magnitude during one specific historical period and not during others, and what are the reasons for the shift from short-term and sporadic incidents of action to a sustained, intensive and wide-scope action. Answering these two interrelated questions will be the theme of the next chapter.

# 4 The *when* question of the Intifada

Why is it, then, that, in spite of ongoing, intense collective hardship and systematic mobilization into organizational frameworks of resistance, the Palestinian uprising crystallized in the specific time context of 1987? In order to understand the overall pattern of contention between Israelis and the Palestinians in the occupied territories and the unprecedented leap in the magnitude of contention, as manifested in the 1987 Intifada, it is imperative to probe the effects of changes in the structure of political opportunities/threats inside Israeli polity on Palestinian strategy: the construction of shared perception regarding an opportunity to act contentiously by Palestinian grassroots activists within the occupied territories.

Analyzing the interplay between the internal Israeli political processes and the Palestinian political processes as manifested in evolving framing processes and contests during the 1970s and 1980s provides added value to the previous analysis of the Intifada. It provides a deeper understanding of the *why* question of the Intifada (i.e., the restructuring of the conflict dynamics as a result of the June 1967 war and the ramifications of such restructuring on the two conflictants), and the *how* question of the Intifada (i.e., the effects of long-term changes in state policy on the formation of a collective actor and on the collective actor's space of action and its strategy). In that sense, the analysis of framing is conducted as a historically embedded process aimed at examining how frames, ideologies, and power relations join to shape political discourse, one that supports participation in contention. In order to account for the *when* question of the Intifada, we will deal with five closely related questions:

1   What were the long-term effects of the occupation on the prospects of, and strategy for contention of, the Palestinian collective actors?
2   Simultaneously, what were the effects of the occupation on the internal dynamics of the Israeli polity?
3   What was the extent of Palestinians' familiarity with the Israeli polity in general and its domestic dynamics in particular?
4   In what ways, if any, did Palestinians interpret such domestic Israeli dynamics in terms of prospects for contention?

5  How did Palestinians' interpretation of these dynamics affect their decisions to *activate* mobilization for, and to select preferred strategies of contention?

## Delineating the Palestinian contentious arena

Students of social movements commonly distinguish two dimensions of political opportunities: *stable* and *volatile* dimensions. As discussed in Chapter 1 the *stable* dimension includes such factors as the strength of state institutions, strength of social cleavages, political cultures or belief systems which are embedded within political institutions and culture, and which change only slowly if at all. The *volatile* dimension consists of opportunities such as splits among elites, increasing access to the political system, elections or legitimacy, and public discourse. These types of opportunity structures shift with events or policies; they are more permeable to political actors' participation and influence (Gamson and Meyer 1996; Tarrow 1994).

Two additional distinctions within *volatile* situations deal with (1) *external* opportunities, that is, political, cultural or economic events and developments that take place outside the nation-state (e.g., war or regional economic crisis) and may affect the rise of challenges by internal political actors (Skocpol 1979; Oberschall 1996), and (2) *long-term/general* versus *short-term/issue or actor-specific* opportunities, that is, authorities' decision rules that may affect a social movement's prospects for, and strategy of, collective action (Tarrow 1994; Meyer and Minkoff 1997; Meyer 2004).

Each dimension is further divided into *societal* and *institutional* aspects. The entire mapping, however, should be seen solely as a series of analytical distinctions among various manifestations of opportunity structures placed on a continuum along which a more *volatile* aspect of opportunity structure (e.g., public discourse) can develop in time into a more *stable* aspect of opportunity structure (e.g., belief system), and vice versa. In like manner, an *external* opportunity (e.g., external war) may lead to an *internal* opportunity (e.g., shifts in political alliances), and an *internal* opportunity may, in turn, develop into an *external* opportunity. Finally, it is important to bear in mind that opportunity is meaningful only in relation to threat, and vice versa; opportunities and threats should not be seen as opposites. Both are meaningful only from the viewpoint of a deprived group and its specific social location, and the meaning constructed for both is always relational.

In light of the above mapping, Figure 4.1 presents a multi-variate distribution of various Israeli repressive measures (shown in lines) used against Palestinians in the occupied territories, together with data on what Israel labeled as "public disturbances" (shown in bars) that took place inside the contentious arena between 1967 and 1987.[1] I shall use the term "contentious events" as I find it to be more representative of the various types of actions and bias-free, as much as this is possible.

The data is telling for two major reasons. First, an interesting inverse relationship exists between the pattern of contentious events and the patterns of

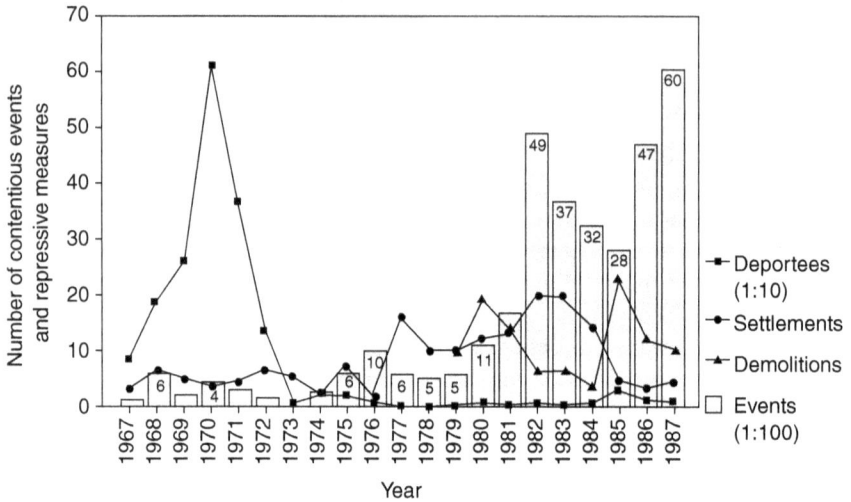

*Figure 4.1* Patterns of contentious politics in the occupied territories.

Israeli repressive measures. It seems that the number of deportees from the occupied territories is at its height when the number of contentious events seems to be lowest. The same goes for the relationship between the number of house demolitions and contentious events. Apparently, a decrease in the number of houses demolished during 1980–4 is followed by an increase in contention. At the same time, however, we see no such relationship between the pattern of settlement rates and the pattern of contentious events. As of 1980, it seems that an increase in the number of settlement events does not predict a change in the number of contentious events.

One possible explanation for such a mixed pattern may be found in Goldstone and Tilly (2001) suggestion of distinguishing between *current threat* (i.e., avoiding harms that are currently experienced or anticipated), and *repressive threat* (i.e., costs of repression if protest is undertaken). In that case, it is possible to account for the positive relationship between the number of settlements and the number of contentious events by treating the Israeli settlement policy as *current threat*. It is also possible to argue, as Khawaja does (1993, 1994), that this mode of Israeli repression resulted in a strengthening of Palestinian collective identity, sense of belonging, and identification with and commitment to social movement organizations, which helps to explain the increase in contentious events.

A second pattern that can be gleaned from the data, however, concerns the striking relationship between public manifestations of divisions inside the Israeli polity over the continuation of the occupation (e.g., Sebastia Settlement of July 1974 and March 1975, and the General Security Service of May 1986), which I label "crisis-events" to denote the deepening process of Israeli polity power deflation, and the pattern of contentious events in the occupied territories.[2] Table 4.1 illustrates the process of linking the conceptual types of political opportunities and the particular crisis-events in the Israeli context, and provides a brief introduction to the various crisis-events. I shall return to these crisis-events in the following section.

Using the climax period of Israel power deflation between 1981 and 1984 (Sprinzak 1995) as a referential point indicates a sharp increase in the average number of contentious events. Whereas the highest number of events during the 1970s reached 1,000 per year (1976–7), from 1981 onward the number of events does not fall beneath 2,000 per year, with a relative decrease during the "iron fist" policy, only to reach the higher level of over 6,000 during 1987.

The overall pattern is just as telling. The series of crisis-events in Israel reveals an interesting correlation between a given crisis-event and the subsequent level of contention between the two contenders. As of 1975–6, seen by various Intifada scholars as the beginning of Palestinian contentious politics (Mishal with Aharoni 1989; Tamari 1988) due to the fact that Palestinians within the territories rather than outside PLO forces started to set the tone of contention, it is possible to see a series of cycles, and that every cycle of contention seems to reach a higher level than its previous one. There is a gradual increase from one cycle to another, indicating a cumulative effect along the sequence.

Returning to Tilly and Goldstone's suggestion of distinguishing between two types of threat or modes of repression, and Khawaja's argument that Israel's increased repression only intensified Palestinian mobilization and collective protest, it is possible to argue that any type of threat/repression whatsoever must be considered in relation to opportunity/facilitation. It may well be that Palestinians experienced changes in Israeli policy for the occupied territories as facilitative, at the same time as they suffered repression. It may be also, as this book argues, that in spite of repression Palestinians have had a growing sense of an opportunity to act because of the series of crises Israel experienced over the issue of the occupied territories throughout the 1970s and 1980s.

In order to substantiate this argument we must engage in an examination of the type of opportunities structure relevant in the case of the Palestinians in the occupied territories. Specifically: *How did the re-structuring of the Israeli–Palestinian conflict, as a result of the June 1967 war, delineate the contentious arena? What were the relevant structures of political opportunities facing the Palestinians in the occupied territories? And, how did the integration of the occupied territories within the Israeli polity structure what became an internally-based Palestinian national movement?*

The Israeli victory of June 1967 resulted in long-lasting effects on the Israeli democracy's framework and contours vis-à-vis its Palestinian antagonist. The expansion of Israeli rule over the occupied territories and the Palestinian population within them shifted the conflict structure and dynamics back to an inter-communal one: two ethno-national communities within one territory. This was so due to the fact that the State of Israel was designed primarily and essentially to have a Jewish character, i.e., to be the state of the Jewish People.

Table 4.1 Operationalizing Israeli political opportunities structure

| Political opportunity | Operationalization | Crisis-event |
|---|---|---|
| Centrality of political system | Extra-parliamentarism | The unprecedented protest of military officer Moti Ashkenazi against the government (1974). The conditioning of military service, vocalized in the Officers' Letter, on Prime Minister Begin implementing peace with Egypt (1978/the foundation of Peace Now). |
| Depth of social cleavages | Political violence among collective actors | Assassination of left-wing activist Emil Grinzweig by right-wing adherent. (1983). |
| Implementation of collective goals | Challenges to authority decision rules | The forceful evacuation of the Yamit settlement in the context of Israel and Egypt peace treaty (1982). The violent struggle over the Sebastia settlement attempt by Block of the Faithful right-wing movement (1975). |
| Resistibility of the rule of law | Illegalism/social control | The uncovering of the Jewish Underground – Jewish terrorism against Palestinians (1984). |
| Strength of state institutions | Lack of legitimacy and trust | Peace Now demonstration against the war in Lebanon and the massacre of Sabra and Shatila (1982). General Security Service (Shabak) – Secret Service and high official involvement in the illegal killing of two Palestinian terrorists before trial, and the public uproar over the concealment of information and perjury during the work of the committee investigating the event (1986). |

Consequently, Israel has defined citizenship within its polity on an ethnic basis, as one mechanism for the preservation of Jewish collective identity and the Jewish character of the State of Israel. Other national or ethnic minorities, while they can be said to enjoy a certain level of civil and political rights, are prevented from expression and fulfillment of their collective rights or a fulfillment of civic duties, such as serving the Israeli army (Hofnung 1991; Peled 1993). Indeed, the dynamics of the conflict between the Jews and the Palestinians are, for Benvenisti (1992), the type of dynamics that characterize inter-communal conflicts:

> In the Israeli second republic a civil war takes place or, in fact – a communal war. It is an ongoing struggle that is not necessarily violent, between the majority Jewish community ... and the minority Arab community ... the dynamics of the Israeli communal war resembles that of inter-communal conflicts ... being conducted through an endless cycle of violence, enforcement, domination, and entrenchment.
>
> (p. 62)

As in every conflict, dynamics are the product and producer of interaction, a relationship of action–reaction and mutual estimation of each other's strength and power. The extension of Israel's domination over the Palestinian population, and given the unprecedented proximity that was reestablished between the two antagonists, resulted in two meaningful processes: a long-term opportunity for the Palestinians, and changes in the stable dimensions of political opportunities in the case of Israel. First, the Palestinians in the occupied territories gained the possibility to learn and to know the Israeli polity. Second, the occupation of the territories and the Palestinian population held within itself the seeds that developed into the Israeli *stasis*, namely, a deep conflict among the citizens that had a far-reaching repercussion on the stability and cohesion of the polity (Bernard 1980). For our purpose, the occupation of the territories and the consequent internal Israeli system-wide conflict over their future status resulted in power deflation that, as I argue, was perceived by the Palestinians in the occupied territories as an opportunity to activate contention. As we will see, the link established among Palestinians in the occupied territories between their conflict with Israel and the domestic Israeli divisions had long-lasting effects on their strategy for contentious politics.

The Israeli "fateful decision," to use Harkabi's concept (1986), to extend its domination over the occupied territories and, later, to integrate the Palestinian market with the Israeli one, brought about not only a change in the conflict structure. This fateful decision also acted as a catalyst for the process of Palestinian politicization of discontent, the development of a collective actor in the occupied territories, and, equally importantly, the restructuring of the relationship between the two antagonists. Thus the Israeli occupation turned out to be the fulcrum, to use Tarrow's wording (1994), of the would-be Palestinian national-social movement. Concomitantly, the Palestinians' space of action became, primarily, contingent upon the Israel military rule's orders and regulations.

The labeling of Israel's fateful decision as a long-term opportunity represents a shift in the structure from the viewpoint of the Palestinians in the occupied territories. This assessment rests on the following economic and political grounds. As we have seen, in spite of various Israeli acts designed to improve the living conditions of the territories' Palestinians, the latter had experienced a multi-dimensional oppression, such as restrictions over the right of association, freedom of movement, freedom of expression, and punitive measures against whoever was suspected of resistance activity. Nonetheless, by deciding to maintain its domination over the territories and allowing numerous Palestinian workers to enter Israel on a daily basis, Israel had practically enabled the Palestinians to gain first-hand knowledge of their occupier. In that sense, recalling Simmel's theorizing on conflict, the occupation provided the Palestinians with a chance to acquire knowledge about what was, to a considerable extent, initially an unknown antagonist, thereby establishing the basis for other forms of contention.

In an article dealing with the sociopolitical status of the Arab minority in Israel, Bishara (1993) contends that the 1967 War influenced the Palestinian issue the most, in that it placed Palestinians in direct confrontation with Israel. Hiltermann (1991) follows suit by arguing that the experience of Palestinians inside the occupied territories, especially Palestinian workers, is unique. This is so according to the author, given the physical proximity with the Israeli polity, which, among other things, enabled those workers to maintain their relationship to their land.

Yet, such physical proximity resulted also in additional processes. Unlike other Palestinians and Arab people residing outside the contentious arena, holding simplistic and stereotyped attitudes and opinions on the conflict in general and on Israel in particular, the Palestinians in the occupied territories gradually acquired a more sophisticated approach with regard to Israel and the conflict. In research conducted among Palestinian refugees as early as 1974, in an attempt to learn about refugees' attitudes towards Israel, Shamir (1974) found that such attitudes developed out of refugees' personal experience with their occupier. According to the author, while the entire Arab world consumes information almost entirely through the mass media located outside the occupied territories and totally expressing the voice of the given Arab ruler, Palestinian refugees can be said to have first-hand knowledge, which is a major reason for their less simplistic perceptions of Israel.

The fact of the matter was that the Palestinians in the occupied territories turned into "specialists" on Israeli society. They learned the essence of democracy, highly familiarized themselves with Israeli social and political institutions, and the values and norms upon which the Israeli society is founded. An Israeli news correspondent to the occupied territories provides his own account regarding the depth and scope of Palestinians' knowledge of Israel:

> Palestinians knew what went on inside Israel in great details. Israeli news were considered more important than Palestinian or Arab news ... as early

as 1968 *Al-Quds* had a special section on Israeli affairs called Israilyat that included editorials, and reports on daily developments inside Israel. Listen, when I am telling you they knew us from the inside I mean they knew more than you can imagine ... during the 1980s, I was amazed by the depth of their familiarity and understanding as they were capable of analyzing social and political developments in a very profound manner. What's surprising, if you ask me, is how little we knew them.

Indeed, as Shalev (1990) points out, among the younger generation the ability to speak and read Hebrew was prevalent. Such competence enabled many Palestinians to learn about Israeli society, becoming familiar with its strengths and weaknesses. In contrast to that, most Israelis knew little about what was going on beyond the "green line." With the exception of the security forces (i.e., soldiers, police or security service officers, whose social location and roles defined their learning), the majority of Israelis had no contact whatsoever with the Palestinians in the occupied territories; the occupied territories were perceived as a remote place that had no connection with the daily life of Israelis. Such uneven curiosity was reflected in the media coverage on both sides of the "green line." An indication of such imbalance, according to Rubinstein (1998), can be traced in the almost complete absence of translated Palestinian articles in Israeli dailies, whereas the proportion of translated Israeli articles in Palestinian newspapers was immense and dealt with almost every aspect of Israeli social and political life.

In short, the 1967 military occupation resulted in two intertwined developments. First, a shift in the conflict's mode from a latent, indirect conflict to an overt, direct conflict between Israel and the Palestinians, as a result of which Israel became the direct target of Palestinian discontent, and, second, an opportunity for the occupied Palestinians to know their occupier.

However, while a combination of political and economic considerations resulted in such a long-term opportunity structure, Israel's rule shaped the bounds of, and alternatives for, action available for the Palestinians. In that regard, Sharon's "strong hand" policy, the dismissal of several West Bank mayors, the abolition of the Gaza Municipality, and the expulsion of the PLO from Lebanon, can be said to have acted as a short-term opportunity for the internally-based grassroots organizations to acquire dominance in the Palestinian movement.

As it turned out, Sharon's policy practically eradicated the last moderating factor between Israel and the Palestinian population (Ma'oz 1984), leaving the stage for the increasingly influential radical forces. As can be seen in the quote below, grassroots activists were already speaking in terms of "we-ness," fully aware of their role in setting the dynamics of contention with Israel. Indeed, as of 1982, grassroots organizations took over the pace and tone of contention, realizing, as put most vividly by a Palestinian grassroots activist who was interviewed, that,

During the years after Lebanon, we understood that continuing to rely on Arab States or any other external force would lead us nowhere ... we must start to rely on ourselves, we are to decide what to do and how because we are the power of the Palestinian question. The PLO is not here anymore, and we should therefore concentrate on what is going on here and not elsewhere ... any assistance must be sought from within ourselves and not from the outside.

The fact of the matter was that an integration of the Palestinian population with Israel had never been treated seriously by the Israeli administration. At best, the practice was to speak of the territories as if no occupied people existed, and at worst, as promoted by extreme right-wing groups, Palestinians were to be transferred from Eretz Israel (i.e., the land of Israel in the biblical sense) to the surrounding Arab States. A full integration, or formal annexation, of the occu-pied territories was rejected for political reasons, which went beyond the con-straints of international law and conventions concerning the status of occupied land and the responsibilities of the occupying force vis-à-vis the local popu-lation. For instance, Kimmerling (1983) contends that the arguments against such an integration rested on political and economic grounds. Politically, a *de jure* annexation was perceived as a threat to the principle of a Jewish majority within the Jewish State. A full integration of the Palestinian population would also be economically detrimental, as the exploitation of the Palestinian market could not be maintained once Palestinians gained Israeli citizenship.

Under such circumstances, where the Palestinians in the occupied territories were systematically obstructed from any form of political participation in, and exertion of influence on, the Israeli political system, the *volatile* aspects of polit-ical opportunity structure seem secondary. Changes in elite alignments, elec-tions, or divided elites within the Israeli political system could hardly have had any effect (let alone act as an incentive) on a contentious strategy from the view-point of the occupied Palestinians. The fixation of the Palestinians as a perman-ent challenger situated outside the Israeli polity made the *stable* aspects of political opportunity structure (e.g., strength of state institutions, political culture or belief system) the primary viable option against which contentious politics might be directed.

Before examining the validity of such reasoning according to various voices within the Palestinian political media discourse, an analysis of the effects of the occupation on the internal dynamics of the Israeli polity, and the depth and scope of the Palestinians' familiarity with the Israeli polity's internal dynamics is in order.

## Cracks in the Israeli second republic

The Israeli polity post-June 1967 is labeled by Benvenisti (1992) as the "second republic," to mark the significant transformation in the Israeli State as a result of the occupied territories' informal annexation to Israel. Indeed, the Israeli second republic experienced profound changes, some of which this book holds as crit-ical to the Intifada's inception.

Given a structural setting within which an occupied national minority faces a "blocked opportunity" situation, to use Merton's concept (1968), the circumstances are ripe to trigger the impetus to rebel because they are rooted in the development of a stable opportunity structure in the occupier's arena. As we will see below, Israel's glorious victory had turned out to be a "pyrrhic victory"; the occupation of the territories resulted in a series of crises inside Israel, the type of crises that found their most profound expressions in the sociopolitical arena.

The seeds of the Israeli polity's power deflation can be traced to the euphoric and invigorating results of the June 1967 War, namely, the taking over of territories that were, and still are, considered to be by the majority of the Jewish People part of the promised land of Israel. Indeed, many Israelis perceive the hoisting of Israel's flag on the Temple Mount and the ability to touch the Western Wall, the holy remnant of the Temple House, as a divine sign of the return to the promised land of the Jewish ancestors.

Yet, with the occupation of the territories there surfaced also, this time with higher intensity, what had been an underlying tension inherent in the mere fact of founding a Jewish State: the politico-ideological cleavage over the territorial boundaries upon which the Zionist vision should be fulfilled (Lissak 1990). What had been a latent conflict for approximately twenty years (1948–67), given the unexpected taking over of the territories, turned into the most profound of sociopolitical cleavages in Israeli polity – the national-ideological cleavage over the territories' future status and the status of the Palestinian population within them (Horowitz and Lissak 1990).

The cleavage's poles can be said to reflect two positions and/or solutions: "the one next to the other," that is, a new division of Israel, west to the Jordan River, with the establishment of a Palestinian State, and "the one instead of the other," that is, deportation of the Palestinians and full annexation of the territories. Such a cleavage, as both Lissak (1990) and Horowitz (1977) suggest, was not a sheer political debate over security issues. Rather, it was, and still is, a conflict over the character, identity, and essence of the Jewish–Israeli State. Thus, while for some the occupied territories were to be used as a bargaining card for negotiating peace with the neighboring Arab States, others claimed the historical and divine right of the Jewish People over the Land of Israel – Greater Israel.

While the ideological conflict, despite few exceptions, remained bounded within the Israeli political system between 1967 and 1973 (Sprinzak 1995), the Yom Kippur War of October 1973 acted as a catalyst for the intensification of the conflict and its spilling over beyond the boundaries of Israeli parliamentary politics. During eighteen days, Israel suffered the loss of nearly 2,600 soldiers and civilians and 7,500 wounded, facing the most imminent threat to its existence by a joint Arab States front. That Israel was, eventually, successful in forcing back the Egyptian and Syrian armies from outside the Sinai Peninsula and the Golan Heights, inflicting serious injuries on both armies, did little to lessen the national trauma Israelis have been experiencing since then.

The October 1973 War represents a watershed in the history of the state.

Despite intelligence evaluations, the Israeli leadership failed to foresee the Arab States' military attack. This misjudgment threw into question the leadership's competence and credibility, a crisis exacerbated by the leadership's misconduct during the war per se; the October War, or, as it is labeled in Israel, "the omission," has illustrated, for some, the possible devastating repercussions of the occupied territories' "creeping annexation" (Lissak 1990). For others, the national trauma and void after the war were seen as a springboard for increasing the struggle for the ascendancy of a new Zionism, a religious Zionism, as an alternative to the state (Peleg 1997).

For the first time in the history of the Israeli State, protest movements and extra-parliamentary groups proliferated, questioning the government's basic competence and authority. True, such questioning was manifested also within the political system. Opposition parties raised profound criticisms that focused mostly on personal responsibility and misconduct on the part of the coalition. Yet, such criticisms abated significantly following the Agranat Investigating Committee's report on April 3, 1974.

Named after the Supreme Court Chief Justice, the investigating committee was established by the government on November 18, 1973, largely because of public pressure. After months of investigation, the committee recommended termination of the ministry of the military chief-of-staff David Elazar and several other high officers. The political echelon, that is, Defense Minister Moshe Dayan and Prime Minister Golda Meir, was found to be only indirectly responsible. Prime Minister Meir resigned from office as a result of public pressure on April 11, 1974, while Dayan was not included in the new government formed by Itzhak Rabin.

What had been unprecedented during the weeks following the war was the widespread criticism expressed by the public, which only intensified by reason of what were seen as mild recommendations in the committee's report. Right-wing groups (such as, the Cnaanim, the Movement for Greater Israel, and The League for Jewish Defense) and left-wing groups (such as Etgar [challenge] and the Clique for Sorting out Social and State Problems) raised a stern critique of the government's decision-making process, demanding full accountability for the failures.[3]

Essentially, the critique raised by these groups, however, was more far reaching than a mere democratic public opposition. To begin with, a large portion of the Israeli public, disappointed with the Agranat Investigation Committee's recommendations, was voicing a deep sense of estrangement toward the political system at large. Perhaps the strongest expression of this trend was the action taken by discharged military officers who protested individually (at first) in front of the government offices (e.g., Assa Kadmony and Moti Ashcenazi). In addition, and from the other side of the political spectrum, right-wing groups, with the Gush Emunim [Block of the Faithful] as their vanguard, argued that the state had veered from its course and needed to correct these acute aberrations. Viewing the situation as an opportunity to undermine the current secular state apparatus in order to transform it into a religious state (*Halakha* State), these groups considered the June 1967 War's results as a divine sign for the embarkation of redemption – *Athalata De'gehula*. It was God's will, and in contrast to the state's positivist law and the government's policy, to engaged in wider attempts at settling the "all of Israel" as was the case in Sebastia in 1975.

Rabbi Eliezer Valdman, one of the Block's leaders, provides a revealing insight into Rabbi Kook, the Block's central spiritual leader. He describes his attitude towards the Liberal-Humanistic tradition,

> [I]t is not according to Kant that he lives, but according to God's words: It is not to Kant that we shall return, but rather to the Dead Sea, to Sinai, and Jerusalem, to Abraham, to Moses, and David ... Kook's concept of progress are not humanistic, they belong to another spiritual sphere, divine-sphere, which may have an empathy to the humanistic morality, yet by no means subjected to it.
>
> (cf. Raanan 1980: 117)

In a systematic research on illegalism and extra-parliamentary phenomena in Israel, Sprinzak (1981, 1986, and 1995) stresses the systematic, persistent and consistent delegitimization and disregard of the law, which Gush Eminum's modes of action embodied. The essence of things, for Sprinzak, is rooted in the inevitable conflict between two legal systems: the secular state system versus the religious *halakhic* system. Thus, as opposed to the belief of several members of Knesset regarding their ability to control the Block's enthusiasm and zeal, reality proved the opposite. In fact, despite the election of Begin, who was elected Prime Minister in 1977 (hence ending decades-long left-wing Labor political hegemony), and the formation of right-wing government, the Block's fervor had not tempered.

Such was the case, for example, with the attempts at establishing a settlement in Alon Moreh. The headstrong attempts by Block activists to settle in Alon Moreh took place between September 1978 and June 1979 and the settlement was finally approved by the government to be located east to Nablus after deciding to confiscate the land on security grounds. The appeal by the Palestinian owners of the land to the Israeli High Court for Justice was accepted after the judges refused to accept the security needs claims. The verdict was unprecedented in terms of questioning the security considerations raised by the government.

As it turned out, despite Begin's declaration that "there will be more Alon Moreh," Block members intensified their acts of delegitimization and disobedience, especially during the Camp David talks of 1978–9. As argued by one of the Block members in an affidavit to the Israeli High Court for Justice, "The act of settling the land by the people of Israel is the real act of security, the most efficient and genuine. But the settlement itself does not stem from security consideration ... but out of vocation ... this is why the security argument, as serious as it may be, has no meaning for us" (cf. Hofnung 1991: 305).

Triggered by the Block's growing influence inside Israeli society and the "corridors of power," a countermovement emerged. A group of reserve officers drafted a carefully worded letter to Prime Minister Begin with a blunt warning: only a peace-seeking Israel that exhausted all possible means for attaining peace would continue to enjoy the support of its soldier-citizens, and thus be capable of standing firm and winning any future war forced upon it (Kaminer 1996). While avoiding any actual signs of disobedience, Peace Now [Shalom Achshav] set a meaningful precedent by which soldiers conditioned their military service on a moral basis, arguing that only unequivocal threats to Israel's existence would receive their full support and personal sacrifice, as future events would demonstrate (Barzilai 1987).

Undoubtedly, the seeds of delegitimization, estrangement, and illegalism sowed during the 1970s fully burgeoned during the first half of the 1980s. The Israeli sociopolitical arena during 1981–4 witnessed a series of crisis-events that reflected the internal conflict over the issue of the occupied territories, such as the evacuation of the Sinai settlements, the Lebanon War, the assassination of Emil Grinzweig, and the uncovering of the Jewish Underground. The intensity of crises during that period has led several Israeli scholars to label it as the apex of political violence in Israel (Sprinzak 1995), or the entire period of 1967–84 as the development of a national consensus of discontent (Wolfsfeld 1988).

As argued by Wolfsfeld (1988), who researched the rise of what was labeled as provocative non-institutional politics in Israel, "The rise in discontent between 1967 and 1984 had reached the point of a national consensus. The fact that such a high level of discontent has been expressed about both governments illustrates that these findings are not based on mere partisan sympathies" (p. 13). The findings to which Wolfsfeld refers are based on public polls conducted during the 1970s that showed a striking increase in the level of Israeli citizens' discontent with the functioning of Israeli government (8 percent to 81 percent), and to a poll conducted in 1984 in which 56 percent of the respondents expressed a negative attitude toward the political system.[4]

Indeed, the crisis-events unfolded between 1981 and 1984 brought to the fore with greater emphasis what Israeli law specialist Moshe Negbi conceptualized as the "conditional and selective obedience phenomenon" (1987). If an Israeli citizen supported or was indifferent to a governmental decision or policy, he would accept it. If he personally resented or disagreed with a decision or policy, however, he would violate it or support such a violation.

This phenomenon was not exclusively a right-wing practice. It seems several left-wing groups passed through the same radicalization process. In addition to various mass rallies and demonstrations against Israel's increasing involvement in Lebanon (1982) and its ongoing rejection of the Palestinian rights initiated mostly by Peace Now, other incidents revealed left-wing groups' willingness to cross the lines. During the Lebanon War, various incidents demonstrated the willingness of left-wing activists to "cross the lines" of the Israeli social contract's norms and values, and to resort to violence and vandalism. The Limits of Obedience corpus published by intellectuals gave legitimization to insubordination within the context of the fighting in Lebanon. The Sabra and Shatila refugee camps massacre accelerated this tendency, as did the case of the scandalous resignation of Colonel Eli Geva from duty.

While trying to restrain their actions within the boundaries of legalism, in line with their social status and political worldviews and beliefs, the contentious dynamics with Block of the Faithful that escalated Peace Now deeds (Peleg 1996, 2000). Block of the Faithful and Peace Now fought simultaneously against each other and against the government, whenever that the government appeared to act in accordance with the preferred agenda of one group or the other. This was the case, for example, during the Yamit Evacuation in April 1982 and during the military invasion of West Beirut in September 1982. On February 10, 1983, the tension between the two movements reached the point of brutal murder as one of the Block's supporters threw a grenade at Peace Now protesters marching towards the government offices in Jerusalem. Several protesters were seriously injured and one Emil Grinzweig, then writing his dissertation on the right to protest, died.

Combining two modes of action, right-wing movements threatened to undermine the cornerstones of Israeli democracy. From "within the system," right-wing movements worked institutionally, using the empathy of right-wing political parties, and the traditional support from the National Religious Party [MAFDAL],[5] which, given the structure of the Israeli election system, enjoyed a disproportionate political power relative to its number of seats in the Knesset. The "Thiya" Party, founded in 1979, entered the Knesset in the 1981 elections with several Block members who became MKs, and was another example of such an institutional mode of action. And the election of the extremist right-wing leader Rabbi Meir Cahana as member of Knesset in the eleventh Knesset (1984) was perhaps the strongest indication of the support right-wing groups enjoyed from a significant portion of the Israeli public.

On the non-institutional level and mostly within the occupied territories, right-wing activists were violating the law on a daily basis, using paramilitary vigilantism against the Palestinian population. The rationale behind their vigilantism rested on the claim that the military was not providing the proper protection against Palestinian attacks. Yet it was aimed also at intimidating Palestinians and forcing them out of the disputed land. For example, in May 1983 Settlers from Shiloh harvested and confiscated the crops of a Palestinian resident of the village of Turmus, claiming they were the rightful owners of the land. In addition, in July 1983 Settlers set a Palestinian public bus on fire in Hebron, in retaliation for a Palestinian attack on an Israeli car.

The seeds of political extremism sowed by right-wing groups, while rooted in their ideology and religious fervor from the outset (Peleg 1997; Sprinzak 1986), found their most lethal expression in the formation of the Jewish Underground, which demonstrated the most potent challenge to the state's legitimacy and to the law. The Underground's formation was a reaction to the peace agreement with Egypt (i.e., Camp David Accord), and indicative of right-wing groups' resentment of any government or administration whatsoever in particular, and Israeli democracy in general. Its members' principle and concept were "breaking the law for the sake of God in order to save the government, parliament, and the Jewish people from their own hands" (Negbi 1987: 131). The Underground engaged in terrorist activities against Palestinians, as was the case with the attempted killing of West Bank mayors in 1980, the attack in 1983 on the Islamic College in Hebron, and the abortive plan to blow up the Mosques on the Temple Mount. Shauli Nir, one of the Underground members, laid down his moral justification for the actions he participated in:

> Unfortunately the State of Israel abandoned its claim for a full sovereignty [over the occupied territories] and the enforcement of law and order, thereby creating a vacuum well used by the Arab public . . . under such circumstances the government has no moral ground whatsoever to demand from its Jewish citizens to give up on their personal security in the name of an unapplied law.
>
> (cf. Segal 1987: 159)

Although several members were brought to trial and sentenced to life imprisonment, it seemed that a broad sector supported the Underground's deeds and avoided condemning its actions. As the State Barrister Yona Blatman wrote,

> Not everyone who identifies with the underground's ideology would give expression to this identification or embrace their methods. Still, it seems that substantial portion, maybe decisive, of the population legitimizes its actions and regards its activists as "fine men," believing they should be released.
>
> (cf. Negbi 1987: 130)

As with the right-wing groups, various incidents illustrated the left-wing groups' lack of support for Israeli policy regarding the Palestinian issue. During the Lebanon War, their defiance was exacerbated, as evidenced by the 400,000-strong demonstration in Tel-Aviv in September 1982 protesting Israel's role in the massacre of Sabra and Shatila. Other examples include the organizing of Without Languor, a group of several thousand Israeli soldiers who rejected the war in Lebanon and called for insubordination; the group held ongoing rallies outside the Prime Minister's house with signs designating the death toll, updated daily. The soldiers' ambivalence toward the use of force spread to wider sectors in Israeli society, and was reflected in the mass media and academia. Indeed, the involvement of the media, academics, poets, and novelists, was demonstrated by their participation in protests and rallies, poetry, literature, petitions in the press, and plays (Barzilai 1987; Ezrahi 1997).

Increasingly aware of the ominous situation facing Israel, the National Unity Government of 1984 aimed, at least in principle, at reconstructing a new consensus for Israeli society. However, as Korn (1994) argued, the Unity Government was more the outcome of a political deadlock than a genuine effort at addressing the maladies ailing Israeli society. The fragile consensus was soon to be shattered against the background of the Jewish Underground members' trial, during which a public debate took place over the morality of the trial and the appropriate verdicts for the Underground members. In addition, the alleged involvement of high public officials, including the Prime Minister, in attempts to conceal the brutal killing of Palestinian terrorists (the General Security Service ["Shabak"] Affair) following the publication of photos taken at the scene proving the terrorists were still alive after Shabak forces took over the bus – resulted in a public uproar that seriously shocked the political, judicial, and security systems.

Ostensibly, it can be argued that the National Unity Government was successful in implementing its declared policy (e.g., the partial withdrawal from Lebanon in 1985, and the emergency program for the recovery of the economy).[6] Yet, the shattered Israeli economy and the Lebanon debacle were the substantial factors behind the formation of the Unity Government in the first place. The fact of the matter was that the preexisting ideological disagreements between the Likud and the Labor Parties had hindered any effort to initiate new policies for the most crucial issue that Israel had been facing, namely, the future of the occupied territories and the status of the Palestinian population within them. It was wishful thinking to expect the extra-parliamentary sociopolitical forces to withhold their action. In the absence of any potent opposition inside the political system, and in the face of the ineffectiveness of the government with regard to the issue of the occupied territories, the extra-parliamentary movements resumed their action with more zeal and tenacity. In fact, it was institutionalized by the movements themselves, and legitimized by both the public and the political parties (Sprinzak 1995). Paradoxically, the unified government only highlighted Israel's power deflation.

In concluding, as of 1967 Israel had run into a developing power deflation situation. The main expressions of such power deflation stemmed from the national-ideological conflict over the issue of the occupied territories' future status and the Palestinian population inside them. The manifestations of this conflict centered on challenges to the authority of the government, any government, weakening trust in, and legitimacy of, the system, and increasing willingness by a wide array of sociopolitical groups to disregard the rule of law and accepted norms and values of Israeli democracy. Consequently, Israeli governments, and again no matter what the specific ideological orientation of the given administration, found it increasingly difficult to generate and implement collective goals or to recover social control and reestablish trust in and legitimacy of the system.

## Knowing your antagonist

The depth and scope of Palestinian familiarity with the Israeli polity is astonishing, demonstrating general knowledge of and familiarity with a range of issues and with the manifestations of Israeli power deflation. It seems that the Palestinians' eagerness to know what was going on in Israel was profound. The fact of occupation and the ongoing uncertainty and lack of control Palestinians experienced acted as a central factor in developing a "need to know." Interview material provides useful insights into this process.[7] According to a Palestinian journalist who was interviewed: "Palestinians put a lot of effort in gaining information of what was going on in Israel; it became almost a "natural" interest of the occupied to know its occupier ... an interest that evolved into a need." Another Israeli interviewee provided the following rationale, saying

> I think that their situation as occupied people led Palestinians to understand how crucial it is to know. Gaining information reduces the uncertainty they are in ... that was a major reason for the interest in learning Hebrew. Hebrew helps you not only in better getting along in Israel, but also in understanding what's going on around you.

Indeed, familiarity with Hebrew, mostly among the younger generation, was an important factor in the accumulation of first-hand information. This process was conducted in two ways: on the inter-personal level and on the mass media level. On the inter-personal level, information came from Palestinian workers inside Israel, prisoners, truck drivers, and Israeli Arabs who arrived at the territories. On the mass media level, Palestinians were earnest users of radio (especially among the illiterate), newspapers, and television (by those who could afford a television set).

Information about Israel came also from Arab radio stations, newspapers and TV programs. However, the majority of Palestinians gradually favored consuming Palestinian dailies, PLO radio broadcasts from exile,[8] and Israeli media. According to an Israeli interviewee who acted as a news correspondent in the occupied territories, "Palestinians in the occupied territories looked for reliable sources of information free from propaganda and indoctrination. Such interest led them, at times, to purchase Israeli papers and watch Israeli programs, and to compare between Israeli and Palestinian sources."

Still, such a flow of information was partial, as a significant portion of Palestinians in the occupied territories, despite an impressive relative improvement during the 1980s, were capable of neither reading nor writing. This fact should not, however, be considered as a hindrance to news circulation, given the Palestinian oral culture. By using oral methods of communication, such as collective sharing of news and discussions, the distribution of information was efficient and unstoppable. Thus, in public places such as town quarters, cafes or teahouses, community clubs, cinemas, and hotels, depending on the specific social strata to which the gatherers belonged,[9] Palestinians shared the news collectively. They discussed recent events, listened to the radio, and read newspapers collectively, a social practice labeled by Longrigg and Stoakes "newspaper recital" (1970).

News was circulated also by teachers, lecturers, and students acting as traveling agents who, through their jobs or social roles, would move from one town/village to another and share the recent news with others. Last, but not least, in some newspapers distributed in the territories there was a particular section dealing with Israeli society and the political system.

The average Palestinian, say in Nablus, was well informed about and attentive to what was taking place within Israel – his occupier and target of discontent. Palestinian newspapers were deeply preoccupied with a variety of aspects
and issues of the Israeli sociopolitical arena (Shinar and Rubinstein 1987),
acting as a primary source for acquiring information about Israel, whereas for
information about what was going on in the occupied territories the Palestinian
newspapers were an after-the-fact source, used mostly for their analyses of
recent events.

To what extent, if any and in what ways did such coverage frame the
domestic Israeli crises-events? To get some sense of the extent to which
the Palestinians were aware of domestic Israeli events and developments and the
ways these occurrences were thought of, I conducted a content analysis of articles that were published in three central Palestinian dailies between 1974 (the
period when all newspapers operated on a daily basis) and 1987 (the onset of the
Intifada). A first step in the analysis of the newspapers' content focused on two
key questions: *were those crisis-events considered an issue*, and *of what type*?
Each question was treated by examining several aspects seen as representing the
nature and content of the Palestinian media discourse (i.e., amount and quality
of coverage) while paying attention to both changes over time and variations
among the different newspapers.

Three daily newspapers were used: *a-Sha'ab* (The People) representing the
radical factions inside the PLO, the Fatah organ *al-Fajr* (The Dawn) representing the more conservative factions inside the PLO, and the traditionally pro-
Jordanian *Al-Quds* (Jerusalem).[10] All three were published and distributed within
the occupied territories and/or East Jerusalem. They were also the most widely
distributed and circulated newspapers in the territories with an overall distribution of approximately 35,000 readers per day (Najjer 1994).

The proportion of stories and space given to Israeli crisis-events are presented
in Figure 4.2. The results offer a helpful summary of the amount of media attention given to the various Israeli crisis-events.

Of the 188 articles sampled, eighty-five articles dealt with Israeli crisis-
events, sixty-seven did not, and thirty-six were considered as "unclear" as they
dealt with issues and events that had only an indirect link with the given crisis-
event. Thus, an article dealing with tension between Settlers and Palestinians
near Nablus due to a settlement attempt seen by the Israeli government as
illegal, was treated as "reference." However, when an article contained no reference to the Israeli government's view of the settlement attempt, it was treated as
"unclear." Such a distribution does not tell us a great deal, however. After all, it
is plausible that a heavier Israeli repression would result in tougher censorship
over the newspapers' coverage, as was the case during the early 1980s following
Defense Minister Sharon's introduction of heavy repressive measures to dimin-
ish the PLO presence in the region.

Of importance is the distribution of cases among the three newspapers and
over time i.e., the sequence of crisis-events. In terms of distribution among the
newspapers, *a-Sha'ab*, the more radical PLO-politically oriented newspaper,

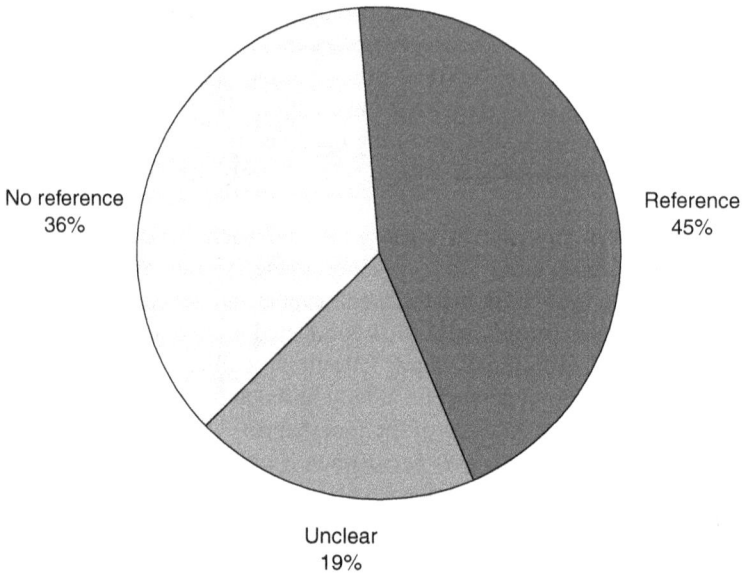

No reference
36%

Reference
45%

Unclear
19%

*Figure 4.2* Palestinian media attention to Israeli crisis-events from 1974–86.

with seventy-six articles dealing with Israel, has the largest portion of articles that make direct reference to crisis-events. *Al-Quds*, the traditionally pro-Jordanian, and *al-Fajr*, the PLO-Fatah news organ, present a similar portion of such references. Revealingly, however, *al-Fajr* has a larger portion of articles (40.3 percent) with no reference whatsoever to the crisis-events in comparison with *Al-Quds* (30.9 percent). As we will see, this pattern is consistent throughout the analysis below; it seems that the newspaper's coverage reflects the remoteness of the Fatah-led PLO and the fact that throughout most of the twenty years of occupation the occupied territories had not been the Fatah's sole and prime focus of attention.

When the amount of attention is examined over time, the results of which are presented in Figure 4.3, it is possible to get a better sense of how the media attention varies along with the Israeli crisis-events. Interestingly, the portion of "unclear" reference steadily decreases along the various crisis-events. As one moves in time towards the Intifada, the portion of articles dealing with crisis-events directly and explicitly increases. This pattern is even more pronounced regarding the articles with no reference at all.

An additional way to learn about the amount of media attention was through asking which of the various Israeli crisis-events (treated as various aspects of opportunity structure) received more coverage. The results of this analysis, presented in Figure 4.4, offer a closer view of how the newspapers' attention is divided by the various types of sociopolitical issues/opportunity structures inside Israel. For example, "foreign policy" (corresponding to "external opportunity")

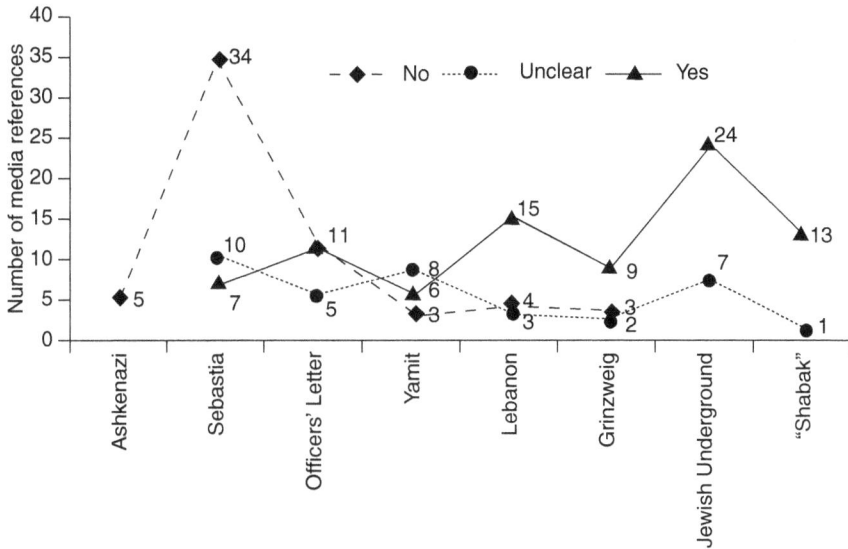

*Figure 4.3* Palestinian media reference to Israeli crisis-events over time.

denotes (and was coded accordingly) a threat of war against Israel or diplomatic issues.

Evidently, domestic Israeli sociopolitical issues receiving the most extensive coverage in all three newspapers are Israeli difficulties with "social control" (e.g., over the issue of illegal settlements), with "collective goals" (e.g., the struggle over the evacuation of Yamit), and with "legitimacy and trust" (e.g., public protest over the Lebanon War and the Shabak Affair). Of importance to note is that while the category of social cleavages shows few column inches this is not entirely representative. Interestingly, almost all articles dealing with the assassination of Emil Grinzweig framed the incident as an issue of "legitimacy and trust," hence coded as such. Also revealing is the relatively small amount of coverage for the categories "political system" (with the exception of *a-Sha'ab*) and "foreign policy." Clearly, manifestations of parliamentary struggles, threat of war against Israel, and international pressure on Israel regarding the occupied territories, integral parts of several crisis-events including the Shabak Affair and the Lebanon War, were considered less newsworthy. It is not only that "political system" issues or "foreign policy" issues received less space. In fact, they were considered less significant from the Palestinian point of view. A Palestinian journalist who was interviewed argued accordingly:

> You have to understand ... we were, as journalists, less interested in news about the possibility of political accords such as the Jordanian Confedera-tion. We were much more interested in covering events and occurrences where critique and challenges were raised against your government.

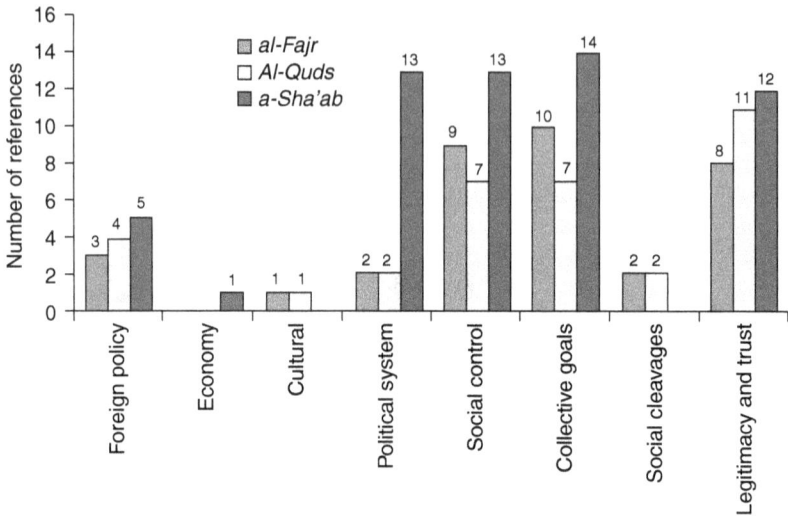

*Figure 4.4* Reference to Israeli sociopolitical issues by newspapers.

An example of this can be found in an *a-Sha'ab* article from March 8, 1978, entitled "The Settlement Swirl," that deals with tension inside Prime Minister Begin's government caused by two developments. First, Defense Minister Weitzman threatened to resign from office in protest at the government's policy toward the settlements. The second development that exacerbated tension inside Begin's government was the pressure exerted by the US Administration on Begin's government to stop the settlements in the occupied territories. After describing these, the article goes on to reveal a much deeper analysis of the issue. After delineating Weitzman's threats to resign, the article deals with the Officers' Letter in the following way,

> The objection to the settlements goes far beyond the U.S. administration ...
> we hear these days of a sensitive sector among Israelis that condemns the
> settlement policy, and thinks it is a hindrance to just peace in the region.
> The letter sent by 300 reserve military officers and soldiers ... is the ulti-
> mate proof of our just cause.

These findings, based on the interviews and the content analysis, suggest that the Palestinians in the occupied territories were highly attentive to the Israeli sociopolitical scene. Such attentiveness was facilitated and nurtured through a variety of communication channels of which the Palestinian print news media acted as a central source of information gathering and dissemination. Concomitantly, the analysis of the Palestinian print news media reveals a deep interest in, and accurate "readings" of the internal Israeli power deflation when translated into various aspects of opportunity structure. Specifically, were one to ask, "*Was there an issue?*" and "*What was the issue?*" from the viewpoint of the Palestinians in the occupied territories, as reflected in the news media discourse, clearly the understanding of the nature and sources of Israel's power deflation is accurate. This is true for all three newspapers, whose coverage shows over time a gradual increase in attentiveness to the developing Israeli power deflation. However, diagnosis is one thing and prognosis is another thing; analyzing how the Palestinian media discourse answered the question, "*How should one think about the issue at hand?*" will be the focus of the following section.

## Constructing political opportunity

Throughout the twenty years of occupation, the Palestinians in the occupied territories had experienced Israeli policy as "carrots and sticks," mixed measures of facilitation and repression. As specified in previous chapters, Israel's policy for the occupied territories and for the Palestinian population within the territories, involved rules of governance that, on the one hand, aimed at improving the lives of the Palestinians so as to promote a Palestinian acquiescence with its rule. The opening of the Israeli market to Palestinian workers or the unprecedented ruling of the Supreme Court's President Shamgar allowing Palestinians access to the Israeli High Court for Justice (Hofnung 1991), represented such policies of facilitation. On the other hand, however, the Israeli government also initiated policies aimed at repressing any sign of resistance; the unbending policy of Defense Minister Sharon between 1981–2 represented this tendency.

It is true also, that some of the facilitative measures were the result of international pressure, based on international law (e.g., The Hague Regulations 1907 and the IV Geneva Convention 1949). This pressure was intended to prevent Israel from unilaterally annexing the West Bank and the Gaza Strip. Traditionally perceiving itself as a member of the international community, Israel realized that a change in the juridical status of the occupied territories would be considered a violation of international law. In order to comply with international treaties regarding the responsibilities of the occupying force it had to enable the occupied population to create its own institutions and to observe the humanitarian provisions of the Convention (Hofnung 1991). As such, and in order to appear as an "enlightened" occupier, Israel enabled the establishment of academic and media institutions, put up with the flow of PLO funds to the territories, and embraced the idea of "personal autonomy" (i.e., autonomy to the Palestinian population and not to their territory) for Palestinians in the occupied territories during the Camp David Accord of 1978–9.

Yet, such facilitative aspects, no matter their causes, had hardly any effect on the Palestinian sense of an opportunity to trigger contention, as they neither changed the blocked opportunity situation the Palestinians faced nor promoted a genuine resolution to the Palestinian situation, one that would have directly addressed the interests and aspirations of the occupied Palestinians. It was not only that diplomatic initiatives (e.g., the Jordanian Option or the Reagan Plan) were rejected. In fact, as Benvenisti argues, international pressure on Israel was, at best, limited to condemnations of the type that Israel had previously systematically ignored. As it turned out, the lack of international sanctions against Israel and the perpetuation of the occupation resulted, ironically, in a situation where any such condemnation came to be perceived by Israel as an interference with its internal affairs (1992: 56).

In order to grasp the dynamics of contention in the territories by a predetermined challenger, the Palestinians in the occupied territories who had no part to play in the Israeli political system, we should move beyond exploring policy measures of repression or facilitation, as both Beitler (2004) and Frisch (1996) suggest, to review changes in the existing power relations inside the Israeli polity. It was these changes that, to a large extent, affected Israeli policy toward the occupied territories.

Palestinian media attention to the Israeli arena and to sociopolitical developments that took place inside the Israeli political system has already been demonstrated in the previous section, showing the prominence of issues such as lack of legitimacy and trust, difficulties in implementing collective goals, and deterioration in capacity for social control, in the newspapers' coverage. It is crucial, then, to move beyond an analysis of the amount of media attention to the quality of media coverage, to ask:

1   In what ways did the Palestinian newspapers frame the overall Israeli internal conflict?
2   Was there any link made between Israeli internal conflict and the Palestinian situation?
3   And, which of the various manifestations of the Israeli internal crisis was framed as favorable to the Palestinian situation?

### *Jews against Jews*

Palestinian journalists made a clear distinction between their impressions of Jewish solidarity during the 1970s and during the 1980s. While impressed by the cohesion of Israeli society during the 1970s, by the early 1980s, Palestinian journalists and their readers became aware of the disintegration of such solidarity. The following excerpt from one of the interviews conducted with a Palestinian who acted as the editor of a Palestinian daily illustrates the growing perception among the Palestinians that domestic divisions over the continuation of occupation were affecting the inner cohesion of Israeli society,

> We understood that your soldiers were afraid as many people in Israel disapprove of their actions ... in the past, each time we did something you disagreed with, we were bitten and even got shot, but later we noticed soldiers were more careful in their reactions ... [asked to clarify what he meant by "in the past"] ... At the beginning of the occupation you were united, we believed Jews do not fight each other, but back each other. But then we recognized that you started to hurt each other and fight over how to behave

with Palestinians and what to do with the territories ... you remember what a mess you had after two Palestinians got shot near the bus around Tel-Aviv and the ongoing scandal over the issue of the settlements inside the territories.

The content analysis described above offers important evidence about the shift in Palestinian shared perception of Israel's internal cohesion, as represented by the three newspapers. Accepting 1981–4 as the most contentious period inside the Israeli sociopolitical arena, during which the most severe manifestations of the system's power deflation occurred (Sprinzak 1995), I classified the various crisis-events accordingly and examined how the three newspapers framed Israel's cohesion across three time periods.

The results in Figure 4.5 show an interesting pattern. While during the 1970s all three newspapers, despite slight differences, framed Israel as enjoying relative social cohesion, it is clear that all three drastically shifted their framing to Israeli divisions during the period 1982–3. Compared with the framing of the 1970s it is evident that the framing of Israeli disunity during 1984–6 is higher in the coverage of all three newspapers. Despite various crisis-events during the 1970s, such as the unprecedented challenge posed by the Block of the Faithful to the government over the settlement in Sebastia (1974 and 1975), and the Officers' Letter, Palestinians nonetheless perceived Israel during 1974–8 as still enjoying a climate characterized by solidarity and unity. However, the framing of events in 1982–3, such as the Yamit Evacuation, the mass protests over the Lebanon War and the assassination of Emil Grinzweig marks a significant shift. The dominance of articles that convey a disunity framing continues throughout the third period, 1984–6, during which the uncovering of the Jewish Underground and the Shabak Affair took place. Clearly, such crisis-events, regardless of their nature and content, were gradually framed as significant manifestations of discord and disunity inside Israeli society over time.

Thus, for example, following the Sebastia events the newspapers' framing of

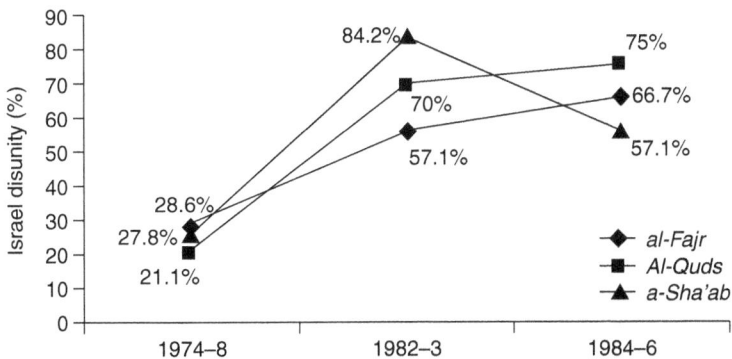

*Figure 4.5* Perception of Israeli disunity by newspapers by time.

Israel's cohesion tended to convey a united image of Israeli society. However, following a similar event such as the uncovering of the Jewish Underground, in the sense that both reflected the activities of pro-occupation Israeli sociopolitical forces, Palestinian newspapers focused on the disunity and lack of solidarity inside Israel. To illustrate such a cumulative pattern, the following two excerpts are taken from the same newspaper. While the first (*al-Fajr*, July 28, 1974) demonstrates a framing of Israel as united, the other (*al-Fajr*, April 22, 1982) provides an example of a disunity framing.

### Wave of protest spurs inside the occupied lands
*Against the settlement attempts in the Nablus area*
Anger and rage intensified yesterday as a group led by Begin, Sharon, and other members of Knesset arrived at Sebastia ... Numerous cars and buses arrived at the area with dozens of Jews aboard ... The number of extremists who plan to settle in Sebastia approximates four thousand people.

### The evacuation of Yamit has begun
*Kahana arrived at the site to sympathize with his followers*
Yesterday afternoon operation "red dove" started, an operation designed to evacuate the Jewish extremists from the Yamit settlement. The Israeli military radio announced soldiers will have to use ladders in order to force their way into the houses in which the strong-holders have concentrated ... the extremists are reacting with violence, and throwing stones and sand bags at the soldiers.

Clearly, while the first article emphasized the parliamentary support for the Settlers' actions and included no reference to opposition to those actions, the second article focused exclusively on the violent resistance to the evacuation of Yamit.

Interestingly, however, in the case of *a-Sha'ab* we see a decrease of such framing when comparing the 1982–3 and 1984–6 periods. While the 1984–6 period still contains a higher portion of disunity framing than in the 1974–8 period, one would expect *a-Sha'ab*, known as representing a more radical, hard line inside the PLO to present a higher portion of Israeli disunity framing during 1984–6 compared with the other two newspapers.[11] How can we account for such a mixed pattern?

Three possible explanations may be offered. First, on the face of it Israel demonstrated a higher solidarity as of 1984 with the formation of the Unity Government. While such unity was fragile and artificial, it surely had an impact on the newspapers' coverage in comparison to the previous period of 1982–3. Indeed, there was a significant decrease in violence between Israelis during this period (Sprinzak 1995). Additionally, *a-Sha'ab*, unlike *Al-Quds* and *al-Fajr* demonstrated a higher interest in the Israeli political system (see Figure 4.4). Second, compared to both *a-Sha'ab* and *Al-Quds*, *al-Fajr*'s framing presents a less differentiated distribution across the three time periods. It may well be that the Fatah-led PLO expulsion from the region as of 1982 by Israel influenced the coverage of *al-Fajr* in such a way that it portrayed Israel as relatively united. This might have been a tactic designed to intensify senses of grievance and solidarity among Palestinians in and outside the territories.

The practice of conveying an image of Israel as homogenous might provide a third closely related explanation for the relative decrease in *a-Sha'ab*'s framing of Israeli disunity and the more moderate increase of such framing during 1982–3 and 1984–6 by *al-Fajr* and *Al-Quds*. At times of increased repression, as was the case during 1985, for example, such a tactic strengthens a sense of belonging and "we-ness" vis-à-vis the occupier. This insight surfaced during one interview with a Palestinian grassroots activist who, when asked whether Palestinians were aware of Israeli groups' struggle against the occupation, recalled,

> We were very much aware of the various factions and groups inside Israel ... hearing news about Israel helped us in that regard ... Such awareness mostly focused on the way you vary in regard to what to do with the territories. You should not be misled to think otherwise despite the fact we usually spoke as if we thought of you as monolithic ... strategically we understood that viewing you as such would be a mistake.

It is clear, then, that Palestinian framers and readers, as demonstrated in the content analysis and supported by the interview material, were highly aware of the disintegration of Israeli unity and solidarity, mindful of the detrimental effects the domestic divisions over the continuation of occupation had on "Israeliness." It is to this linkage between the Israeli internal conflict and the Israeli Palestinian external conflict that we now turn.

### *A perceptual linkage*

As indicated in the first article from *al-Fajr* (above), Palestinians had realized the interplay between the two conflict cycles – the Palestinian–Israeli and the domestic Israeli divisions. In fact, in all crisis-events the Palestinian newspapers' coverage made such a link. The proportion of articles where such a link was made is represented in Figure 4.6. To get a more nuanced view of how such a linkage varies with changing political circumstances, the crisis-events are presented in their concrete manifestations.

Extremely revealing is the growing proportion of articles that link internal Israeli events and developments and the Palestinian situation (i.e., Palestinian reaction to the events or the events' effects on Palestinians) as we move along the series of crisis-event episodes. Between 1974 and April 1982 (the Yamit evacuation), the first manifestation of the Sebastia crisis-event (July 1974) is the only incident during which the newspapers' coverage involves such a link in a meaningful manner. An insignificant portion of such links represents coverage of crisis-events such as the Officers' Letter (March 1978), initiated by Israeli actors opposing occupation. In fact, in March 1978, a considerable proportion of

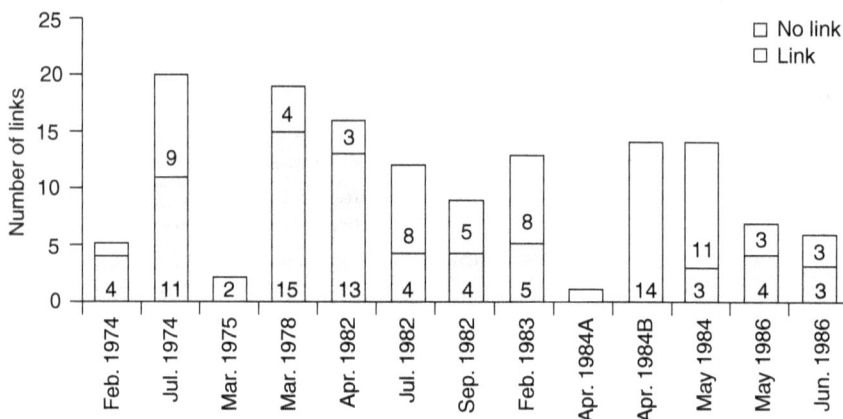

*Figure 4.6* Linking Israeli sociopolitical issues with Palestinian situation by date of coverage.

the coverage in all three newspapers revolves around the "cost road" incident, during which several Palestinian terrorists took over a bus and engaged in deadly fighting with Israeli security forces, in which thirty-five Israelis died and over seventy were injured.

Conversely, during the 1980s the proportion of articles containing such a link grows significantly. As an example, in late April and May 1984, the period during which the activities of the Jewish Underground were exposed, *Al-Quds* published an article dealing with Peace Now's condemnation of the Underground, whereas *a-Sha'ab* (April 29, 1984) made such a link differently, by emphasizing the threat of the Jewish Underground to Palestinians in the following manner,

> [O]n the arrest of the group that is accused of trying to detonate seven buses in Kalandia refugee camp, Israeli officials say that these attempts are related to what is called "the Jewish Underground in the West Bank" which is a serious organization to which Jewish residents of Hebron and a group of people who were evacuated from Yamit belong.

The nature of such perceptual linkage is, however, of greater importance. Palestinian activists in the occupied territories gradually realized the influence of their actions on the Israelis and started to adapt their actions accordingly. Revealing evidence in that regard is a memo sent in May 1983 by the Israeli Advisor on Arab Affairs in the Ministry of Defense to the coordinator of military operations in the West Bank and Gaza Strip.[12] According to the Advisor, whose analysis was based on the Arab press, it is possible to detect a profound, deliberate shift in the Palestinian mode of action within the territories.

Apparently, Palestinian activists became fully aware of the ways of influencing the Israeli arena. Thus, the Advisor argues,

> Stone throwing inside the territories has turned into a declared PLO tactic for managing the "armed struggle," realizing the Israeli Defense Force has no adequate reaction to such tactic ... stones throwers have gained the status of warriors ... stone throwing is a means for fermenting wider participation and support as such action entails less risk in comparison to terrorist activity, the means are simple and the results are effective in terms of both disrupting the daily routine and receiving standing in the Israeli and international media.

As it turned out, the Advisor's analysis was realistic and accurate. Palestinian grassroots activists in the occupied territories, according to a grassroots activist who was interviewed, were indeed mindful of such a linkage. Asking whether Palestinian activists were interested in internal Israeli reactions to the broadening contention in late 1987, I was struck by the depth of such linkage and the strategic thinking that accompanied it,

> It actually started after Lebanon ... we realized that if we use deadly weapons we will fail to cause a divide inside your society, we wanted to keep the momentum of fights and conflict inside Israel and not to cause you to reunite by using guns. This would not work under a regime like that of Saddam [Hussein] ... this was our way to strengthen those groups inside Israel that rejected the occupation.

The final analysis of the newspapers' content in this section offers a closer look at the nature of the linkage. As already shown in the previous analysis, the newspaper coverage that linked internal Israeli sociopolitical issues and the Palestinian situation increased after 1982. Interestingly, when such a link was analyzed according to whether the link was framed as "encouraging" or "discouraging" to the Palestinian situation supportive results surfaced, as can be seen in Figure 4.7. An example for "discouraging" link is the following article from *Al-Quds* published on February 15, 1974: "Threats to attempt to kill Teddi Kolak [the mayor of Jerusalem] after promising to compensate three Palestinian–Christian centers that were set on fire." An example for "encouraging" link is found in the following article from *Al-Quds* published on July 28, 1974: "Nablus calls for a general strike; rage and anger throughout the West Bank cities and villages ... [in response to] ... Jewish extremists' intention to settle in Siluwan, Jericho, and Ma'ale Edomim; it seems that the Settlers will be called off and that the government will consider their actions as challenging its power." And, an example for what was coded as "unclear/informative" is found in the following article from *a-Sha'ab* published on April 29, 1984: "Sarid: this proves the existence of a Jewish underground on the West Bank; Israeli MK, Yossi Sarid, said yesterday that the exposure of the attempt to attack Arab buses in

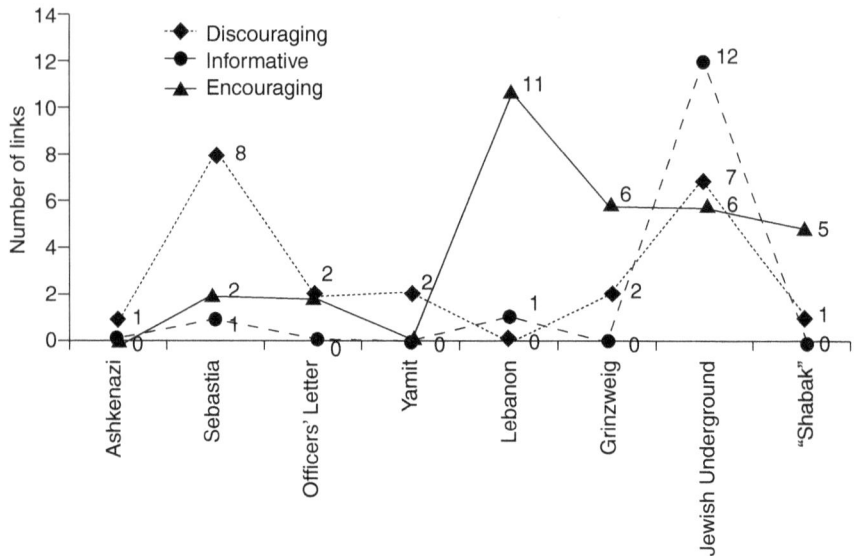

*Figure 4.7* Nature of Palestinian link by Israeli crisis-events.

Jerusalem revitalizes his arguments, expressed six months ago, concerning the existence of a well-trained and dangerous Jewish underground on the West Bank."

It is clear that as of 1982 the proportion of "encouraging" coverage is far greater than "discouraging" coverage. Also of importance is the "unclear/informative" coverage over the Jewish Underground affair. It is revealing that even when confronted with an Israeli phenomenon so threatening to their situation and facing a heavier crackdown during Rabin's Iron Fist policy of 1985, the Palestinian newspapers' coverage refrained from framing the linkage as discouraging. A possible explanation for this might be rooted in the depth of understanding of Israel that the Palestinians held; that despite increased repression and threat, the Palestinians' reading of the sources of Israel's power deflation balanced the picture from their own standpoint.

### *Threat/opportunity – beyond repression and facilitation*

Throughout the 1980s, the Palestinians in the occupied territories were highly interested in both types of challenges to the Israeli government. The ascendancy of left-wing opposition to government policy and the growing magnitude of such opposition had balanced the picture from the viewpoint of the Palestinians. Trying to explain the influence of the various types of crisis-events on Palestinians' perception of the events and developments inside Israel, one Palestinian interviewee argued that Palestinians

... understood that the left-wing groups inside Israel are interested in maintaining a moral society and state ... we also understood what the right-wing groups are interested in, and that really infuriated us, as their calls and actions intensified the injustice we were experiencing ... it was always this combination of "against us" and "for us.."

According to another Palestinian interviewee, Palestinians realized also that this was not a mere opposition to government policy as is the case, and should be the case, under a democratic regime:

We understood that there is a strong opposition in Israel to the occupation, and paid careful attention to the conflict between those that wanted to continue the occupation and those that rejected it and their struggle with your governments ... [but isn't there an opposition in every democracy, I asked] ... indeed so, but the prevalent perception among Palestinians was that the scope of challenges and opposition inside Israel cut across any government whatsoever, and that there were several groups such as Kahana and the settlers that actually challenged the cornerstones of your democracy ... their ideology stood in opposition to the rules, values, and norms of the democratic regime.

Figure 4.8 presents a bivariate distribution of the ways Palestinian newspapers framed the various Israeli crisis-events, classified according to their germane opportunity structures. The categories of "discouraging" and "encouraging" acted as indicators for the Palestinians' shared perception of threat and opportunity respectively, as constructed by the newspapers. For example, an article in *al-Fajr* (May 24, 1984) was coded as "discouraging" for citing the Israeli Knesset Chairperson saying, in the context of the Jewish Underground exposure, "we must puncture the eyes of Arabs and slay their bellies." Another article in *Al-Quds* (May 26, 1984) coded as "encouraging," emphasizes that "Peace Now strongly condemns Jewish Underground activities in the occupied Arab lands."

All in all, Palestinians, as reflected in the newspapers' coverage, considered the domestic divisions in Israel favorable to their situation. In accordance with previous analyses, the framing by the various newspapers portrays the challenges to the Israeli government as going beyond the political system, revolving around lack of legitimacy and trust, and around the government's difficulties in implementing collective goals and dealing with illegal activities. Extremely revealing, in this regard, is the newspapers' framing of what is "discouraging" or "encouraging" to the Palestinian situation. Clearly, Palestinians drew no encouragement from Israeli foreign policy issues. Nor did they draw any meaningful encouragement from oppositional voices within the Israeli political system. For example, in an editorial by *a-Sha'ab* on February 13, 1982, dealing with Sharon's resignation from office following the recommendations by the Kahan Investigating Committee on the Sabra and Shatilla massacre, a cynical reference

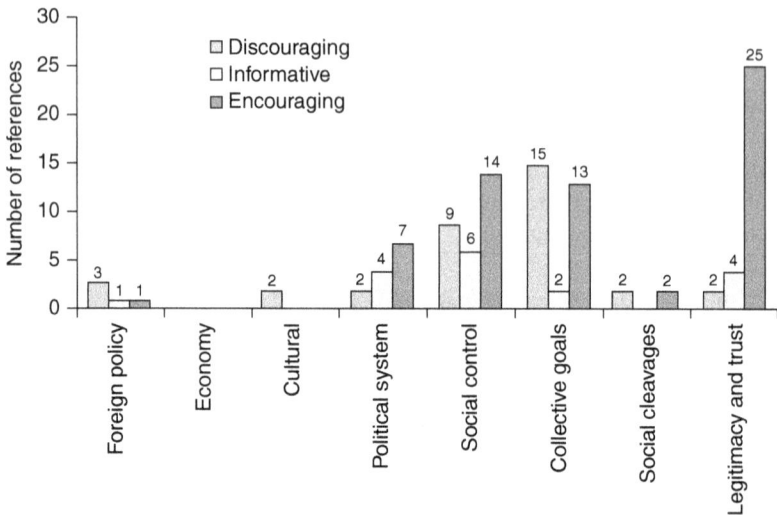

*Figure 4.8* Prognosis of Palestinian situation by references to Israeli sociopolitical issues.

is made to the joy Egypt and European States feel and that such joy will lead them to do nothing except believe that Sharon's resignation will bring about a progress in the American-led peace process. The editorial ends with the conclusion that no change is to be expected, especially in the face of US support for the Likud Government, and despite the growing militancy of the government.

Also revealing is the mixture of encouragement and discouragement within the categories of "social control" and "collective goals" (involving mostly challenges by right-wing groups, such as the struggle over the evacuation of Yamit, and Sebastia). Encouragement for the Palestinian situation is found mostly within the category of loss of "legitimacy and trust" in Israeli governance by both left-wing and right-wing groups.

It seems conceivable that these types of domestic Israeli sociopolitical issues demonstrated to Palestinians the developing disunity inside Israeli society, and accordingly were framed as encouraging for Palestinians. The results of this analysis are presented in Table 4.2, demonstrating that "encouraging" framing is more likely to be associated with "disunity" framing than with "unity" framing (68.2 percent compared to 15.4 percent).

The crucial point is that the "encouraging" framing was present in all three newspapers even when the threat to Palestinians from the Jewish Settlers' vigilantism was at its height and government repression of Palestinians had increased, as Rabin's Iron Fist policy of 1985 suggests. One Palestinian interviewee argued that Palestinian confrontations with the army were not indicative of the processes and developments that took place inside the Israeli sociopolitical arena, e.g., the processes and developments Palestinians perceived as encouraging. The "Iron Fist" policy, according to him, was perceived as a "paper tiger":

*Table 4.2* Perception of Israeli unity by prognosis of Palestinian situation

| Prognosis of Palestinian situation | Unity | | Disunity | |
|---|---|---|---|---|
| | *no.* | *%* | *no.* | *%* |
| Discouraging | 25 | 64.1 | 12 | 13.6 |
| Informative | 8 | 20.5 | 16 | 18.2 |
| Encouraging | 6 | 15.4 | 60 | 68.2 |
| Total | 39 | 100 | 88 | 100 |

Notes
a $P < 0.05$.
b $N = 127$.

...an army is always firm ... it is its job to look like that. But, the territories' population understood that the army's support from Israeli society and government is partial ... [the developing notion among Palestinians, argued another interviewee, was that a growing portion of the Israeli public did not want the occupation to last] We were constantly analyzing Israeli society, learning about the fights that you had over the territories and that many of you don't really want the territories and reject the occupation ... we were encouraged by that...

A final step in this section analyzing the newspapers' content reconnects with the multi-variate distribution presented at the beginning of this chapter, looking at how the newspapers' prognosis of the Palestinian situation varies, first, with the pattern of contentious events (Figure 4.9) and second, with the number of Jewish settlements in the occupied territories (Figure 4.10). The time axis in

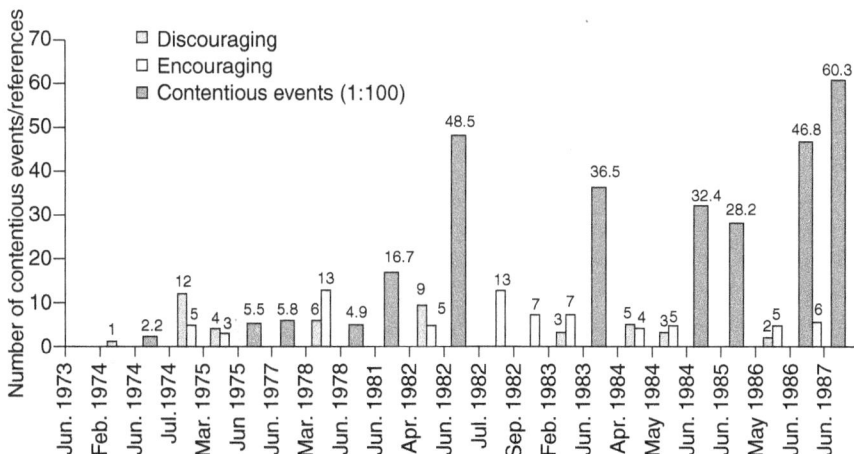

*Figure 4.9* Contentious events by prognosis of Palestinian Situation.

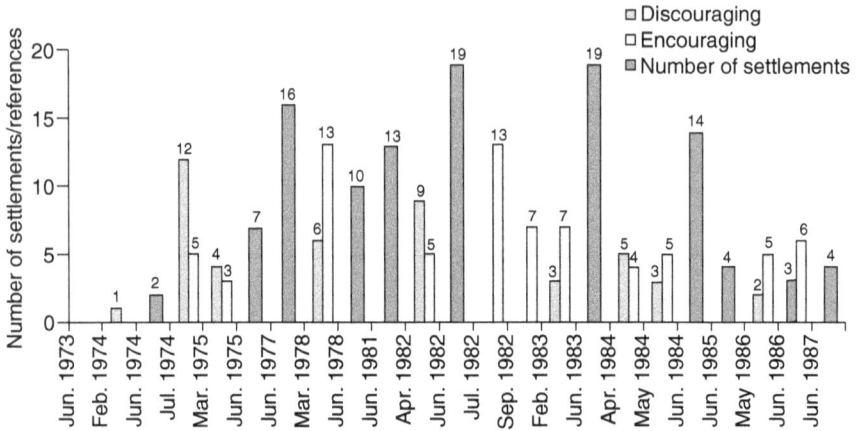

*Figure 4.10* Number of settlements by prognosis of Palestinian situation.

both figures includes the various manifestations of Israeli crisis-events and the number of contentious events or Jewish settlements respectively. For every crisis-event, I have placed the preceding and the ensuing data on number of contentious events, as is the case in Figure 4.9, and data on number of Jewish settlements in the occupied territories as is the case in Figure 4.10, by using the mid-year as a representation of the overall pattern of a given year. Lastly, Figure 4.9 also includes a secondary count axis (although not shown) for contentious events: this axis graphically adjusts the ratio between the different data sets.

The two figures examine a general pattern. While no test of statistical significance is possible, and while other factors unquestionably affect both sets of data, the overall pattern is revealing nonetheless. As can be readily seen in Figure 4.9, there is a positive relationship between the gradual increase in number of contentious events and the rise in "encouraging" framing in the Palestinian print media discourse. In fact, with the exception of April 1984 (the uncovering of the Jewish Underground) and April 1982 (the Yamit Evacuation as part of the implementation of the Camp David Accord, rejected by the majority of Palestinians in and outside the occupied territories), "encouraging" framing seems to dominate the newspapers' coverage even when the number of contentious events decreases. Figure 4.10 supplements the overall pattern. Despite the marked increase in Jewish settlements (an indication of what Tilly and Goldstone might label as *current threat*) no parallel dominance in "discouraging" framing appears as of 1977. Rather, the opposite is true, as can be seen, for instance, in March 1978, and, in a more striking manner, in July 1982.

In short, the Palestinians in the occupied territories, as reflected by the print media discourse, were highly aware of and attuned to the deepening domestic Israeli divisions. They were also aware of their role as the focus of the Israeli system-wide crisis. Not only were such domestic Israeli sociopolitical divisions seen as an ongoing and worsening issue inside Israel; Palestinian framers and readers were just as precise in their reading of the nature and consequences of these internal divisions. As was constructed by the three newspapers, the series of crisis-events were perceived as an expression of such a system-wide crisis, the consequence of which was the disintegration of the sources of Israeli governmental and state authority. All three newspapers emphasize the connection between the lack of Israeli unity and solidarity, the link between Israel's internal divisions and the conflict between Israel and the Palestinians, and the conduciveness of Israel's power deflation to their situation as an occupied national minority.

The final section of this chapter deals with how the Palestinians' framing of Israel's power deflation as structural opportunity affected their attempts at activating mobilization to contention. The established context for examining the third task of framing processes – *what should be done about the issue* – is Palestinian attentiveness to, and shared perception of, the events and developments that took place inside Israel, the impacts of Israeli policy of repression and facilitation on Palestinian space and modes of mobilization, and the Palestinians' sense of grievance. Given these, I shall demonstrate first, the Palestinian attempt to activate mobilization, that is, to spread the perception of developments inside Israel as ripe for the triggering of contentious politics and second, the Palestinian preferred strategy for action, that is, a promoted dominant mode of action that evokes a preferred solution to their hardship.

## Activating commitment – discourse in contention

In speaking of a Palestinian strategy of contention, it is suggested that dating the beginning of the Intifada as December 9, 1987 may be misleading and inaccurate. Such dating portrays the Intifada as a sudden outburst of anger and frustration, thereby serving, paradoxically, the interests of both Israel and the Palestinians alike. Such a portrayal serves Israel's attempts to frame the Palestinian insurgency as an issue of *law and order*. For the Palestinians, the portrayal of the uprising as an authentic, spontaneous explosion of rage serves their promoted frame of *injustice and defiance* (Wolfsfeld 1997). Such a Palestinian framing should not be surprising. As Polletta (1998) suggests, such a framing fits the activists' interest in trading on the image of protest as unplanned, thereby scoring more points in the struggle of who achieves victim status in the eye of "third parties." Both antagonists purposively constructed their frames to promote their cause in the international arena, as will be analyzed in the next chapter.

As shown in the beginning of this chapter, patterns of contentious events between our two antagonists seem to contradict this image of spontaneous combustion. As systematically shown by Khawaja's review of contentious events initiated by the Palestinians in the occupied territories, as of 1982 the proportion of events that could be characterized as representing a non-violent mode of action far exceeds the proportion of events that represent a violent mode of action (1991). Such findings and the overall pattern of contentious events between our two antagonists seem to fit with the line of argument that this book promotes, specifically, that speaking of a Palestinian strategy of contention is not too far fetched. Furthermore, this strategy was affected, to a large extent, by Palestinian framing of Israel's power deflation as representing ripe conditions for triggering contention.

Viewed from this perspective, the pattern of contentious events in the territories suggests that the Intifada was certainly not a sudden outburst of contention dated December 9, 1987. Several Intifada researchers labeled 1987 as the "year of discontent," referring to the rise in contention that took place in the occupied territories (Urban 1993; Robinson 1997). During 1987, the Palestinians were indeed engaging in an unprecedented level of intense confrontation with Israeli soldiers and Jewish Settlers (Rekhess 1989). Through confronting the Israeli military, Palestinian activists tested whether conditions were ripe to trigger contention practicing what turned out to be the dominant mode of action during the Intifada: disruptive action.

In early 1987, under the lead of Shabiba activists, Balata refugee camp's residents planned to take over the refugee camp, to release it from the control of the Israeli military. For several weeks, every Israeli military force that ran into the camp area was heavily stoned and prevented from patrolling the camp. At the end of May 1987, a massive military force raided the camp to regain control over it. A siege was implemented and over 3,000 men were held in the camp's square for an identification lineup. Their detention was disrupted by a women's riot, which, together with the men, forced the soldiers to back off. The taking over of the biggest refugee camp in the West Bank made an enormous impression on Palestinians throughout the occupied territories, and acted as a model for other attempts, as was the case for instance in Jibalyya camp in the Gaza Strip in November 1987.

Data from the Palestinian newspapers served me also in examining how Palestinian framers and readers provided answers for the question "*what should be done about the issue?*" I analyzed the Palestinian media coverage according to two types of rhetoric (rhetoric of action and rhetoric of reaction (Gamson and Meyer 1996)), and the relative prominence of various promoted solutions to the occupation along a series of three protest events and among the various newspapers.

At this stage of the research a fourth newspaper was added: *al-Ahad* (The Covenant) a news organ of the Islamic organization, the Hizbollah. Although *al-Ahad* is a weekly, was affiliated with a political organization located outside the territories, and was not an integral part of the Palestinian movement, I included it because it was the only newspaper available that reflected an Islamist voice, specifically the Islamic Jihad, within the territories, given the ideological affinity between the two organizations (Hatina 2001). A summary of these solutions can be found in Chapter 2 (Table 2.1). The various themes constituting the two rhetorical packages are detailed in Table 4.3.

The analysis of the media coverage was carried out on 84 news articles sampled at random from the subsequent coverage of three waves of protest during 1987: May 7, October 7, and December 8.[13] Each protest wave represen-

*Table 4.3* Action/reaction rhetoric

| Rhetoric of action | Urgency | Agency | Possibility |
|---|---|---|---|
| | One must act promptly as any delay would make things worse. | Action is the way and through it, things can get better. | Change is possible and within reach; this is the time to act since the conditions are ripe. |
| *Rhetoric of reaction* | *Jeopardy* Let's stick to what we have; things are not necessarily bad. | *Futility* There is no sense or utility in action. | *Perverse effects* Conditions are not ripe; action may turn out to be a self-defeating strategy |

ted an intense period (more than three days) of clashes and involved a variety of incidents ranging from strike through demonstration to terrorist attack.

The analysis looked at the relative prominence of a given rhetoric as it changed across the three protest waves and among the various newspapers. The results of this analysis are presented in Figure 4.11. They show that as we move along the protest waves the dominance of "reaction rhetoric" decreases whereas the relative proportion of "action rhetoric" increases. An additional interesting finding that can be gleaned from Figure 4.11 concerns the variation in each newspaper's coverage. Evidently, while *al-Ahad* presented absolute "action rhetoric" across the three protest waves a converging trend supporting rhetoric of action emerged among the other three newspapers.

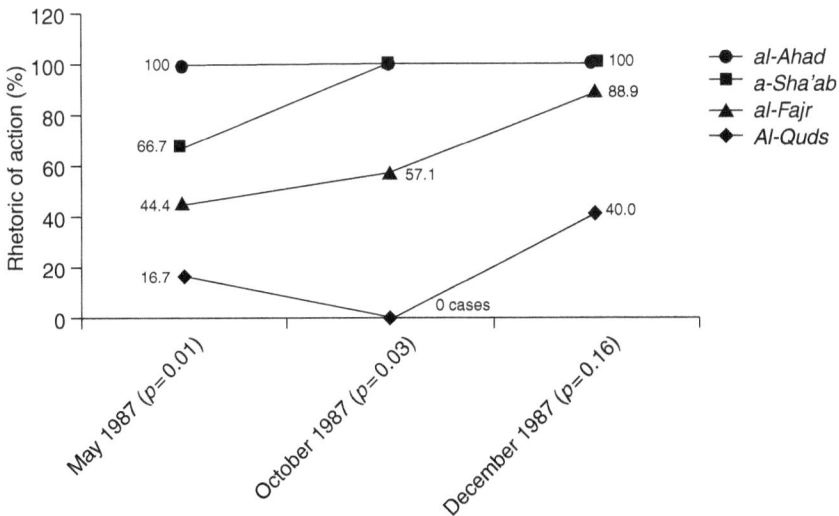

*Figure 4.11* Palestinian varying rationales for contention.

The newspapers' treatment of the escape of Palestinian activists from an Israeli prison in the Gaza Strip provides a useful example of the differences in the quality of coverage according to the two types of rhetoric. An article by *Al-Quds* (October 10, 1987) was treated as promoting reaction for its emphasis on "perverse effects" based on its coverage of the activists' escape and the ensuing armed confrontation with Israeli forces, during which several of them were killed. The following is an excerpt from the newspaper's coverage.

### Broad scope military measures and search activity in the Gaza strip
*Military sources: we shall check under every rock and in every corner*
Wide reaching operations were initiated in order to capture the remaining fugitives.

On the same event, *Al-Fajr* used a different coverage emphasizing "agency," which I therefore treated as promoting action:

### Armed confrontation in Gaza
Palestinian spokesperson: many Israelis were killed; Israeli spokesperson: four Palestinians and an [Israeli] intelligence man were killed
...during a confrontation between Israeli forces and armed Palestinian squad of the Islamic Jihad organization.

Clearly, the article by *Al-Quds* is not promoting action; it stresses the military's threatening reaction and uses an Israeli source. The article by *al-Fajr* promotes action; it relies on a Palestinian source and reports on the death of "many Israelis" during a confrontation following the escape, a confrontation not mentioned by *Al-Quds*.

It is important to bear in mind, however, that the prominence of calls for action did not occur in a vacuum. The newspapers' emphases on action framing were largely related to the reaction within Israel to the confrontations and less related to the actual military reaction on the battlefield. Palestinian activists fully grasped that the army reaction to the confrontations was a by-product of the events and developments within the Israeli sociopolitical scene; they realized the uniqueness of the Israeli army, that there could be no real separation between Israeli politics and Israeli army, and that the Israeli society *is* the army. In that sense, Palestinian activists understood that they should look beyond the immediate reaction of Israeli soldiers, and that, in their calls for action, they should attend to the dynamics of events and developments inside Israel. One Palestinian interviewee put this most vividly, arguing that "We certainly sensed and understood that during the months before the uprising the IDF's actions and activities were far from enjoying a full backup by the Israeli public ... we simply acted against the soldiers in a provoking manner as an indicator for what was going on behind them..."

However, Palestinians were experiencing violent attacks by Jewish Settlers as well. Such was the case with attacks by a Settlers' militia on the city of Kalkilia in May 1987, during which armed patrols were initiated on a daily basis, aimed at intimidation and at destruction of property. The newspapers' coverage constantly referred to Israeli responses to the events and suggested various modes of action to bring a certain solution to the occupation. On December 11, 1987, for example, *al-Fajr* published an article emphasizing a favorable Israeli response, stating:

### The Israelis wonder about the utility of their presence in the Strip
Tel-Aviv – Observers think that the worsening of the situation in the occupied Gaza Strip, which has continued for months, leads many Israelis to doubt the utility of their presence in the Gaza Strip. . . .

In the context of broadening contention and attentiveness to Israeli responses to the deteriorating situation, a final analysis looks, first, at how different Israeli responses to the events influence the relative prominence of the two types of rhetoric and, second, how these Israeli responses are associated with various solutions to the Palestinian situation.

The three possible solutions/modes of action are "moderate" (acceptance of peace conferences or any other political arrangements that do not necessarily entail an independent Palestinian political entity, such as a Jordanian Confederation), "radical" (a call for ending the occupation, recognition of the genuine needs and interests of the Palestinians in the occupied territories, and the PLO as the sole representative of the Palestinian People), and "extremist" (a total rejection of Israel and calls for the destruction of the Zionist Entity). The following article excerpt is taken from *a-Sha'ab*. Published December 13, 1987, the article was coded as promoting a "moderate" solution to the occupation.

### Who will respond?
While the outcries of Palestinians in the occupied land continue to be heard a deadly silence prevails in Arab cities ... The call of the UN general assembly to convene a peace conference on the Middle East expresses a genuine desire for peace and to redeem humanity from fear and uncertainty, but Israel and the United States defy the world to reject such a conference. They keep challenging the international consensus, a challenge that necessitates Arab unity.

The results of the first analysis are presented in Figure 4.12. Despite a relatively small proportion of references made to internal Israeli reactions, the mere existence of references to whether Israeli reaction favors or disfavors Palestinians is telling, suggesting that Palestinians were attuned to the impact that increased contention was having on Israeli politics.

Evidently, action rhetoric is strongly related to Israeli responses framed as favorable to the Palestinians. Closely related, and as can be seen in Table 4.4, it is clear that "radical" solution/strategy is more likely to be associated with those

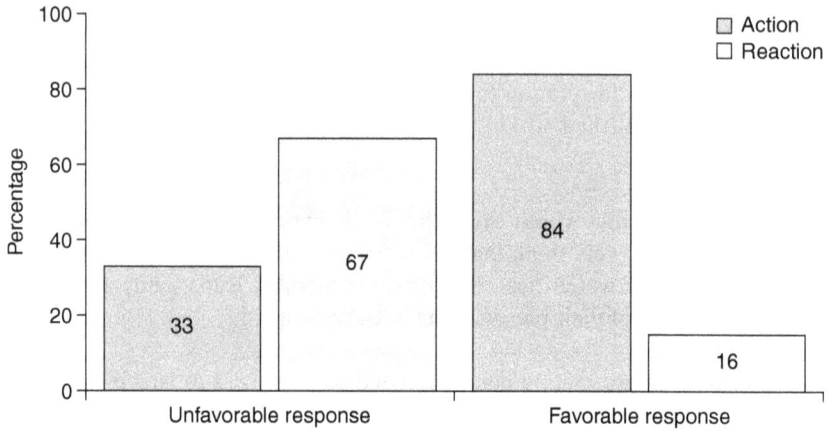

*Figure 4.12* Types of rhetoric by interpretation of internal Israeli reactions.

same references to Israeli responses framed as favorable to the Palestinians. It is important to note also the absence of any reference to the Israeli arena within the category of "extreme" solution, which the Islamic voice, *al-Ahad*, most represented.

In concluding, the Intifada was far from being a mere outburst of frustration. Nor was it spontaneous in the sense that a perceptual infrastructure was absent before December 9, 1987. As previous chapters have elaborated, such perceptual processes were grounded and embedded in an already developed mobilizing infrastructure, which united a variety of Palestinian movements under the Nationalistic action frame, that of "ending the Israeli occupation." The Intifada, then, did not erupt, rather it consolidated; such a consolidation involved a pro- moted and favored strategy for action, deeply embedded in the Palestinians'

*Table 4.4* Promoted solutions by interpretation of internal Israeli reactions

| Framing solution to occupation | Disfavor of Palestinian | | In favor of Palestinian | |
|---|---|---|---|---|
| | *no.* | *%* | *no.* | *%* |
| Radical | – | – | 4 | 66.7 |
| Moderate | 7 | 100 | 2 | 33.3 |
| Total | 7 | 100 | 6 | 100 |

Notes
a  $P < 0.05$ (Fisher Exact Test).
b  n = 13.
c  No reference to Israeli arena within extreme solution category.

structural conditions within the occupied territories. As the following chapter will show, the dynamics of the Intifada represent an attempt by the Palestinian insurgents to capitalize on such a strategy. Yet, we will also see that intentions are one thing and that the dynamics of contention involve processes and developments that may pose serious challenges to such a strategy.

# 5    The Intifada

## Tactics for expanding political opportunities

It is one thing to trigger contentious politics; it is a totally different story to sustain contentious politics. Unlike former challenges during the twenty years of occupation, the 1987 Intifada should be distinguished chiefly by the Israeli incapacity to curb the challenge. Over six years, the Palestinians in the occupied territories succeeded in mounting a wide spread and intensive revolt sustained by a well-established and coordinated organizational infrastructure, unprecedented commitment, and a calculated use of contentious repertoires. Two closely related questions should be raised: why was Israel incapable of repressing the uprising, and, conversely, why were the Palestinians capable of promoting such a challenge?

In contrast to both Israeli and Tunis-based PLO evaluations, the widening contention was not another sporadic, short-term wave of protest (Peretz 1990; Shiff and Yaari 1990). Both sides soon realized that the daily increasing contention was something new – different in its mode of action, type of actors, and scope. The magnitude of the 1987 cycle of contention is illustrated in Figure 5.1, the data for which is taken from Israeli sources such as the Israeli Defense Force's Spokesperson Department. Contentious events include stone throwing, roadblocks, tire burning, mass gatherings, and riots; excluded are incidents of firearms, bombs, grenades, arson, and gun firings.

Although it is not possible to differentiate between specific types of action (e.g., stone throwing and mass demonstration), Figure 5.1 readily shows that in comparison with the period of 1988–90, during which the number of contentious events within the occupied territories steadily increased, the year 1991 indicates a sharp decrease in the level of Palestinian contention. Indeed, the level of contention in the occupied territories continued at much higher levels than in the years preceding the Intifada, but much lower than the four-year period with which this book is mostly concerned. By contrast, the Intifada witnessed a steady increase in the use of deadly weapons by Palestinians, which continued through 1992 and on. We will return to the contentious 1990s in a postscript which follows the concluding chapter.

Israeli publications make it clear that the proportion of disruptive events (i.e., stone throwing, mass gatherings, demonstrations, etc.) predominates over other violent activity involving the use of deadly weapons.[1] Moreover, it is reasonable

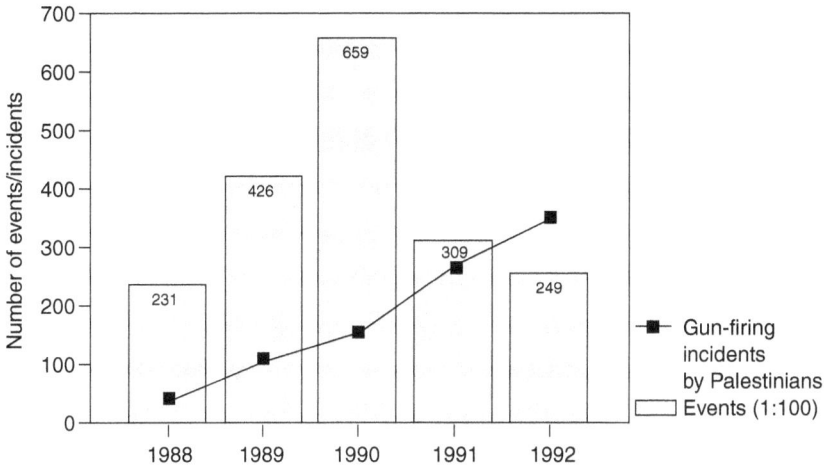

*Figure 5.1* Contentious events in the occupied territories.

to argue that a considerable proportion of the gunfire incidents involving Palestinians resulted from Palestinians shooting at Palestinians collaborating with Israel, a differentiation not made in the Israeli statistics. The overall picture, nonetheless, demonstrates that by 1991 the level of contention was abating.

This chapter by no means provides an in-depth analysis of the Intifada. Nor is it an attempt to evaluate whether the Intifada represented a successful challenge. This is so for the simple reason that I see the Intifada as successful on narrow grounds: the sheer ability of the Palestinians to generate and sustain such a challenge should be seen as a central aspect of a successful cycle of contention. This chapter, rather, analyzes how the Palestinians were able to sustain such voluminous contention. It analyzes the trajectories of the contention phase, exploring possible links between the Palestinian strategy rooted in the shared perception of developing opportunity structures inside Israel and Palestinian tactics of contention. Specifically, it examines the Palestinian insurgents' attempts to capitalize on such a strategy by using specific tactics of contention for taking advantage of the Israeli opportunity structure, thereby increasing Palestinian prospects of political gains.

As we will see, to sustain a widespread and intensive challenge, Palestinian activists attempted to act within the bounds of the perceived Israeli political opportunity structures in three major ways. First, they systematically limited the use of deadly weapons, instead employing a disruptive mode of action aimed at increasing both internal solidarity and cohesion and Israel's sense of uncertainty. Second, they constructed unprecedented mobilizing mechanisms for broadening participation and managing the uprising. Third, they successfully framed their struggle both internally to maintain the commitment of the population and externally to gain international support. These three tactical "powers," to use

Tarrow's concept (1998), were implemented, but not without difficulties or mistakes. As we will see, the Israeli crackdown on the uprising, contingent events, and leadership misdeeds, complicated the trajectories of the Intifada.

## Repertoire of action: innovative action and innovative repression

To sustain contention a social movement centers on tactical power, its ability to employ specific types of actions that both express its challenge and promote its goals.[2] It is useful here to distinguish between two modes of contention: the *contained* mode of contention (in which all parties are previously established actors employing well-established means of claim-making) and the *transgressive* mode of contention (in which at least one party is a newly self-identified political actor, and at least one party employs *innovative* action) (McAdam, Tarrow, and Tilly 2001). The authors also argue that *innovative* action involves the incorporation of claims, objects of claims, collective self-representations, and means that are either unprecedented or forbidden within the regime in question.

The reader should know by now that the value of the above analytical distinction between *contained* and *transgressive* modes of contention is heuristic, as *transgressive* contention was the only available mode of action for Palestinian insurgents. The question then, is what type of *transgressive* contention did the Palestinians introduce during the Intifada and, concomitantly, how did Israel cope with such a mode of action? In a way, this book is about how the Palestinians in the occupied territories *innovated* contentiously to force their way into the arena of *contained* politics.

Intifada scholars share the argument that, throughout the uprising, most Palestinian groups and organizations made systematic efforts to restrain their contention (JMCC 1991; Kaufman 1990; Shalev 1990). From the early phases of the Intifada, the Nationalist Movement inside and outside the occupied territories consciously limited the use of violence, not using deadly weapons such as gun firing, throwing of grenades, and firebombs or limiting violence to specific occasions and/or locations. At certain times and as a reaction to specific events the use of violence was called for in leaflets and other channels of communication. Such was the case in reaction to the Nahhalin event of April 13, 1989, during which an Israeli military force raided Nahhalin village near Bethlehem, as a result of which four Palestinians were killed and thirty were injured (Kaufman 1990).

The tactic of limited violence was embedded within a larger approach, the non-violent resistance that Mubarak Awad introduced into the occupied territories. A Palestinian American, Awad founded the Palestinian Center for Non-Violence in Jerusalem in 1983, and was deported by Israel on June 1988. Limited violence meant that despite the possession of other means of action (see below) the non-violent tactic was preferable. Thus, for the purpose of disrupting the Israeli military order, Palestinians were practicing acts of refusal to co-operate with Israel (e.g., non-payment of taxes, withdrawal of labor or strikes), acts of disengagement from Israel (e.g., setting clocks independently of official Israeli time or renaming streets and schools), and acts of support and solidarity (e.g., mass funerals or popular education).

Indeed, according to Israeli statistics, between 1988 and 1991, the relatively small number of fourteen Israeli soldiers were killed and twenty-nine Jewish civilians were injured by Palestinians both in Israel and in the occupied territories. By comparison, according to reports by Israeli information center B'Tselem, between 1988 and 1991, Israeli security forces in the occupied territories killed 790 Palestinians, and eight Palestinians were killed inside Israel.

This is not to say that deadly weaponry was not present or that no use of deadly force occurred. Rather, it means that the prevalent conception among Palestinian insurgents was that limiting violence would better serve their goals. One Palestinian interviewee, a Fatah activist, put it in the following way,

> The Intifada was a symbolic struggle to a large degree, a performance, in the sense that we were avoiding any call or act that could have been inter-preted as an interest in the destruction of Israel or the Jewish people ... after all you could not really fight the Israeli army with the weapons we had ... it was our will against yours ... and the soldiers we confronted daily had been mostly influenced by that. All in all, I can tell you that deadly weapons were everywhere but we deliberately refrained from using them.

Arguably, based on data provided by the Israeli Defense Force's Spokesper-son Department, between 1988 and 1992 there was a steady increase in gun firing incidents. However, other statistics also reveal that during the same period shooting at Palestinian collaborators by Palestinians increased at a similar pace. Further, it is not possible to know (and no systematic data exists) whether inci-dents of gun firing or stabbings were the initiative of Nationalist groups or Islamic groups.[3] Such differentiation is important since it can provide a more accurate analysis of variations between the modes of action employed by the Nationalist organizations within the overall existing repertoire of contention. Still, and despite the absence of systematic data, scholars agree that the use of deadly weapons and violent activities was far more prevalent among the Islamic groups (Paz 1992; Mishal and Sela 1999).

As argued, the tactics of employing non-violence and limited violence actions were not new to the Palestinians in the occupied territories. As demonstrated in previous chapters, prior to the Intifada Nationalist grassroots activists in the territories presented a much more pragmatic and realistic approach both in their actual activities and in political claims, as compared to Islamic groups and also, during most of the period under analysis, to the exter-nally based PLO.

According to Khalidi (1988), who uses results from public polls conducted during 1986 and 1987, such pragmatism regarding what can be achieved was far more dominant among grassroots activists than among the population at large. While it is difficult to estimate the extent to which Awad's ideas and teaching had influenced the Palestinian populace in the occupied territories, clearly the use of limited violence and the practice of non-violent tactics had been more dominant than other modes of action, shared by the leadership and the population alike.

The decision to limit violent acts and to focus mostly on disruptive tactics included the majority of political groups and organizations. Such a decision was arrived at during the early phases of the uprising. Despite the availability of deadly weapons, both the PLO and the Unified National Leadership of the Uprising (see below) explicitly urged that Palestinians not use "hot" weapons. However, as both Shalev (1990) and Mishal with Aharoni (1989) denote, PLO leaders added that the option of deadly weapons remained; that their decision to refrain from the use of deadly weapons was for a limited time, and that the Intifada was only a first step of an all-out uprising against Israel.

From the viewpoint of Israel, such a threat received ample expression as signs of unrest started to appear throughout the region. During the first months of 1988, Palestinians inside Israel, Lebanon, and Jordan expressed solidarity with the Intifada by raising calls of support and through the initiation of demonstrations, disruptions, and violent acts against Israel. On the Israeli–Lebanese border, an escalation of confrontations consolidated during the first half of 1988 under the direction of PFLP leader George Habash, who argued that while the Intifada should not be transformed into an armed struggle, it was important to back it with firepower (Kaufman 1990).

In Jordan, where Palestinians comprise nearly two-thirds of the population, the King's anxiety had significantly increased as growing unrest surfaced within Palestinian refugee camps on the outskirts of Amman, and rumors spread about transferring the Intifada into Jordan. Israel, also anxious about waning Jordanian influence in the territories, was attentive to this possibility. Hussein's reaction to such developments was to sever administrative and judicial ties with the West Bank and to recognize the PLO as the sole representative of the Palestinian people, an act that further intensified Israel's own anxiety about the PLO taking over the vacuum thus created.

From within Israel, the fear that Israeli Palestinians would join hands with the Palestinians *within* the occupied territories brought Sharon, at the time a Likud member of Knesset, to argue, "They want to destroy us instead of fighting with us as loyal citizens of the state" (Benvenisti 1992: 83). Sharon's words came as a reaction to the call of Israeli Palestinian public figures – already in December 1987 – for a day of general strike as an expression of Palestinian nationalism. This coincided with a wave of clashes and confrontations with Israeli police, hoisting of PLO flags, assistance to Palestinian activists from the West Bank and Gaza in photocopying and distribution of leaflets, money transfers, and the like. Still, in spite of the interest of the PLO, Israeli Palestinians' widening involvement in the Intifada was contained by a combination of harsh Israeli reaction and the fact that the majority of the Israeli Palestinians favored the approach, "Yes to sympathy – No to violence" (Rekhess 1992b: 112).[4] As it turned out, Israeli Palestinians' support soon became symbolic sympathy, with the exception of a small radical group named the Sons of the Village, which had long called for unification of the Palestinian People writ large.

The local leadership core had another rationale for limiting the violence of the uprising. Hanna Siniora, editor of *al-Fajr*, called for non-violent resistance to the occupation that stressed the importance of influencing internal Israeli politics. Fully aware of the election year in Israel (1988), Siniora wrote the following:

> Palestinians must talk to the Israeli populace, the Israeli electorate ... this is an election year in Israel. The Palestinians should not simply hand victory to the right-wing parties ... we are simply repeating what was done by Gandhi in India ... the importance of this movement is that it is long-term, people can participate in it at various levels, and it does not alienate the international community or the Israeli worker.

Siniora's strategic thinking was associated with that of Awad. The promotion of a non-violent approach did not necessarily rest on moral ground. Rather, it was a strategic understanding of its effectiveness. For Awad, the non-violent approach, among other things, would neutralize important sectors of Israeli society, those sectors that were possessed by the irrational fear of Arab joint attack on Israel and the subsequent elimination of the Jewish State (1984).

Not all PLO factions shared Siniora's line of reasoning and the elections in Israel resulted in yet another Unity Government, showing a stronger right-wing orientation than the former administration. Still, in line with Siniora's approach, the most central actor of the uprising – the United National Command of the Uprising – made serious and systematic efforts to limit the use of violence and to practice non-violent techniques, as will be further elaborated below.

In support of Siniora's approach, it is possible to suggest four additional reasons. First, disruptive actions had proven effective in the past. In 1986–7 when Palestinians successfully took over refugee camps, mass participation proved a fertile tactic for forcing the Israeli army to back off. Cumulative experience suggested that the army was incapable of coping with this mode of action. Second, as mentioned above, non-violent approaches undermined the Israeli army's justification for using heavily repressive measures. Indeed, many Israeli soldiers found themselves in a state of cognitive dissonance when responding with live ammunition to children and women throwing stones (Peretz 1990). Palestinian activists were aware of Israeli soldiers' moral doubts: as one interviewee put it, "... a soldier is first and foremost a human being and we 'played' on that ... by using stones and sticks we knew his doubts became stronger." Third, Palestinians recognized their military resource inferiority vis-à-vis the Israeli army. Grassroots activists were aware that using their weapons arsenal would result in bloodshed on their part, ending the uprising in a matter of weeks if not days. The decision, in that sense, to focus on disruptive actions and to limit the use of violence was perceived as a tactic that would better serve the Palestinian struggle. One of the Palestinian interviewees, a DFLP activist, reveals,

> We wanted to show you [Israelis] that what you were taught about the Palestinians is not true, to show you that we are not interested it the destruction of Israel, but simply to stop the occupation ... had we used deadly weapons the Intifada would probably have lasted no more than a week ... had we used deadly weapons we were fools.

A fourth rationale behind the decision to employ such modes of action was rooted in the understanding by grassroots activists that using simple techniques not requiring serious skills would facilitate broader participation. According to Peretz (1990), such a rationale was central to Awad's understanding of the effectiveness of the non-violent approach. Indeed, said one of the Palestinian interviewees, "We wanted everyone to participate. Had we used deadly weapons this could not be achieved, coupled with providing Israel with the excuse to use all its military capacity ... with stones we provoked Israel, pushing her to make mistakes so that the world see how violent the occupation really is." Indeed and as will be analyzed below, media presence was crucial for the symbolic aspect of the Intifada.

An example of the self-restraint tactic occurred in December 1987. During a confrontation near the Shifa hospital in Gaza, Palestinian protesters managed to isolate an Israeli soldier. Makhul, a Palestinian journalist who documented a day of confrontations in Gaza and witnessed the incident, writes the following:

> The captive was stripped of his clothes ... and all his equipment was taken. Nobody touched his body, and he was released wearing only a pair of torn trousers. Some of them started to dance, with the rifle magazine in one hand and a "V" sign on the other. I asked them "What are you so happy about?" "It is the greatest humiliation for the Israeli occupation."
>
> (1988: 97)

The Israeli attempts to crack down on the Intifada provided numerous situations that put this Palestinian approach to the test. At times, as a reaction to certain acts by Israel, the Palestinians were divided regarding the appropriate mode of response. Such was the case with Israel's assassination of Halil al-Wasir (Abu-Jihad), Fatah's second-in-command, in April 1988. While the Tunis-based PLO called for the use of arms as a reaction to the assassination, the local leadership of the uprising refused to comply. A declaration published after the assassination included no extreme calls, but rather calls stressing "we-ness" and determination to continue the uprising; no matter what Israel's deeds, the declaration stated, the link between the local and external command of the uprising would remain inseparable, adding that the Israeli crimes and assassinations would only strengthen the Palestinians' adherence to the PLO and their determination to continue with the popular uprising.

The Israeli assassination of Fatah's second-in-command represented Israel's rapid awakening from the notion that there was "no cause for concern ... There is nothing new in this ... We have overcome this kind of thing in the past and we will do so now and in the future," explained Prime Minister Shamir in a December 1987 *Guardian* interview (JMCC 1991: 26). Such awakening in the face of wholesale demonstrations and confrontations and the threat that the Intifada would spill over to other arenas brought about a harsh policy aimed at suppressing the uprising by using brute force and live ammunition, as illustrated in Figure 5.2.

The reader should note that the data in this figure does not include statistics on East Jerusalem, and is based on statistics gathered by the Israeli Defense Force. An analysis of the first sixteen months of the Intifada in East Jerusalem, conducted by Shalev (1990), shows that in comparison with Gaza and the West Bank the overall level of contention had been significantly lower in East Jerusalem. According to the author, the reason for this can be found in the use of trained police forces (unlike in the West Bank and Gaza Strip), the smaller area to control, and the interest of Arab religious leaders in excluding the Temple Mount from the struggle, following a deadly incident that occurred on January 1988. Still, as we will see, such interest did not last for long, and in October 1990 a deadly confrontation broke out on the Temple Mount.

Returning to Figure 5.2, it seems that the first two years of the Intifada witnessed high numbers of Palestinian deaths at the hands of Israeli security forces. There is, however, a marked decrease starting during 1989 and continuing throughout. The same pattern holds when examining numbers of Palestinians injured by military forces. Data, when gathered by non-Israeli organizations,

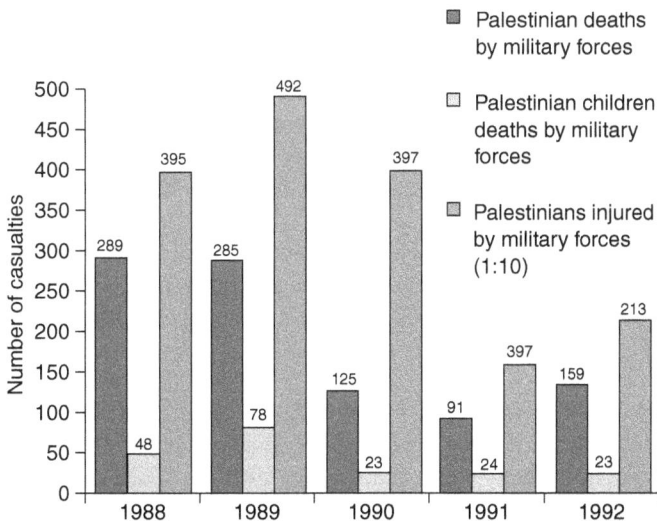

*Figure 5.2* Patterns of Israeli crackdown.

such as Palestinian Human Rights Information Center (PHRIC), reveals that the overall gross numbers were far higher. According to PHRIC annual reports, during 1988, 390 Palestinians died as a result of Israeli forces' shooting, beating, burning, and stoning, or as a result of the use of teargas. During 1989, 345 Palestinians were killed by the same causes.

The much higher numbers when data was collected by non-Israeli agencies or organizations surfaces also in data on Palestinian injuries. Although injuries by Jewish Settlers are also included, data by PHRIC and UNRWA (UN Relief and Works Agency) shows that the numbers of Palestinian injuries are far higher than the IDF's data indicates. According to UNRWA, 26,820 Palestinians were injured during 1989 alone because of live ammunition, beating, plastic bullets and rubber bullets, and other reasons. PHRIC provides an estimate of 34,000 Palestinian injuries during 1989 and 46,000 during 1988.

Such patterns are not surprising given Israeli Defense Minister Rabin's announcement on December 22, 1987, only a day after UN Security Council Resolution No. 605 strongly deplored Israel's "merciless policy" for controlling the Intifada in the occupied territories. Rabin's policy entailed deployment of massive military presence, extensive arrests, threats of mass deportation, and administrative detention. Moreover, when the extensive use of live ammunition only fueled the uprising (and led to media portrayals of Israel as an inhumane occupier, as will be discussed below), Rabin changed the policy to one of "might, power, and beatings." As it turned out, seeking more direct physical contact with Palestinians led to unprecedented brutality by Israeli soldiers – what Shiff and Yaari labeled as the "Intifada brutalization symptom" (1990: 149). A telling example was the case of Lt. Col. Yehuda Meir, who ordered his soldiers in January 1988, to bind and gag twelve Palestinian detainees from the village of Huwara.

An indicative example of Israel's attempt to innovate repressive measures came in the face of "non-lethal" "plastic bullets" and later "rubber bullets," both developed for use in dispersing street demonstrations. Aware of international criticism of its repressive measures and the growing internal dissent, Israel looked for ways to increase the number of injuries but decrease the number of killings during confrontations or incidents considered as non-life-threatening. Attempts, however, to clearly define what a life-threatening situation was and what it was not were far from being successful. Being aware of the ongoing interrogation they would face in cases of using live ammunition instead of rubber bullets, many soldiers simply decided not to shoot at all. Others, standing in the face of raging Palestinian masses, decided to use live ammunition and faced trials.

Thus, in September 1988, live bullets with a hard plastic tip were introduced. Yet, in the face of the still high numbers of Palestinian deaths, Israel began to use rubber bullets (steel marble covered by a thin layer of rubber, fired at lower velocity) as of January 1989. The use of rubber bullets did lower the number of Palestinian deaths; the use of live ammunition, "rubber" or "plastic" bullets remained, however, the major cause of Palestinians deaths over the first two years of the Intifada. It also brought about an increase of injuries as shown in Figure 5.2.

Other measures of repression included collective punishment. While trying to avoid using collective punishments during the first few months of the uprising, Israel was soon to adopt punitive measures in face of its inability to take over the situation (Shiff and Yaari 1990). One such punitive measure was curfew. A curfew means forcing a total community to stay indoors for a specific period. It usually lasted for days and often weeks, with occasional one hour breaks for food provisioning. According to FACTS, a Palestinian information center, the total days of curfew as of 1987 show a steady increase both in towns and in refugee camps, reaching the height of 1,560 days in 123 places by July 1988. Whereas in December 1987, thirty-six days of curfew were reported in the local press, January 1988 shows a rise to 112 days, and between February and July 1988 the total number of curfew days does not go below 200. Table 5.1 presents data on some of the collective punishments between 1988 and 1992, based on a report by PHRIC (1994).

Based on the above analysis, it is possible to argue the following. First, regardless of the source and the specific indicator used, the level of overt, direct Israeli repressive measures (i.e., gun firing, beatings, etc.) was decreasing after the first two years of uprising. Second, the mode of indirect repressive measures (e.g., land confiscation), while steadily growing and substituting for direct repressive measures (e.g., curfew), nonetheless decreased after 1990. As of 1991, it is possible to discern also an overall decline in the mode of collective repression (e.g., curfews, and military house demolition – see Figure 5.1). Last, but not least, while the level of Palestinian contentious events sharply decreased after 1990, the use of deadly weapons and other forms of violent actions by Palestinians was rising gradually, with a marked peak in 1991 and 1992.

How can we account for the overall patterns of contention between 1987 and 1991? Several explanations can be provided, some of which will be treated in more depth in the following sections.

First, while the sense of threat during 1988 undoubtedly influenced the

*Table 5.1* Types of Israeli collective punishment

| Type of punishment | 1988 | 1989 | 1990 | 1991 | 1992 |
|---|---|---|---|---|---|
| Curfew days (not including E. Jerusalem) | 3,091 | 3,192 | 5,704 | 896 | 953 |
| Trees uprooting | 25,000 | 52,698 | 10,000 | 34,000 | 19,898 |
| Land confiscations (dunam) | 10,000 | 75,000 | 227,335 | 80,594 | 14,660 |
| Administrative demolitions* | 423 | 347 | 102 | 227 | 160 |
| Military demolition | 112 | 163 | 143 | 75 | 12 |

Note
The difference between administrative and military demolition is the declared justification, not the end-product. Military demolition is done as a punitive response to involvement of Palestinians in violent action (whether proved or suspected). The reason for administrative demolition is unlicensed building of houses.

forceful reaction by Israel, as of late 1989 a policy of lowering the profile of repression was implemented. The new policy for controlling the Intifada involved a systematic attempt by military forces to keep away from main streets and population centers, to avoid engaging in clashes with Palestinians in their population centers. Instead, Israel began to rely more on the use of covert modes of repression. This meant increased reliance on intelligence for tracing Palestinian individuals suspected to be the key activists responsible for sustaining the momentum of the uprising. It also meant ordering the military to minimize direct contact with the Palestinian population, and to monitor activities in refugee camps and towns from rooftop observation posts.

According to a report by the Jerusalem Media and Communication Center (JMCC), the new policy's central facet was the large-scale and frequent use of undercover squads within the territories. Soldiers of special units named *Doovdevun* (Hebrew for cherry) and *Shimshon* (Samson in Hebrew), disguised in traditional Arab garb and heavily armed, would travel around the territories in local cars. At times, they even tried to join a crowd of stone throwers to identify the "hardcore" activists. Other modes of repression were heavy taxation and ID card confiscation. The idea was simple, yet proved efficient, designed to force Palestinians to interact with the authorities on procedural and bureaucratic grounds. During a concerted campaign of tax collection, ID cards were taken from any Palestinians who did not pay tax, facing them with two options: either to pay the sums demanded or to serve a prison sentence.

A similar mode was the introduction of new ID cards, and then of magnetic cards, which the Palestinians were forced to carry with them, otherwise risking arrest. At times, the simple act of collecting the new ID card was sufficient for arrest as the Israeli authorities had a list of "wanted" activists. The new policy proved successful in significantly lowering the Palestinian death toll; it succeeded also in creating confusion and distrust among Palestinians and, consequently higher numbers of shootings at alleged collaborators with Israel.

Second, the Palestinian insurgents were capable of forming a coordinated leadership that most competently directed the uprising and widened the scope of participation. Yet the level and extent of such coordination slowly deteriorated as Israel became more sophisticated in its modes of repression. Indeed, by the end of 1988 the ability of the coordinated leadership to continue its guidance and control of the Intifada had weakened significantly. Moreover, the ability of the Palestinian insurgents to maintain a high level of coordination was contingent, to a large degree, upon the prospects of political gain. As these prospects became imminent, internal conflicts surged.

In this regard, the Intifada witnessed the rise of an Islamic political action-oriented movement, Hamas, introducing a more militant and violent approach that soon began to rival the Nationalist Movement. As will be further elaborated, intra-conflict surfaced even among PLO-oriented grassroots organizations aligned with the United National Command of the Uprising (UNCU), as the PLO began engaging in a dialogue with the US administration. Intra-conflicts resurfaced in a more ferocious fashion during 1990 amidst the suspension of the dialogue and the Gulf crisis. As will be demonstrated also, although coordination had been established more or less between the Nationalist and Islamist Movements during the first months of the uprising, political achievements and the prospects for further achievements brought about a fierce contention between the two groupings.

Third, prospects of political gains were highly contingent upon the visibility of the confrontation with Israel in news media. The news media, mostly the international news media, played a crucial role in the Intifada; the Palestinians saw news coverage as a means for broadening the scope of contention. The practice of limited violence and the preferred frames were designed, to a large extent, to promote the Palestinian cause to the international community. Palestinians were willing to endure the Israeli crackdown and maintained a high level of coordination as long as their non-violent actions proved efficacious. In that sense, the combination of news media presence and the visibility of Israeli repression was a "winner." As already mentioned, in 1989 the Israeli mode of repression went through a significant shift, which had a broad impact on the symbolic struggle in front of the media. The use of undercover squads and other techniques of covert, less visible repression that were less dramatic and newsworthy, practically meant no media show, and no media show meant deteriorating international involvement.

Fourth, the Gulf Crisis of 1990–1 was a serious blow to the Intifada. It was a critical, transformative event in the sense that it posed a stalemate in US involvement. The centrality of the US in influencing the outcome of the Intifada had increased considerably following the Soviet Glasnost and Perestroika and the ensuing changes in Moscow's foreign policy in general and its policy towards Israel and the PLO in particular (Golan 1991). Thus, after almost three years of promising progress and physical and mental sacrifice, it appeared that the fate of the Intifada would be largely determined by developments elsewhere in the region (Litvak 1990). The political stalemate and the resulting shared frustration translated into a process of radicalization, weakening coordination, and tense internal conflicts among PLO factions and also between Nationalist and Islamist groups.

Finally and closely related, the Gulf Crisis shifted the media spotlight from the Israeli Palestinian battlefield. The Palestinians, argue Wolfsfeld (1997), were a relatively minor story compared with the drama of the Scuds falling on Tel-Aviv, and the ongoing war in Iraq. Israel used the opportunity to take complete control over the occupied territories, and indeed, throughout the actual fighting during early 1991, a total curfew was imposed; not even one riot or terrorist attack occurred during this period. While this might have accounted for the deteriorating *standing* of the Palestinian Intifada in the international news media, Arafat's declaration of unconditional support of Saddam Hussein in August 1990 had broader repercussions. The immediate result was a negative coverage of the Palestinian struggle that threatened to shatter the painstaking achievements reached by the internally-based leadership core.

## Mobilizing structure: coalition formation, competition and intra-conflict

During cycles of contention, argues Sidney Tarrow (1998), social movements must bring people together in the field, shape coalitions, confront opponents, and assure their own future after the exhilaration accompanying the peak of mobilization has passed. A mobilizing structure, Tarrow continues, should be distinguished from formal or grassroots modes of organization, and "refers to the connective structures that link leaders and followers, center and periphery, and different parts of a movement sector, permitting coordination and aggregation between movement organizations and allowing movements to persist even when formal organization is lacking" (p. 124).

Thus far, we have analyzed the development of both formal and informal grassroots organizations and leadership cores, showing how the internally-based grassroots organizations gradually formed issue/action-specific coalitions. The purpose of this section is to analyze the ways Palestinian grassroots organizations acted to broaden the scope of the challenge to Israeli rule during the Intifada. In order to bring about a popular uprising that would mobilize the entire Palestinian population, it was crucial to increase the density of the mobilization infrastructure, which had already developed throughout the 1980s.

As was demonstrated in previous chapters, the mobilization infrastructure was fairly impressive and efficient. However, numerous Palestinians were still unaffiliated with any of the grassroots organizations. Moreover, in the face of the Israeli crackdown and the existence of Palestinian collaborators, a further strengthening and thickening of this mobilizing infrastructure was imperative, especially in light of the potentially conflicting ideologies and the developing tension between the well-established Nationalist camp and the increasingly influential Islamic camp.

As described previously, Israeli attempts to quell the broadening clashes were harsh and unbending. Yet, the Israeli repressive repertoire was not limited to protest policing only. Israel disrupted the daily routine of the occupied territories. To do so, Israel shut down the gasoline supply, schools and academic institutions, cut off phone services, and gradually started to impose a total curfew over the occupied territories. Additionally, the scope and intensity of detentions increased substantially, a fact that forced Israel to create new detention facilities, such as Ansar II in Gaza, and Ansar III in the Israeli Negev area. In fact, to control the situation, Israel was forced to recruit up to five times more military forces than had usually been the case (Vitullo 1988).

In spite of the Israeli crackdown, the Palestinians managed to form and sustain a mobilizing structure. The Intifada's mobilizing structure, an illustration of which is presented in Figure 5.3, was the product of nationalist grassroots activists, an additional phase of organizational infrastructure to the one established during the mid-1980s as analyzed in Chapter 3 (Figure 3.1).

The willingness of the Palestinian population to participate in the broadening uprising was so high that even central grassroots activists who acted as the first

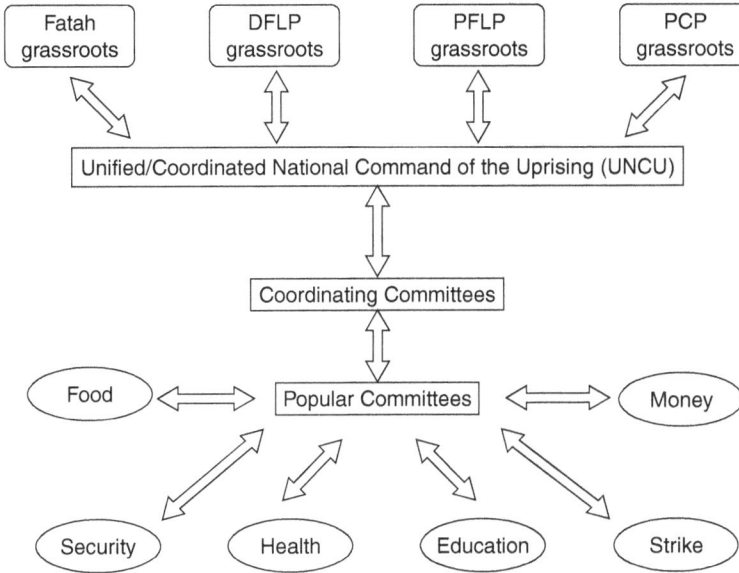

*Figure 5.3* Nationalist Movement structure of mobilization.

members in the UNCU were overwhelmed by the scope of the participation (Hass 1996). The following first-hand account describing the ways Palestinians organized locally[5] exemplifies the willingness of the population and devotion of grassroots activists. The speaker is Odai, a PFLP grassroots activist:

> I went home to Hebron, and the primary concern in my mind at that time was to keep this thing alive ... We had an emergency council of young leaders from different factions to force the city to move. We began to organize young people. They used to bring them to me to talk to and I would tell them, "There is nothing to talk about. The only thing we have to do now is to kick the Israelis out of our cities ... There was coordination between the leaders of youth factions at a local level and we decided how to implement the orders between us. This was very easy. I had a friend who was from Fatah ... another friend was from the PCP ... we called each other, discussed things, and agreed to tell each others' people and got back to each other.

Ubiquitous as such participation was, it nonetheless necessitated the formation of an organizational framework that could simultaneously sustain the widespread participation and assist the population in coping with the Israeli crackdown. As can be seen in Figure 5.3, the mass mobilization took the form of popular committees designed to provide the basic daily needs of the population in the towns, villages, and refugee camps. In every neighborhood or apartment building, tenants – usually members of one of the grassroots organizations – organized action-committees responsible for various missions such as food supply, provisional teaching facilities, first-aid treatment, shelter for "wanted" activists, collection of donations, or security from Settlers' attacks or vandalism (Nassar and Heacock 1990). For example, temporary classes were established in churches and mosques and teachers taught voluntarily. Health treatment teams coordinated visits to residents injured during confrontations and, on occasion, circulated lists of required blood types. The committees also harvested crops and initiated local markets for free distribution.

The devotion of the popular committees was so high that when one region was under military curfew, those committees operating in other areas made additional efforts to deliver supplies to the "internal" committees, which then distributed the supply. Such was the case when a closure was imposed on Gaza in December 1987, and popular committees had sent food and medical supplies from East Jerusalem and the West Bank. The popular committees write Nassar and Heacock, "...established a shadow administrative structure for a society that had decisively rejected the one in place for over twenty years. They therefore institutionalized and legitimized the Intifada at the grassroots level" (p. 202).

The proliferation of the popular committees indeed represented the institutionalization of the uprising; a fact fully grasped and realized by Israel, declaring that membership in popular committees was illegal on August 18, 1988. Still, this Israeli attempt to outlaw the committees had hardly any influence on their ability to operate, let alone on Palestinians' willingness to participate in such activities.

The United National Command of the Uprising (UNCU), which systematized this widespread participation, accomplished the proliferation of the popular committees during the early phases of the uprising. The formation of the UNCU took place during December 1987, the product of secret meetings initiated by grassroots activists from the variety of PLO factions. With the publication of its first leaflet in January 1988,[6] the UNCU became the informal, clandestine leadership of the uprising. The immediate aim of the UNCU was the coordination of the first popular committees, for which coordinating committees were formed in several areas. Comprised of grassroots representatives of the PLO factions, but also of the Islamic Jihad (Kuttab 1988), the UNCU began on the West Bank and only moved into Gaza towards the end of January 1988.

The UNCU (known also as the United Nations Leadership) was an informal, clandestine coordination of the grassroots organizations in structure and mode of operation. It was not hierarchically structured or based in a fixed location. Rather, the UNCU was a forum for decision-making convened frequently, yet not at fixed times or in a systematic manner, at random locations (usually an apartment). The participants in these meetings could well have been any grassroots activists, with no formal status of leadership. Concomitantly, the process of decision-making had no fixed procedures, and the decisions reached were never mandatory in the sense that no autonomy was vested in the UNCU members. Indeed, and as will be elaborated below, in addition to the leaflets published by the UNCU, each organization formulated and published its own leaflets. Other leaflets were local leaflets, the initiatives of grassroots activists, and sectoral leaflets by voluntary committees. In that sense, while signing the leaflets as the "unified" leadership, the UNCU was in fact an expression for a coordinated mobilization that rested on the grassroots activists' understanding of the necessity to join forces in order to maintain and increase the uprising's momentum.

The UNCU operated in several ways. Attempts to direct the Intifada were conducted through serialized leaflets mostly printed in East Jerusalem and distributed throughout the territories with a frequency of two or three per month during 1988, and later at a slower pace due to Israel's crackdown. The serialized leaflets consisted of specific directives, public calls for action, or weekly or biweekly schedules; they thus practically organized the uprising's daily contentious routine. They provided the population with a reassurance that the struggle against the occupation was guided and supervised. In fact, as Johnson, O'Brien, and Hiltermann maintain (1988), people were constantly trying to spot the latest statement from the UNCU. The following excerpt from leaflet 13 (April 11, 1988) gives a sense of the style of and guidance provided by the leaflets:

> No Voice Rises above the Voice of the Uprising; O struggling people! You have shaken the ground under the feet of the Zionist occupiers ... making our shining future through your heroic struggle ... so let us continue with civic disobedience. The Israeli oppressive measures have failed because of your unity ... They have only increased our determination to continue ... We salute our people and our national institutions, and especially the economic institutions, who refused to pay taxes ... Fridays, Sundays and Tuesday 12th April are days of demonstrations and national activities ... Thursday 21st April is to be the day of the Palestinian Molotov, as an answer to the policy of the authorities to shoot the throwers of Molotov [cocktails]. It will be a day for general strike. O great people! Continue your forward struggle...; The Palestine Liberation Organization; The Unified Leadership of the Uprising in the Occupied Territories.

When the distribution of leaflets was successful, getting a copy was easy. Yet, this was seldom the case. Israel put considerable efforts both into detecting the members of the UNCU and, consequently, into stopping the publication of leaflets. Detecting the members of the UNCU was a complicated task and, as it turned out, ineffective in terms of stopping the leaflets' writing and distribution. While the use of a covert mode of repression and undercover squads proved relatively successful for detecting the uprising's "hardcore" activists, it did not stop the flow of leaflets. The reason was simple. There were no fixed activists responsible for the writing of the leaflets, just as any activist could take the temporary role of a UNCU member. In fact, each time Israel announced it had arrested the writers of the leaflets a new leaflet came out.

Frustrated by Israel's inability to track down the leaflets' writers, Israeli

Minister of Police, Bar-Lev, issued a false declaration claiming their arrest in early 1988. According to an Israeli security official who was interviewed, the grassroots activists' ability to write and distribute leaflets amazed Israel. When asked about the attempts to stop the leaflets, he said,

> It was simply unbelievable. We simply were unable to take control of this. Every time we traced a place from which leaflets were distributed, it took two or three days, at the most, for new leaflets to come out. We started to joke about that and played with guessing how successful we would be this time.

Still, Bar-Lev's false declaration was also a part of a manipulative Israeli policy of repression. According to Kuttab (1988) and Nassar and Heacock (1990), Israel gradually started to publish fake leaflets to muddle the directives of the genuine leaflets, thereby hoping to generate confusion among the Palestinians. Palestinians, however, were quick to identify the false leaflets for two reasons and warned the population about them. First, leaflets were usually distributed collectively, that is, piles of leaflets were put in various locations for people to take, and sometimes, in their full version, they were aired on the radio, written as graffiti on walls, recited over the mosques' speakers, or transcribed as tape recorder cassettes. For example, radio Al-Quds, Monte-Carlo or the Voice of Jerusalem (broadcasting from abroad) were broadcasting the leaflets in full (Vitullo 1988), in addition to other contents such as national songs and specific learning programs on how to make Molotov cocktails. Ironically, many Palestinians were capable of getting the most recent leaflet by purchasing Israeli newspapers, as some of the leaflets were published in the Israeli press. Leaflet number nine (March 2, 1988), for example, was published in the *Jerusalem Post* verbatim.

Second, the flow of communication was based upon an organic solidarity in which the level of personal ties, involvement by the Palestinian populace, and familiarity with each other facilitated the identification of such fake leaflets. As one of the Palestinian interviewees argued, "...it took less then a day for everybody throughout the territories to know what was happening ... it is not like in Israel, here everyone knows each other ... the society here is based on *Hamulas* [big family]."

Apparently, the level of familiarity and personal ties translated into high efficiency when initiating action. Makhul's account of the role of a grassroots activist and the ways he took control over the daily routine of confrontations is a useful illustration of this efficiency:

> Every half hour he received up-to-date information from his people on what was going on in the Gaza Strip ... [although] the distribution of leaflets from any organization was forbidden ... if he wanted to he could organize the distribution of leaflets every day without problems ... yesterday, five hundred women went on to Bayt Hanun, and they only knew of the planned

trip five minutes before they left ... When we want to operate through the whole Strip, our short experience has taught us that within a few minutes we can block the main traffic route leading out from the Strip.

(1988: 945)

While such commitment originated in the 1980s and further thickened during the Intifada, serious challenges to this commitment were mounted nevertheless. The Israeli crackdown, coupled with the prolongation of the uprising, necessitated a judicious leadership highly attentive to the abilities of its constituency and capable of long-term planning. Specifically, for the uprising to continue with widespread participation and coordinated action, it was imperative that this leadership both cope with the difficulties experienced by the overall population and form a joint front of all the organizations and political forces.

To get a better sense of the Palestinians' ability to sustain the uprising it is important to specify several major reasons for such competence, but also to learn about the difficulties and contingencies that threatened to thwart and undermine the collective endeavor to maximize participation and commitment.

Not surprisingly, money played a central role in enabling the Palestinians to sustain the Intifada. Throughout the uprising, calls for support from Arab States had been a permanent feature in the serialized leaflets, together with local initiatives for fund-raising. In various leaflets, the UNCU addressed the owners of the "national capital" to assist the needy as an integral part of the national struggle. Still, the externally-based PLO played a central role in transferring money to the occupied territories for the purposes of both the PLO and the UNCU. According to Shalev (1990), the PLO transferred considerable amounts of money for assisting any family who experienced loss, whose house was demolished, whose son or daughter was in prison. The monies were also used for paying central grassroots activists and financing resistive actions.

Main channels for transferring funds were tourists who, by reason of their ability to bring into Israel unlimited amounts of money, delivered funds for the territories; moneychangers in East Jerusalem, to whose foreign bank accounts the PLO delivered funds; through Palestinians' bank accounts in Israel to which the PLO transferred funds;[7] and by Israeli Palestinians. Israel was only partially successful in coping with the flow of funds to the occupied territories. While being able to restrict the amount of money coming from Jordan or Egypt, there was no way to control the activities of moneychangers, or to capture those who tried to bring in more money than permitted.

In terms of the UNCU's control over the uprising and level of autonomy in decision-making, as of the second half of 1988 it became clear that the PLO, through its funding, took over the controlling of the Intifada. Shiff and Yaari (1990) argue that the ability of the UNCU to operate was also significantly weakened as the army gradually hardened its operation and captured many of its members, which consequently increased the latter's dependency on the PLO. Indeed, as of late 1988 the frequency of published leaflets by the UNCU was much lower.

Still, the PLO was far from able to support the Intifada indefinitely. Many of the promises of funds made by Arab States went unfulfilled and by 1990 the financial resources of the PLO were such that the allocation of money went to resistive activities rather than supporting the needy population in the local communities (Litvak 1990). Further, as it turned out, the PLO "investment" in Saddam Hussein as of the Arab Summit in Baghdad, in May 1990, and the ensuing Iraqi financial support, not only alienated many of the Gulf States, but also, by February 1991, had proven detrimental to the Intifada.

Second, throughout its leaflets the UNCU, fully aware of the difficulties the population was experiencing and, therefore, avoiding extreme demands, had been calling for support from various sectors. It was clear that the disengagement from Israel and the desire to show self-sufficiency required cooperation from relatively well-off Palestinians. Indeed, scholars who studied the uprising share the argument that the UNCU was highly attentive and realistic in assessing the population's ability to endure the ongoing struggle (Abu-Amr 1988; Hiltermann 1990; Mishal with Aharoni 1989; Pressberg 1988). As will be detailed below, already at the end of 1988 it is possible to discern a decrease in the frequency of calls for disengagement from Israel.

Calls directed to Palestinian employers to take on unemployed workers, to factories to lower their prices, or to shopkeepers to remain open at specific times even during general strikes, were a recurrent theme in the leaflets. In leaflet nine (March 1988), the UNCU provided a list of directives aimed at strengthening the uprising's ability to stand by its goal of self-reliance. The list included a call for shops to open every day for one hour, a call for factories to increase production, and a call for property owners to cede rent from the preceding three months. At other times, the UNCU called also for the population to refrain from excessive expenditures. For example, in leaflet 22 (July 1988), the UNCU provided the following rules to guide behavior during the feast of *al-Adha*,[8] ". . . on Friday and Saturday 22nd and 23rd July, all stores will be opened from the morning until 7 pm, and until 2 pm on Feast days. We urge you to restrict your celebration of the Feast to religious rites only."

At the same time, the UNCU had been intimidating collaborators, also referred to as informers or *wastonaries* (Arabic for broker or pimp). Collaborators were usually given many opportunities for repentance. Additionally, Palestinians who refused to resign from their jobs and positions in Israeli institutions (e.g., the civil administration) were seen as collaborators. The UNCU saw collaborators as a serious threat to the uprising, and put considerable effort into forcing them to sever their links with the Israeli authorities and to repent publicly. At the same time, leaflets included calls for the public to detect collaborators and to punish them. A full section of UNCU leaflet 25 (September 1988) extolled the action of the deterrence (or strike) forces against the collaborators in Hebron, Jenin, Qabatia, and other places in which collective "purification" took place, and to continue and purify the internal front of the uprising from those who sold their souls and dignity to the occupier, thereby betraying their people.

One of the first cases of lethal punishment of collaborators took place in the village of Qabatia in February 1988 and was documented by Johnson, O'Brien, and Hiltermann (1988: 10):

> A small boy threw a stone at the house of Muhammad Ayad, an alleged Shin Bet informant. He opened fire on the crowd, killing a child. Villagers stormed the house several times ... When Ayad's ammunition was exhausted, villagers entered the house and killed him with an ax. They dragged his body to the street where virtually the entire village spat on it including his relatives. His body was hung up on an electricity pylon ... The next day at a gathering in the mosque, four other collaborators handed their guns over to the mukhtar and formally apologized to the village.

However, the growing number of collaborators reflected the increasing internal problems and discord in the territories, the result of the ongoing struggle and the lack of satisfactory political gains, along with Israeli policies designed to maximize collaboration. By 1990, the weariness of the population was clearly felt and the massive participation which characterized the early years of the Intifada was on the decline.

Fully aware of the population's laxity in complying with its directives and calls, the UNCU tried to ease the burden by introducing more flexibility into its demands. According to Litvak (1990), despite extension of the number of hours that shops were allowed to remain opened, and heavy pressure on employers to hire more employees and to pay them fairly, inertia was on the rise, along with growing noncompliance with the UNCU directives.

The rise of warlords and factionalism within the UNCU provided two additional measures of the difficulties facing the resistance. The strike forces, initially a grassroots development aimed at guarding Palestinians from Jewish Settlers and other manifestations of vigilantism, took over the neighborhoods and villages, routinely terrorizing the population. While the strike forces took advantage of the situation for their own personal benefit, others engaged in factional strife. Indeed, 1990 also witnessed the aggravation of conflicts between the four member factions of the UNCU, primarily over the appropriate means to revive the Intifada. This conflict precipitated the further radicalization of the PFLP and the DFLP. We will have more to say about this in the following section.

The third factor accounting for Palestinian ability to sustain the uprising was the attempts to form and maintain coordination between the Nationalist and the Islamic forces. The importance of this coordination was fully recognized by both the Nationalist and the Islamic camps, and genuine attempts were made to form a *modus vivendi*. Coordination between the Nationalist movement and the Islamic Jihad had been relatively successful; the effort built on past collaboration and Fatah's support of Jihad's operation, which were translated into joint efforts and actions during the uprising.

Similar attempts with the Muslim Brotherhood, however, were far more

complex.[9] Attempting coordination with the Muslim Brotherhood and its political arm Hamas (acronym of the Islamic Resistance Movement), eliminated, at
least temporarily, a central factor that could have jeopardized the ability of the
UNCU to sustain the uprising. This fragile coordination disintegrated, ironically,
amidst the first signs of political gains. Ideological tension and the struggle
between the movements resurfaced and resulted in a *radical flank effect*
(Gamson 1990). In other words, the radicalization of the Muslim Brotherhood
and the following collapse of the inherently fragile coordination with the UNCU
turned the Nationalist Movement into a viable partner for negotiation from the
Israeli viewpoint.

Among the many Intifada researchers, there is unanimous agreement concerning the reluctance of the Muslim Brotherhood to participate in the popular
insurgency, primarily due to its traditional ideological emphasis on personal,
passive sacrifices (Hunter 1991; Litvak 1991; Paz 1992; Shiff and Yaari 1990).
In fact, only in January 1988 did the movement find a way out from the growing
contradiction between its ideological creeds and the daily events. Facing a combination of internal pressure, expressed mostly by young activists who kept
pushing for action, and anxiety that the "street" was slipping out of its control
especially given the Islamic Jihad's participation, the Brotherhood's leadership
succumbed to internal pressure to form Hamas.

Such a decision came as a response to the formal formation of the UNCU and
its first signed leaflet. It reflected an understanding by the Muslim Brotherhood's
leaders that they must present a distinct action-identity in order to preserve their
sociopolitical power. This was so especially in face of the active involvement of
the Islamic Jihad and the growing popularity it acquired (Jaradat 1992; Litvak
1991). Forming Hamas was a formal expression of what had been already happening in the streets. As elaborated in previous chapters, throughout 1987 Brotherhood activists participated in the escalating clashes together with nationalist
activists. Hamas's formation, then, did not change the overall picture, though it
demonstrated a growing notion of pragmatism on the part of the Muslim Brotherhood.

In order to present a united front vis-à-vis Israel, the UNCU and the Muslim
Brotherhood established a kind of *modus vivendi*, that is, a latent understanding
to avoid confrontation and to try to lessen ideological disagreements. Throughout most of 1988, Hamas, despite critique on the Nationalist methods and
tactics, did not openly oppose the UNCU. In fact, as Paz (1992) contends, there
were several attempts to coordinate strike days and to modulate the distinct
leaflets. In Hamas's leaflets, before the Palestinian declaration of independence
in late 1988 (see below), one could find different emphases in style, values, and
modes of action, yet one could also detect two consistent features. There was no
call for attacks on nationalist activists coupled with a call for unity to maintain
the momentum of the Intifada.

The significance of this relative coordination should be gauged in light of the
Israeli attempts to hamper it. In relating to Palestinian sociopolitical forces in the
occupied territories throughout 1988, Israel had tried to continue its traditional

policy of "divide and rule"; during the first few months of the uprising Israel had regarded Hamas as a potential counterforce to the Nationalist forces. Nonetheless, the publication of the Hamas Charter in August 1988 resurfaced the tension between the Muslim Brotherhood and the UNCU. It was a public declaration of the Muslim Brotherhood as a political power competing with the PLO. The Charter was triggered by King Hussein's declaration of Jordan's disengagement from the West Bank and the Arab States' decision at the Arab Summit of June 1988, in Algeria, to allocate funds for the PLO. Still, as two Palestinian activists argued, "The problem will only come if Hamas's leaflets say 'Don't listen to the UNL, don't follow its leaflets, and don't face the occupation as the number one goal'" (Hunter 1991: 208).

In mid-1988 this was not the case. Israel, however, anxious over the growing role of Hamas in the uprising and alarmed by the publication of the Charter, reacted by arresting several Hamas leaders. The Charter expressed the Islamic solution to the occupation, but this time with an action-orientation entwined with a Palestinian nationalist flavor. However, as al-Jaro notes (1990), the first Hamas leadership, arrested soon after the Charter publication, was opposed to armed struggle. Only after Arafat's speech in the UN in which he renounced terrorism, and the increased Israeli repression of the movement, did the Hamas-led Muslim Brotherhood start to engage in armed struggle, including terrorism, against Israeli targets and to challenge the UNCU, simultaneously.

Indeed, in leaflet 29 (November 1988) the UNCU urged the Palestinian fundamentalist groups to "... prefer the general national interest, the national interest of our people, over their sectarian interests and premises, and to stop with the manifestations of negative positions ... since they serve the enemy." This leaflet was issued five days after the nineteenth Palestinian National Council (PNC) in Algeria, during which Arafat proclaimed the establishment of an independent Palestinian State and the willingness to embrace the idea of two states in Palestine. This declaration was followed up and expanded later on, on December 13, 1988. During the UN session in Geneva, Arafat recognized Israel, renounced terrorism, and accepted UN Resolutions 242 and 338 as a basis for an agreement with Israel.[10]

The shift in Hamas's mode of action was manifested in the leaflets issued immediately after the PNC declaration of independence. In leaflet 31 (November 1988), Hamas metaphorically used the Balfour Declaration to denigrate the declaration of independence and its implicit willingness to compromise over Palestine, "This is a warning to people so they will know ... the shahid Al-Kasem: No to the Balfour declaration, yes to the blessed uprising. Let the blessed uprising continue fighting the occupier. Let's fire the land underneath their feet."

This was the first time that the Muslim Brotherhood, through Hamas, explicitly and publicly called for a struggle against Israel. In a matter of days after Arafat's UN speech, leaflet 33 unequivocally expressed this shift, "Struggle and confrontation on Sunday the 25th of December memorializing the establishment of the Jihad groups in Palestine by the shahid Abd al-Kader al-Husseini ... let the uprising continue in Jihad."[11] The following months witnessed terrorist acts by Hamas, such as the kidnapping and assassination of Israeli soldiers. Whereas until early 1989 the Israeli crackdown was aimed mostly against the Islamic Jihad, from then on Hamas and the Muslim Brotherhood became the primary target (Paz 1992). In May 1989, Israel initiated a wide-scale operation arresting Hamas and the Brotherhood activists and leaders; in September of that same year, the movement as a whole was officially declared illegal.

The break between the Islamist and the Nationalist Movements that took place after the UN declaration is our primary concern here. As Shiff and Yaari (1990) argue, the declaration caused a huge wave of protest by Hamas activists. Throughout the territories, numerous handouts, petitions and graffiti by Hamas called for denouncing Arafat and the UNCU altogether. In various instances, confrontations broke out between Hamas and UNCU activists. Litvak (1991) similarly describes the bitter struggle between the parties, manifested in the significant expansion of Hamas's presence in the West Bank – the traditional PLO/Nationalist stronghold. Disruption of peace initiatives by Israeli and Palestinians activists demonstrated an additional form of contention. On March 24, 1989, during a conference in Beita, Hamas activists arrived at the scene and violently prevented a planned peace demonstration from taking place.

Continuing confrontations between the two camps characterized late 1989 and most of 1990. During that period, however, the intensity was lower for two reasons. First, the international status of the PLO was seriously damaged during the Gulf Crisis. The suspension of the PLO–US dialogue in June 1990 amidst the developing crisis in the Gulf and after a terrorist act against Israel on May 30 by PLO forces contributed to the deterioration of Arafat's status. The US decision to suspend its dialogue with the PLO threatened to annul one of the Intifada's greatest gains. In the face of such a threat, Hamas's approach began to appear more realistic and attractive to a larger portion of the Palestinian populace (Mishal and Sela 1999).

Second, the PLO's unconditional support for Iraq and Saddam Hussein in August 1990 brought about a significant decrease in the flow of funds coming from the Gulf States. Facing the threat of both financial and political bankruptcy (i.e., the suspension of the dialogue with the US for which internal critiques were mounted by the DFLP, the PFLP, and hard-line Fatah members), Arafat resorted to the traditional vision of a pan-Arabic Community in the hope of applying the necessary pressure on Israel and garnering assistance in funding the uprising.

The PLO's need for unity at that specific time resulted in a September 1990 agreement with Hamas to re-coordinate their activities so as to avert deterioration into an all-out internal war. However, as Litvak (1991) contends, the agreement did not end the struggle for dominance. What actually lessened the struggle this time was Hamas's weakening status within the territories. Fully aware of the potential danger from Hamas – a danger that was, to a large extent, the product of its own creation, Israel engaged in a systematic repression of the Muslim Brotherhood's organizational network. Israel's familiarity with Hamas leaders, the result of traditional fostering of the Brotherhood activities and operations throughout the early 1980s, facilitated the crackdown. Throughout 1990 the arrest of most activists and of the Muslim Brotherhood spiritual leader, Ahmed Yassin, brought about a significant decrease in the movement's strength. From that period onward, Hamas acted solely through terrorist activities conducted by its military arm, Izz al-Din al-Qassam. The only conspicuous political actor left in the scene was the UNCU, with a firm alliance to the PLO. The growing militarism of the Brotherhood made PLO forces in the occupied territories if not desirable at least a reasonable partner for possible resolution of the conflict from the Israeli point of view.

## Framing contention: diffusion, events and radicalization

In order to maintain the zeal and momentum of contention it is imperative to construct meaning for the contention and to diffuse it among participants in many social and geographic locations. The role of a social movement as a signifying agent is twofold: internal as well as external. Internally, vis-à-vis their constituency, social movement framers conjure up and transform an array of symbols, images, historical exemplars, metaphors and other cultural themes that inspire and legitimate the movement's activities and campaigns. By doing so, a social movement encourages its members to continue their activity, coupled with an effort to attract other, as yet non-mobilized, potential constituents to join the challenge. Externally, vis-à-vis authorities, other rivals, and third parties, social movement framers construct collective action frames to punctuate or signal some existing social condition or aspect of life and define it as unjust and intolerable, thereby necessitating corrective action. It is the way each framing effort was carried out and the interplay among both that most concerns us here.

The uprising, Wolfsfeld (1997) argues, was, above all, a struggle for international public opinion. Yet, the Palestinian insurgents' attempt to "market" their national struggle to the international arena was embedded in and contingent upon their ability to seize and expand the opportunity on the state level (i.e., Israel), to capitalize on the Israeli structure of political opportunity in order to be able to create an opportunity on the international level. For the Palestinians, winning the struggle for world opinion would increase the likelihood of political gains. For Israel, winning the contest over world opinion would result in foreclosing the opportunity for the Palestinian insurgents at the state level.

The uprising's leaflets acted as a mechanism not only for calls for action, but also for diffusion of frames. Through the leaflets, the UNCU and Hamas addressed the Palestinian insurgents as well as other actors such as the Arab States and Israel. Yet, unlike Hamas, the Nationalist Movement invested considerable effort to market the Intifada to the international arena, specifically to the European Community, the Soviet Union, and most of all the United States.

As we have already seen, the Palestinian insurgents in the occupied territories systematically attempted to discipline their contention and form an impressive division of labor among a vast array of political groups and factions. What types of frames were constructed for the purpose of shaping Palestinian contention?

What types of frames were constructed and amplified for gaining the support of the international community? In dealing with these two closely related questions attention must be paid to Israeli's parallel counter-efforts to win the battle over international public opinion, as well as to the influence of contingencies (e.g., the Gulf Crisis) on the ongoing contention.

### Inward framing: the local level

The UNCU was the central actor framing the Intifada primarily on the local level, that is, the occupied territories. It acted as the voice of the Palestinian insurgents for delivering their calls to the outside, thereby complementing – albeit not without tension and discord – the activities of the PLO and several of its spokespersons located within the occupied territories. As such, UNCU's attempts to construct the meaning of the struggle had to confront various actors simultaneously with different modes of action and reaction to the ongoing confrontation with Israel.

Basing its framing efforts on previous systematic trends that accentuated a distinct Palestinian culture and tradition, the UNCU embarked upon a process that designated as the Intifada's core frame the popular struggle for national liberation. All leaflets introduced the Intifada as a genuine, self-sustained, collective endeavor of a deprived people fighting against an unjust authority to gain recognition of its national rights and aspirations. Most leaflets accentuated this theme. In fact, almost every leaflet began and ended with a series of slogans reiterating the popular character of the uprising, the glorification of the Palestinian people, the importance of the uprising's continuation, and the imperative of shaking off the occupation. In addition, it was customary to start every paragraph with a header that underscored the popular nature of the struggle, as can be seen in the following excerpt taken from leaflet 15 issued on April 30, 1988:

> No Voice Rises Above the Voice of the Uprising; No Voice rises Above the Voice of the People of Palestine; the People of the PLO ... O great people of Palestine! ... We will continue the struggle with you until we reach our aim of independence, and we affirm that the PLO is the only party to address any dialogue concerning our legitimate national rights ... We salute our steadfast masses, and salute the Arab and international support for our victorious uprising. May we continue the uprising! We shall be victorious! The United National Leadership of the Uprising in the Occupied Territories; The Palestine Liberation Organization.

Based on this fragment and other leaflets, several points should be noted. First, *the* prime voice is the voice of the Palestinian insurgents of the occupied territories. Second, the UNCU serves this voice, it speaks *to* and *for* the people and not in their stead. Third, the UNCU positions itself as an intermediary between the people and the PLO, which is the only representative of the Palestinian people. Fourth, the uprising is a national struggle and aims accordingly at the realization of such national aspirations. Finally, it is implied, by thanking the Arab world and the international community, that the Palestinians are striving for their own collective, national rights, that is, they have a unique national identity, and that the implementation of these rights and aspirations does not necessarily collide with Israel's existence.

It is worth noting, also, that the UNCU's leaflets stressed coexistence between Palestinian Muslims and Palestinian Christian-orthodox. It is possible to assume that such a theme was important, especially in light of the deadly conflict that took place in Lebanon during the late 1970s and early 1980s with its notorious incident of the Maronite massacre of Palestinian Muslims in Sabra and Shatilla. It would not be far fetched to argue also that such an emphasis was linked to the traditional support the Soviet Union had been lending to the PLO, and the interest of the UNCU not to alienate the international community.

Contrasting Hamas and UNCU's leaflets is useful for getting a sense of the way the latter prudently refrained from eliminating prospects for gaining the support of third parties. Scholars who studied the call to arms in the leaflets argue that during 1988 (Mishal with Aharoni 1989) and 1989 (Gangnath and Assaily 1989) the proportion of non-violent action calls in both camps' leaflets (e.g., general strikes, boycotting of Israeli goods or memorial days) aimed at disengaging from Israel and increasing solidarity were far greater than violent action calls such as exhortations to arson, shootings, or using Molotov cocktails. It also shows that compared to Hamas, the UNCU engaged in a considerably smaller proportion of violent action calls. Yet towards 1989 there is a gradual decrease in disengagement calls for boycotting or withdrawal of labor in both camps' leaflets, a pattern that can be explained by pragmatism and adaptation of the two camps as they avoided extreme demands from the population.

Comparing the frames raised by Hamas, UNCU frames illustrate meaningful differences between the two movements. Indeed, the differences between the UNCU and Hamas are clearly discerned in the elevation of historical exemplars and heroic figures recontextualized for the purpose of the Intifada. Hamas's leaflets, while recognizing the popular nature of the uprising and praising it accordingly, portray the Palestinian insurgents via different historical exemplars than do UNCU leaflets. While UNCU's leaflets portray the insurgents as the sons of *Fida'yyin*, as the descendants of the national uprising of 1936 (the Palestinian rebellion against the British Mandate between 1936 and 1939), or as Salah al-Din, who vanquished the Crusaders, the leaflets of Hamas used the exemplar of *Haybar*,[12] and referred to the insurgents as *Mujahidun*[13] or *Murabitun*[14] stressing the religious character of the uprising in particular, and the conflict in general.

Interestingly, both UNCU and Hamas used the historical exemplar of Izz al-Din al-Qassam. Yet, while Hamas stressed his role as a religious preacher who participated in the struggle against the British during the 1930s, the UNCU stressed the national features of Al-Qassam's actions, positioning him as a vanguard of the armed struggle. A similar difference between the UNCU and Hamas can be discerned also in the selection of symbolic archetypes from

Palestinian and Islamic history to provide meaning for the action of the individual Palestinian participating in the uprising. Whereas Hamas's leaflets elevated mostly, yet not exclusively, one symbolic archetype, the *Shahid*, the UNCU provided two additional such archetypes: the *Fida'y* and the *Sahmed*. The combination of these three symbolic archetypes was crucial for inspiring the various insurgents in their daily confrontations with Israeli forces. Yet, their relative importance and prominence in the leaflets reveals, again, the UNCU's systematic attempt to both consolidate the insurgents' stamina and broaden the scope of the conflict through gaining the support of third parties, thereby preventing the closure of the political opportunity. While the *Sahmed* was used by the Hamas as well, it was less dominant than in the UNCU's leaflets.

Wearing a Palestinian cap (*Kafiya*) on his head and with a rifle at his hand, the Palestinian national warrior, the *Fida'y*, was a modern transformation of the Jihad warrior who threw himself into the battlefield, willing to sacrifice even his life. In contrast, the *Sahmed* (i.e., the steadfast or unwavering person) symbolized the passive heroism of the Palestinian peasants who stubbornly cling to their land at all cost. The equal glorification of both modes of action reveals the UNCU's awareness of the necessity to emphasize the contribution of each segment within the population. Indeed, the women were portrayed as the "creators of warriors," and the children as the "sons of the fida'yyin." Passive resistance was as important as active; both were perceived as true heroism.

Promoting the Intifada as civil disobedience and the practice of non-violent resistance meant that heroism was not contingent upon the use of deadly weapon or the sacrifice of one's life. In the face of asymmetry of resources and military skills vis-à-vis the Israeli army, the elevation of the *Sahmed* as genuine hero was critical. To be a *Sahmed* did not require specific skills, enabling the mobilization of the majority of the population. This prudent framing gained full implementation in the children's activity – the "children of the stones." As Kuttab denotes, "To throw a stone is to be 'one of the guys'; to hit an Israeli car is to become a hero; and to be arrested and not confess to having done anything is to be a man" (1988b: 15).

A third heroic figure adapted to the uprising context was the *Shahid*, demonstrating the growing convergence between the Nationalist and Islamic Movements, and the attempts by the former to form and maintain coordination with the latter. The *Shahid* was the young man who gave his life for the sake of Jihad, incarnating his mission as an Islamic warrior. Consequently and following the Islamic myth, both he and his family are guaranteed an eternal life of pleasure in paradise. Although this feature was not formally embraced in UNCU's leaflets, the daily situation necessitated such a usage.

The adaptation of the *Shahid* figure served two additional purposes. On the one hand, it gave a cultural cognitive justification to the death of insurgents, coupled with assisting their families in coping with their loss. On the other hand, it was used as a means of further strengthening the population's solidarity and perseverance. Regarding the collective ritual created after the death of a

Palestinian combatant, Makhul (1988: 93) provides the following description given by one grassroots activist,

> The new system is that we snatch the body from the hospital and bury it and turn this into a sort of spontaneous demonstration. We also forbade the doctors to give the bodies to the military authorities and anyway ... we have no difficulty in snatching the bodies. In the past few days we have snatched four bodies and organized night funerals which have turned into demonstrations.

Last, but not least, the uprising's framers appropriated a historical exemplar from their antagonist's mythical heroic history. Taking into consideration the ancient rivalry between the two People might help us to grasp the Palestinian use of the Jewish myth: David and Goliath. The myth is embedded within the wider context of the Hebrew People's nationalist claim over the "promised land" and their struggle against the Philistine menace. "The leader told me..." writes Makhul (1988: 97), "...that in addition to the stone and the Molotov, they had returned to an ancient method: the sling and stone like David." Thus, just as young David, against all odds and using handmade weapons succeeded in bringing Goliath down, so do the Palestinians, so evidently inferior to the Israeli army, cause the army to retreat.

This transference of Israeli *text* into the Palestinians' *context* was useful in several ways. First, it strengthened the hands of the insurgents facing a well-equipped army, indicating that spiritual resources can be as good as material ones. Second, just as David preferred to use weapons to which he was accustomed, thus rejecting King Saul's advice to use armor and deadly weapons, so too the insurgents should use familiar methods that gave them the upper hand in the daily battlefield. They should not be too quick to use deadly weapons that might thereby play into the hands of the Philistines (i.e., Israel). And third, it was newsworthy; the most newsworthy aspects of the uprising concerned the violent confrontations in which Palestinian youth were throwing stones or burning tires, and Israeli soldiers, standing in front of tanks, were aiming and firing tear gas or rubber bullets. For the international news media there was no question who was the underdog David and who was Goliath. The international news media was the prime outlet through which the Palestinian insurgents made an international opportunity for themselves.

### *Outward framing: from the state level to the regional level and to the international level*

Until 1990, the UNCU's leaflets had systematically and specifically refrained from advocating the use of lethal weapons against Israel. While such a practice might not have influenced the entire Israeli public as to the genuineness of the Palestinian goals (Kaufman 1991), it had certainly forwarded a process in which (1) the conflict's resolution was seen as both feasible and desirable by a larger proportion of Israelis than before, (2) amplified the importance and urgency of the issue of territorial compromise, and (3) added an important measure of realism to the thinking of both "left" and "right" wingers in Israel (Tessler 1990). In fact, growing numbers of Israeli peace groups and left-wing political parties slowly yet gradually engaged in scrutinizing Israeli repressive measures, while also promoting dialogue with the PLO and the establishment of a Palestinian State.

It should be stressed that, all in all, the UNCU had been fairly realistic in its demands. In comparison with Hamas, who treated the Israeli arena as monolithic and ascribed demonic traits to Israel, the UNCU demonstrated a pragmatic approach and demands, such as the removal of the Israeli army from Palestinian settlements or cessation of punitive measures. These demands suggested that the Palestinian aspirations need not necessarily come at the expense of Israel. In some leaflets, the UNCU went so far as to explain to the Israeli public why the Intifada had broken out and why there was no alternative to peaceful resolution. In leaflet 28 (October 1988), for example, the UNCU writes:

> The United National Leadership stresses to Israeli public opinion that our blessed uprising ... was not out of a desire to shed Palestinian or Jewish blood. Rather, it was a revolution against the injustice, oppression and fascism of the occupation and a determination to establish peace in our region.
>
> (cf. Lockman and Beinin 1989)

In fact, the UNCU's flyers included numerous calls to specific Israeli sectors. Examples of such calls can be found in leaflets 10, 23, and 25. Leaflet 10 (March 1988): "...acclaim those freedom-loving people, and those progressive forces in Israel, who have supported us in our struggle for our right of return, our right to self-determination..."; leaflet 25 (September 1988) addressed the Jewish Settlers, urging them to acknowledge that the solution to the "stone problem" would not come from rampage and repression, but only when "...you remove yourself from our lands and recognize our legitimate national rights." Indeed, while during the uprising's first few weeks the Israeli "peace camp" – both parliamentary and extra-parliamentary – had reacted carefully before realizing the nature of the Palestinian struggle (Kaminer 1996), it was nonetheless quick to respond.

On the parliamentary level, the Israeli political party Ratz (the Movement for Civil Rights and Peace) played a central role in criticizing the government for its repressive measures and for the violence exerted by Jewish Settlers. Such was the case with a letter sent to Defense Minister Rabin and to the Israeli press on February 14, 1988, warning Rabin of the ominous collaboration that was taking place between Settlers and military forces, as the latter occasionally connived at the Settlers' brutal action against Palestinians.

On the extra-parliamentary level, groups such as Peace Now, Tikkun (Hebrew for amendment), Israelis by Choice, the Confederation for Peace and

Coexistence and the Committee for Israeli–Palestinian Dialogue, were highly active in initiating acts supporting the Palestinian struggle. For example, on December 15, 1988, Peace Now and Israelis by Choice (an organization of veteran Jewish immigrants) issued a press release, in which the following call was made:

> Peace Now and Israelis by Choice are co-sponsoring the first in a series of encounters between Israelis and Palestinians based on the principle of visits between guests and hosts rather than rulers and ruled ... To our hosts, Many thanks for inviting us ... We are happy to be here today not as occupiers ... We accept your right to an independent Palestine, and to choose your own leaders and representatives ... We come to hear from you how you envision the future of our two peoples.

Still, as noted previously, the Palestinians were also facing frequent attacks by Jewish Settlers and other Israeli civilians, attacks ranging in severity from killings, raids, abductions, and gunshot wounds to crop damage or attacks on religious property. According to a 1989 PHRIC report, between December 1987 and December 1988 Settlers shot thirteen Palestinians, three were burned as a result of arson initiated by Israeli civilians, and Settlers were suspected of being indirectly responsible for the deaths of nine other Palestinians. During 1989 alone, and by Settlers only, twenty-two Palestinians were killed, sixty-five beaten and thirty-two abducted. This was in addition to 170 incidents of raids on Palestinian towns and villages. The declared justification for these acts was the impotence of the Israeli government and the IDF in controlling the Intifada.

Nonetheless, and despite a misperception of the UNCU's messages or an assimilation of such messages into a pre-existing belief system by the majority of the Israeli public during the first three years of the uprising, signs that a shift in the overall acceptance of a resolution to the conflict was slowly percolating. Signs started to take root that the Israeli public was exploring compliance with the notion that any resolution of the Palestinian issue must go through the territories and that the PLO was the sole representative of the Palestinians (Lissak 1990). A useful indicator of such a trend could be found in the shift in Israeli citizens' opinions. As shown by Arian (1999), based on a longitudinal survey, the percentage of Israelis accepting the notion of a Palestinian State in the territories doubled from 1990 to 1994.

Another arena constantly addressed by the UNCU was the regional Arab States. In almost every leaflet, the UNCU praised specific Arab States for their support of the uprising or criticized other Arab States for their support of diplomatic initiatives that did not directly address the needs of the Palestinians in the occupied territories. For example, in leaflet 4 (January 1988) the UNCU criticized King Hussein for his willingness to negotiate around the idea of Jordanian Confederation, and in leaflet 6 (February 1988) Egyptian President Mubarak was harshly attacked for suggesting a plan that would "lead to the elimination of the Palestinian question" (Mishal with Aharoni 1989: 73).

The UNCU's systematic calls to reject any political resolution that would circumvent the genuine aspirations of the Palestinians in the occupied territories, coupled with the imminent threat that the Intifada would transgress into additional arenas, led to the significant decision by King Hussein to relinquish Jordan's administrative and judicial claims to the occupied territories and to recognize the PLO as *the* sole legitimate representative of the Palestinian People.

The Intifada demonstrated and framed accordingly that the Palestinians' decision to take their destiny into their own hands was a pure act of national maturity. After a long period during which the Palestinian issue had been ignored in the region, the Intifada, at least until mid-1990 with the Gulf Crisis, reestablished the Palestinian question as the central focus of the region's politics.

According to the UNCU, three possible, yet interrelated, positions for the Arab States to take stemmed from the frame of Palestinian national maturity. The first called for "united Arab endeavor as a prerequisite for the continuation of the uprising" (e.g., leaflet 11, March 1988). Indeed, Arab States were seen as the central source for symbolic and material (i.e., funds) support. The second urged Arab States to correct their relationship with the PLO and to avoid "creating an alternative leadership to our sole legitimate leadership, the PLO (e.g., leaflet 6, February 1988). Here, an appeal was made to specific Arab States that had refused to accept either the role of the PLO (e.g., Jordan) or the policy of the PLO concerning the ways to fight Israel (e.g., Syria). The third called on Arab States to stop all "attempts and plans that aim to impose surrender on us ... those who appoint themselves as spokesmen for the uprising ... trying to bypass the PLO or give Jordan a mandate to negotiate on behalf of the Palestinians" (leaflet 6, February 1988). This position was mostly aimed at Mubarak's proposal recommending a freeze on violence and repression, and Israeli settlement as a prelude to a UN-sponsored peace conference and to international involvement. An indication of the Arab States' recognition of the centrality of the Palestinian question and the role of the PLO was their June 1988 decision during the Arab Summit in Algeria to allocate additional funds to the PLO for the uprising.

Yet, both the PLO and UNCU were highly aware of the centrality of international involvement to their cause. Indeed, the most central arena was the international one. Through the Intifada's deeds and the framing of those deeds, the Palestinian insurgents gained the international "crowd's" attention and sympathy, to use Schattschneider's metaphor (1975). In doing so, they narrowed the Israeli space of action, thereby preventing Israel from constricting the scope of the Palestinian challenge and, in the process, promoting intervention.

The ability to get the world's attention for their struggle was facilitated by numerous factors that have been studied elsewhere. Among such factors, it is possible to detect: (1) the traditional, disproportional centrality of the Israeli–Palestinian conflict in general and the Palestinian struggle in particular in the international media; (2) the symbolic importance of Israel/Palestine; (3) the presence of news agencies in Israel; (4) the legitimacy of the PLO as a political entity, accorded by numerous countries, most of which were UN members; (5) the exceptional drama that was taking place – national insurgency is always newsworthy; (6) the well-organized Palestinian news services; and (7) Israel's inability as well as reluctance to close off the occupied territories to the news media (Lederman 1992; Cohen and Wolfsfeld 1993; Weimann and Winn 1994; Wolfsfeld 1996, 1997).

Access to the news media, or *standing* (Gamson and Wolfsfeld 1993), is not necessarily, however, correlated with "good news." Newsworthiness may buy you media time, yet not necessarily favorable coverage. The attempt of the Palestinian insurgents to promote their frame in a favorable fashion to the international arena through the news media and the symbolic actions innovated that accompanied and supported such a frame, are of importance here.

Constructing favorable international news media coverage was a collective effort among grassroots activists, the UNCU, PLO Spokesmen within the territories, and the PLO. Perhaps the most meaningful symbolic action taken, as early as January 1988, was the press conference during which Nationalist figures defined the events in the territories. The press conference commenced with the following introductory statement:

> The uprising has come to further affirm our people's unbreakable commitment to its national aspirations. These aspirations include our people's firm national rights of self-determination and of the establishment of an independent state on our national soil under the leadership of the PLO, as our sole legitimate representative.

The purpose of the press conference was to present the Intifada as a genuine popular struggle of the Palestinian People in the occupied territories, aimed at the fulfillment of their national rights in face of an unjust and intolerable Israeli occupation. Labeled as "The Palestinian Fourteen Demands," the document, approved by the PLO, was presented by Palestinian public figures and PLO supporters such as Sari Nusseibeh (a professor at Bir-Zeit University) and Mubarak Awad. Also participating were Mustafa al-Natshah (former mayor of Hebron) and Gabi Baramki, the president of Bir-Zeit University.

The demands included: an international peace conference in which the PLO would participate as the sole, legitimate representative of the Palestinian People; release of all Intifada prisoners; lifting of the Israeli closure over the territories; a moratorium on Jewish settlements, and the like. Of importance, however, is what was *not* included in the document; what is omitted has a greater meaning than what is included. In that vein, it is extremely revealing to note that no explicit or implicit threat to Israel was raised, no claim of a Palestinian State over the entire disputed land was mentioned, the issue of the Palestinian refugees was unvoiced, and no reference was made to the issue of Jerusalem as the capital city of a future Palestinian State.

It should be noted, however, that the demand for Jerusalem as the Palestinian State's capital was raised in several of the leaflets published by the UNCU. The different recipients or audiences can explain such a discrepancy. Doubtless, the UNCU was engaged in a more radical framing of the Intifada as its main calls were directed to and read by the Palestinian population within the territories. The UNCU played, as was already demonstrated, a central role in structuring the repertoire of contention in a meaningful fashion, that of popular, non-zero-sum Intifada. Still, within the context of marketing contention, it is worth mentioning several additional aspects that demonstrated the zeal and discipline of the population.

Fully aware of the uprising's symbolic aspects, and the nature of their proclaimed goals, grassroots activists adapted their behavior to convey their message to the outside more effectively. For instance, specific instructions were sent out allowing army vehicles and news media crews to enter the refugee camps. The goal was to let both enter the camp and then to initiate confrontations in front of the media cameras (Vittulo 1988). Another interesting tactic was the practice of leaving damage inflicted by the army until the media crews arrived at the scene. As one journalist mentioned, "We came to the place about two days after this happened and they had not touched anything ... They said 'We were waiting for the television to come, we were waiting for somebody to take pictures of it' " (Wolfsfeld 1996: 12).

On other occasions, the media presence only intensified the zeal of activists, pushing them, at times, to the extreme. Experiencing a confrontation near Shifa Hospital in Gaza, during which the activists were entrenched inside, Makhul became an eyewitness to an unforgettable incident. He writes: "The soldiers started to fire at a youth on the second floor. The youth tried to escape but saw a soldier facing him. He stopped running, stood facing the soldier, opened his shirt, bared his chest and said 'Shoot!' The soldier pointed the gun at him and from a distance of fifteen meters fired" (1988: 96). Makhul's report appeared on the Israeli newspaper *Ha'yir* on December 18, 1987.

These types of incidents were not frequent, yet the question of who was the victim in the Intifada became clear. Often, the superior military force of the Israeli army worked against it, since, in numerous confrontations in which provocative Palestinian activity resulted in casualties, it acted against Israel on the television screens. As Shalev (1990: 50) admits, televised "...incidents in which Israeli soldiers acted violently against youth and women ... sharpened the image that the Israeli military is an army fighting civilian population that struggle for its political rights of self-determination." Unquestionably, the Palestinians' effort to present their struggle as defiance against unjust authority easily resonated with the cultural themes so prevalent in the West.

In order to further demonstrate their defiance, the UNCU initiated what was, perhaps, the most important symbolic act of the uprising: the declaration of independence based on the Husayni Document during the nineteenth session of the PNC in November 1988. The Husayni Document was based, in part, on secret talks held during the summer of 1987 between members of the Israeli Likud Party and Faysal al-husayni the senior West Bank Fatah activist who nevertheless enjoyed high prestige among all faction in the Nationalist movement.

In a joint effort with Husayni, UNCU's leaflet 24 (August 1988) raised a blunt, unequivocal demand to the PLO to take on the initiative and implement the achievements of the Intifada by recognizing the Husayni Document. On November 15, 1988, after three days of intensive meetings and debates over the precise version of the Document, and with symbolic participation of several of the UNCU members, Arafat declared the independence of the Palestinian people in the territories, based on the UN Partition Plan of November 1947 (Resolution 181). On December 13, 1988, during the UN session in Geneva, Arafat went further to recognize Israel, renounced terrorism, and accepted UN resolutions 242 and 338 as the basis for an agreement with Israel. Following the declaration, and for the first time in the history of the PLO, a dialogue between the US and the PLO began.

The commencement of a US–PLO dialogue was the most significant achievement of the Intifada, the direct product of a deliberative, strategic framing of the Palestinian struggle to shake off the Israeli occupation. In fact, with the first signs of disintegration of the Soviet Block during early 1988, Arafat, although critical of US relations with Israel, acknowledged that the US was, from a practical point of view, the most important international player, a player whose sympathy would enhance the Palestinian cause most significantly. Table 5.2 is taken from Wolfsfeld's illuminating work on the framing contest between Israel and the Palestinians during the Intifada (1997).

The table illustrates the ways our two conflictants framed their story to the international news media throughout most of the Intifada, structured according to what Gamson and Lasch (1983) called a signature matrix. Each story is packaged according to various framing devices, and can be categorized by our three framing questions/tasks: *what is the issue* (suggested by: meta-frame/core frame), *how to think about the issue* (suggested by: metaphor, depiction, etc.), and *what should be done about the issue* (suggested by: roots, consequences, and appeals to principle). Despite variations for each "story," the table captures the frames promoted by both Israel and the Palestinian Nationalist movement. Still, as far as the Palestinians' framing of their struggle goes, meaningful changes had taken place, threatening to jeopardize their prior gains.

The causes of such changes should be familiar by now. The shifts in the Israeli repressive mode; the continuing attacks on Palestinians by Jewish Settlers and other Israeli citizens; the perpetuation of right-wing government in Israel; the cumulative burden experienced by the population; the increasing drain on funds for supporting the population; the increased fundamentalist challenge; the suspension of the US–PLO dialogue following a deadly PLO terrorist attack on Israel; and the shift of media attention to the developing Gulf crisis – all had concatenated to bring about a significant radicalization that threatened to undermine the UNCU ability to shape their contention in a concerted way and, consequently, the favorable international climate they had managed to cultivate.

Thus, as of early 1990 it is possible to trace numerous expressions of

Table 5.2 Israeli and Palestinian competing framing of the Intifada

| Meta-frame | Law and order | Injustice and defiance |
|---|---|---|
| Package | Palestinian violence | Intifada (Shaking off) |
| Core frame | The issue is whether Palestinians who break the law and use violence will be stopped. | The issue is whether Israel will end the occupation of Palestine. |
| Core position | Israel must bring a halt to the violence in the territories and protect the lives and properties of Israelis and Palestinians. | The Palestinians must stand up and fight for their rights against the Israeli oppression. Israel must leave the occupied territories. |
| Metaphors | Time bomb/Fire. | The rock/Zionism as cancer |
| Historical exemplars | Palestinian terrorism/Arab–Israeli wars. | Vietnam/South Africa/Dire-Yassin*/1936 uprising. |
| Catchphrases | No prizes for violence | With blood and fire we will liberate Palestine/Allah is great. |
| Depictions | PLO as terrorist organization initiating local population to acts of violence against Israelis and Palestinians. | Israel as brutal, imperialist, and racist/Palestinians as victims fighting for their legitimate national rights. |
| Visual images | Masked Palestinians attacking cars with rocks and Molotov cocktails/Armed Palestinians in military march. | Soldiers beating Palestinian youth/Palestinian youth throwing rocks/Dome of the Rock mosque. |
| Roots | Arabs' attempt to destroy Israel/Outside agitation of local population. | Israel's brutal occupation of West Bank and Gaza. |
| Consequences | Increased political violence against Israel/A Palestinian State. | The liberation of Palestine/A Palestinian State. |
| Appeals to principle | The need for law and order/Never surrender to violence. | Self-determination for the Palestinian people/Justice. |

Source: Gadi Wolfsfeld, Media and Political Conflict – News from the Middle East (Cambridge University Press, 1997).

Note
Israeli soldiers, members of the paramilitary units the "Etzel" (Warring Military Organization) and "Lehi" (Israel Freedom Fighters), attacked the Palestinian Village of Dir-Yassin and killed over 120 people on April 9, 1948.

radicalization that took place at both the internal level (the UNCU) and the external level (the PLO). First, amidst the growing signs of the population's weariness and the lack of funds to further support the population, the PFLP and the DFLP were calling, in joint leaflets with Hamas's local activists, for the escalation of the Intifada by using deadly weapons and for raids on Israel from Arab States.

Second, the shared perception among the Palestinians regarding the fruitless bilateral talks between the US, Israel, Egypt, and the PLO during late 1989 and early 1990, coupled with the siding of the US with Israel on the issue of undermining the PLO role in the proposed Israeli–Palestinian dialogue resulted in an unequivocal rejection of the plans (known as the Baker first plan and Shamir plan)[15] by the UNCU (Litvak 1990).

Third, following the suspension of the US–PLO dialogue in May 1990, the establishment of a right-wing Israeli Government (June 11, 1990), and the Rishon Le'Zion massacre in May 1990 during which seven Palestinian workers were gunned down and eleven were injured by an Israeli citizen while waiting to be hired as day laborers, a leaflet issued by the UNCU labeled the Israeli government as a terrorist government, and called for burning the ground under the feet of the occupation's army, urging the populace to have confidence in the Intifada, "until the troops of the occupation are killed in the streets ... of our independent Palestinian state (Litvak ibid.: p. 259).

The fourth sign of radicalization was the unconditional support for Saddam Hussein expressed by Arafat, followed by Palestinian populace support and, although to a lesser degree, by the UNCU, which echoed the Iraqi line in an unnumbered leaflet. In a similar vein to the UNCU's stand, several West Bank public figures, mostly Fatah proponents, issued a joint statement on August 15, 1990 in which they rejected the principle of occupation by force (i.e., Iraq's invasion to Kuwait), but decried the double standards of the UN Security Council, which was prepared to enforce its resolutions against Iraq but ignored similar motions against Israel (JMCC 1991).

Last, but not least, was the event of the Temple Mount (al-Haram al-Sharif) in December 1990, demonstrating the diffusion of the previously latent religious aspect of the framing efforts. The event began with an announcement by the Temple Mount Faithful, an extremist Jewish group whose stated aim is the reconstruction of the third Jewish Temple, of a march onto the Temple Mount on the Jewish holiday of Sukkot. The Israeli Supreme Court issued an order to bar their intended entry to the Mount and ordered the deployment of police forces to implement it. More than 3,000 Muslim worshipers gathered on the Mount to thwart any such attempt. According to Litvak (1990), although the Israeli police notified the Muslim Waqf (i.e., the Islamic sacred sites) of the group's route, apparently notification that the group would not be allowed to enter the Mount was not conveyed to the worshipers. While the reasons for the shootings are debatable, the fact of the matter was that within minutes nineteen Palestinians were killed and over 200 Palestinians and eleven Israelis were injured (p. 266).

Whether it was reckless shootings by the Israeli police in face of thousands of Palestinians shouting *Allahu Akbar* (God is great), or whether it was an imminent and genuine threat sensed by the police in the face of a heavy barrage of rocks by the Muslim worshipers who had been misled by the mosque preacher at the nearby village of Silwan that Jews were approaching the Mount – it is evident that the ongoing and painstaking attempts by the Palestinian insurgents throughout most of the Intifada to limit their actions and frames were disintegrating. Arafat's support of Saddam Hussein and the cheering of Palestinians from the rooftops with every Scud missile falling on Israeli cities had unquestionably caused serious cracks in the issue of who was the victim in the Intifada.

Early in the Intifada (March 1988) two grassroots activists were asked, "If the uprising were to end today, what would it have achieved?" They replied, "First, it has gained world attention ... Second, it has united the factions as never before ... there is no one now who plays around with the Reagan plan, the Jordan option, a joint federation or 'raising the standard of living.' "[16]

Later developments in the Intifada raised serious threats to these achievements. Nonetheless, and despite such challenges, the fact of the matter was that the Intifada had gained world attention and forced Israel to come to terms with the notion that any political initiative must address the claims of the Palestinians in the occupied territories, and that the Nationalist forces, despite disagreements, remained united in a more far-reaching manner than had been the case during the 1970s and early 1980s.

The period post "Desert Storm" manifested no significant changes in the developments within the territories. It did, however, force the local activists to take the initiative, given the all-time low status of the PLO after the Gulf War, and raise various political plans for the occupied territories. Such was the idea to reconstruct the Palestinian National Council so that the weight of the local forces would increase, and to revive the idea of Jordanian confederation. While such plans – the product of what Rekhess calls "new thinking" (1992) – were rejected, it was also clear that time was not on the side of the Palestinian insurgents. The joint American–Soviet announcement in July 1991 regarding their intent to convene what came to be known as the Madrid Peace Conference in October practically set the agenda for the two contenders.

As it turned out, in October 1991 the Palestinians and Israelis sat down together for the first time in the history of the conflict to discuss a possible resolution to the conflict in bilateral negotiations within the framework of the Madrid Peace Conference.[17] In retrospect and in line with the analysis developed thus far, the Madrid talks marked an unprecedented shift in the attitudes and behavior of both conflictants; it set the ground for a change in the structure of the conflict.

Nonetheless, the actual process of peace talks and preparation for self-rule elections in the territories, a major product of the conference, generated a renewal of clashes between Hamas and the PLO's supporters. During July and

August 1992, numerous confrontations broke out between the movements, leading the editor of the Palestinian daily *a-Sha'ab* to comment, "What is happening . . . is frightening. It threatens not only the Intifada, but our whole social framework." Intimidating as it was, the balance of power was clear. The PLO had the upper hand as it held the promise of the desired solution. Not only was Arafat accepted by the international community as the legitimate Palestinian representative; Israel also recognized the Fatah-led PLO as the only conceivable – although far from desirable – partner.

# 6    Conclusions and the future of the Israeli–Palestinian conflict

We are left with three tasks to accomplish. Our first task is to summarize the basic argument of the book and to present the conclusions. The second task involves a discussion of our case study in terms of theories of collective action, suggesting several contributions our study makes to the field. Our third task will be to suggest several observations concerning the future of the Palestinian–Israeli conflict and prospects for its resolution. This third task may seem unrealistic as clashes and mutual infliction of damage are still an ongoing matter, and in spite of the recent Israeli pullout from the Gaza Strip no foreseeable systematic and genuine resolution to the conflict is in sight. The postscript which follows this final chapter supplies a provisional analysis of the "new" or "second" Intifada which began in 2000 and demonstrates the validity of, and need for in heeding the observations offered.

## Task one: bringing it all together

We began our journey by asking how to account for the unprecedented shift in the magnitude of the Palestinian politics of contention as manifested in the 1987 Intifada. We argued that the conventional wisdom – that every national minority, facing systematic oppression and lack of possibility to fulfill its human needs, eventually rebels – does not take us far in understanding why a minority succeeds in mounting such massive contention during one specific historical period and not another, what influences its strategy, and why it is that one form of contention succeeds in achieving political goals where others fail. This book argues that a promising point of departure is an analysis of the effects of the restructuring of the conflict created by the June 1967 military occupation not only on the relationship between Israel and the Palestinian minority, but also on each side separately.

To validate this perspective, I drew insights from the extensive body of literature on collective action and conflict written by Simmel, Marx, and Weber, and recent social movement writers in sociology. I used those insights to suggest a conceptual synthesis between *structuralist* and *culturalist* approaches in the study of collective action. Specifically, I tried to substantiate the conceptual bridging between, and beneficial integration of, the structurally-laden Political

Process Model and the culturally-laden Framing Processes tradition. I argued that such integration has the potential for capturing the dynamics of collective action.

By integrating framing processes with the study of individual grievances and discontent, the study of mobilization processes, and, most importantly, the study of the effect on contention wrought by changes in the structure of political opportunities, I developed a model that illustrated the possible trajectories of contention within one distinct conflict. The model requires answers for three interrelated guiding questions: the *why* question (dealing with the *willingness* of individuals to rebel), the *how* question (dealing with the process whereby individuals' *readiness* to act contentiously is shaped), and the *when* question (dealing with the possible influence of political *opportunity* on strategy and tactics of contention).

The potential to capture the dynamics of the Intifada arises from equal attention paid to both *structure*-oriented and *agency*-oriented modes of analysis, and, equally importantly, from the interplay between the two, a give-and-take, inherent in each of the three guiding questions. As such, I attended to the multifaceted structural oppression experienced by the Palestinians in the occupied territories, their shared grievances and discontents. I also examined the process through which their hardship was politicized through interaction with Israeli domination. I called this politicization the *willingness* to act contentiously.

Similarly, in analyzing the process of Palestinian *readiness* to act contentiously, I attended not only to modes of Israeli repression and facilitation but also to Palestinian mobilization through the development of various organizations and ideologies. Here again, I explored how contention with the Israeli authorities affected the internal relationships among the numerous Palestinian organizations.

Finally, I analyzed how changes in the structure of political *opportunities* faced by Palestinians affected patterns of contention within the occupied territories. I considered as crucially important the ways that Palestinian activists constructed the meaning of structural changes, and the effects of these meanings on their strategy of contention. Here again, I attended to the interplay between *structure* and *agency* by probing the influence of both dimensions on the tactics Palestinian activists employed during the Intifada.

In accomplishing this, the book brings together insights from past research about the Intifada with broader data on patterns of contention between Israel and the Palestinians in the occupied territories, to show how an intersection between a preexisting *willingness* and *readiness* (representing the Palestinian shared discontent and sense of injustice, together with commitment and solidarity) and an *opportunity* dimension – demonstrating a power deflation situation inside the Israeli polity – triggered the inception of the Intifada. Specifically, I argued that a growing Palestinian shared perception of ripe conditions – domestic Israeli division over the continuation of occupation – was translated into contentious tactics that generated a sustained, intensive, and widespread challenge. Concomitantly, the Palestinians' use of such tactics successfully, yet not without difficulties, promoted the possibility of a peaceful resolution of the conflict among the majority of the Israeli public and the international community.

It is possible to unpack this argument as follows:

1   The 1967 restructuring of the Israeli–Palestinian conflict profoundly affected the prospects of, and modes of action chosen by the Palestinians in the occupied territories;
2   The occupation of the territories triggered a deep, ongoing, and widening conflict within Israel regarding both the issue of the ongoing occupation and the treatment of the Palestinian population in the territories. I call the cumulative effects of this conflict Israel's power deflation;
3   As a result of the occupation, the depth and scope of Palestinian familiarity with the Israeli polity in general and its internal dynamics in particular increased considerably;
4   The Palestinian public at large (measured by media discourse) and Palestinian grassroots activists understood the systemic Israeli domestic crisis as a favorable condition for action;
5   This framing affected not only their readiness to act, but also their willingness to rebel, and their ability to agree upon a preferred strategy of contention; and
6   The tactics employed for contention were rooted in a deliberate attempt to capitalize on such a strategy of contention that satisfied Palestinian actors, sought to provide the least pretext for Israeli crackdown, and played well to world opinion.

A useful way to present the conclusions is provided by the three guiding questions or, alternatively, the three vectors of analysis used: the *why*, *how* and *when* questions of the Intifada.

Palestinians' *willingness* to act contentiously was unquestionably rooted in the Israeli occupation of 1967. The Israeli occupation of the territories restructured the dynamics of the conflict. It not only compartmentalized a considerable portion of the Palestinian People, situating them in direct confrontation with their age-old antagonist, but their presence as occupied people and the collective hardship they experienced, engendered a profound cognitive development. The Palestinians *within* the occupied territories gradually realized that their salvation would come about only through their own initiatives. While, at first, such an understanding was anchored in disillusionment with the vision of a joint Arab front that would solve the Palestinian question, it gradually evolved into recognition that Palestinians in the occupied territories "are the people on the land," to recall the words of NGC member Ibrahim Daqqaq. As such, their position and "saying" in managing the conflict with Israel is at least as important as that of the PLO or any other externally-based Palestinian organization.

Indeed, being the people on the land meant confronting multi-faceted hardships. Regardless of Israeli attempts to construct the appearance of an "enlightened occupation" (as was the case during the Israeli Labor Administration between 1967 and 1977), the majority of occupied Palestinians experienced hardship both individually and collectively. The collectivization of their grievances resulted from Israeli crackdowns on any resistance, coupled with structural oppression of their daily lives and needs. Simultaneously, the growing Jewish Settler presence within the occupied territories concretized for many Palestinians that their continuing presence on their land was being called into question. The collectivization of grievances and the framing of shared discontent were the product of action-oriented political consciousness, the initiative of externally-based organizations and, later, local grassroots activists, who promoted the idea of a distinct Palestinian identity and agency.

The analysis of Palestinian *readiness* to act demonstrates the significant shift in the mode of Palestinian mobilization that took place in the late 1970s and early 1980s. During this time period, the mode and pace of Palestinian commitment was driven by Palestinians *within* the occupied territories, as local grassroots activists took the initiative in forming an organizational infrastructure. The causes of this shift toward activists within the occupied territories can be found in the continuing conflict between the externally-based organizations, but also in Israel's policy favoring control of land over control of population (Frisch 1996). Such a policy was translated into various decisions that, as a practical matter, facilitated Palestinian organization within the local arena of the West Bank and Gaza Strip.

Yet, Israel's "letting the Arabs run their own affairs" (Abu-Shakrah 1986), as expressed in, for instance, the renewal of the right of association, was contingent upon Palestinian compliance with what Israel accepted as "restricted radicalism." This was accompanied by a significant increase in Jewish settlement initiatives in the West Bank and the Gaza Strip. The result of this double-headed policy and the subsequent crackdown of Palestinian Nationalism inside (the dismissal of West Bank mayors and Gaza Municipality and the crackdown of the NGC) and outside (i.e., the Lebanon War) was the ascendancy of local grassroots radical forces in the contentious arena: the occupied territories.

The Palestinians' shared experience of oppression and repression, and their continuing frustration not only made the Nationalist ideology resonate better with the collective experience of the majority of the Palestinian populace, but also brought about a lessening of ideological tensions among grassroots activists, regardless of their respective organizational affiliations. They united around an action-frame, that of ending the Israeli occupation. As demonstrated, the prioritization of the Nationalistic action-frame was rooted in the recognition by Palestinians within the occupied territories that they could challenge Israel by using their knowledge of their occupier.

In terms of *opportunity*, being the people *on* the land meant an unprecedented proximity between the two antagonists and growing familiarity on the part of Palestinians with the Israeli polity. The Israeli policy of *de facto* integration, while purely an attempt to further Israeli interests, enabled a large proportion of Palestinians to familiarize themselves extensively with their antagonist. The Palestinians' need to acquire knowledge and their emerging ability to know what was going on inside their antagonist's arena provided Palestinians with rich information and understanding of Israeli society.

The Palestinians' familiarity with and awareness of Israeli domestic developments extended to understanding the conflict developing inside Israel over the future status of the occupied territories. This conflict tore the Israeli polity apart, a conflict manifested in governmental instability, inability to generate and/or implement collective goals, growing instances of disregard for the rule of law, lack of trust in and legitimacy of the system, and deepening social cleavages. Such a system-wide crisis – in which the occupied Palestinians played a central role and were highly aware of their role – gradually stagnated the Israeli political system. This was manifested in a series of crisis-events, expressing the deepening and the diffusion of the Israeli power deflation.

My analysis of the Palestinians' awareness of and framing of the Israeli power deflation reveals interesting results. Palestinian grassroots activists and the media discourse showed a high level of accuracy and sophistication in their "reading" of the developments inside Israel: attentiveness to the deterioration of Israel's internal cohesion; a perceptual link between the external Israeli–Palestinian conflict and the domestic Israeli conflict; and a growing sense of encouraging, favorable conditions to act contentiously. Moreover, my analysis of the Palestinian media discourse throughout 1987 shows the construction of rationale for contention, demonstrating a gradually evolving and systematic media discourse openly discussing whether conditions were ripe to increase contention. Additionally, this process of activating commitment to contention resonated with the diagnosis and prognosis of internal Israeli developments during preceding years. It became clear also that grassroots activists were fully aware of awaiting the right moment to trigger contention; to test Israeli reactions they undertook attempts to initiate confrontations during the months preceding December 9, 1987 – the date on which many Intifada scholars suggest the Intifada presumably "erupted."

The Intifada, however, was far from being a mere outburst of frustration. Nor was it "spontaneous" if one considers the perceptual and organizational infrastructure established throughout the 1970s and 1980s. As demonstrated, the Intifada was grounded and embedded in a specific historical context and was the initiative of a consolidating collective actor with a clear strategy of contention. However, the development of this strategy or, alternatively, the reason for the specific time context of the Intifada's inception, rested on a strategic framing of changes in the political conditions faced by the Palestinians. My analysis of this framing process, as represented in the media discourse, showed a converging trend among various Palestinian voices/political groups that conditions were ripe for triggering contention. In that sense, the Intifada did not erupt, rather it consolidated; this consolidation involved the favoring of a specific strategy for contention, a strategy deeply embedded in astute collective perception of the Israeli opportunity structure.

My analysis of the Intifada action phase demonstrated grassroots activists' attempts to employ specific tactics perceived as appropriate for capitalizing on the developed strategy. These tactics were designed both to keep the opportunity structure at the state level open (i.e., to influence internal Israeli politics) and to broaden this opportunity structure in order to create a favorable international climate for their struggle. Such a collective endeavor went through serious challenges, some of which were caused by erroneous leadership decisions and acts, others rooted in conflicting ideologies, and still others were unexpected externalities such as the Gulf War. Regardless, by deciding to limit the use of deadly weapons and to avoid militant calls against Israel, by forming a solid and efficient mobilizing structure that was capable of mobilizing almost the entire population, and by constructing collective action frames to maintain the population's zeal and stamina and to promote their struggle in ways that resonated successfully with the international community, the Palestinian insurgents successfully advanced their cause.

## Task two: theories of collective action

The analysis of the Intifada generates several theoretical contributions to the study of collective action. Let me specify several such contributions in succinct form.

### *Political processes and dynamics of contention*

The study of collective action has long been divided between structural-oriented and cultural-oriented perspectives. The Political Process Model's proposition that changes in the political conditions serve as incentive for social movement activists to trigger contention is problematic, as it both underplays the role of *agency* and, concomitantly, rests solely on a *post factum* analysis. To explore the influence of changes in the structure of political opportunities (POS) on a movement's strategies and the triggering of contention, we should examine whether movement activists recognize such changes, and then the ways that they use such knowledge to frame strategies.

The insistence on maintaining the separation between *structure* and *agency* promises an analysis of collective action that captures its dynamics in a profound manner. For a research agenda to capture the dynamics of contention, attentiveness to the role of the agent and to the specific historical context of contentious politics must act as the starting point. Failing to preserve the distinction between the actor, the context, and the phenomenon under study (i.e., contentious politics), might lead to reification of contentious politics. Social movements become phenomena, and consequently, the social movement as actor is blurred. To avoid reification, we should link issues of power, inequalities and injustice with their origins rather than acknowledging that injustice is ubiquitous and treating oppression only when it is challenged. At present, the thrust of analysis is far too often to explain contention only after protest-events surface, stressing external factors, primarily shifts in political opportunities. Yet, in various situations, and our case study is a case in point, the mere ability to challenge authorities, let alone to trigger contention of such a magnitude, must not be taken for granted and thus, should not act as the starting point of analysis.

The work of Charles Brockett (1991) is a case in point in the sense that it questions the proposed effects of POS on contention in non-industrialized democracy, in his case the peasant mobilization in Central America, without paying careful attention to the role of movement members' perception of opportunity. While no systematic measurement of such perception of opportunity is provided, Brockett's work nonetheless contributes by emphasizing, just as this book does, the need to be attentive to the historical embeddedness of opportunity structures by showing how, when analyzed from the perspective of movement members, other types of opportunities surface.

### Framing processes

It is equally crucial to avoid the overemphasis on social construction. While much of contention is about collective interpretation and attribution, the proposed integration of framing processes with political processes calls for attentiveness to other factors that influence movement activists' interpretation, which, in turn affects the politics of contention. A central aspect in the proposed integration provided in this book rests on the idea of event(s) as possible catalysts for individuals to engage in reframing of their existing perceptions and beliefs. For a discontented challenger who lurks, awaiting signs of weakness in an antagonist, an event may act as a trigger, as incentive. In that case, it is reasonable to expect a process of reframing. As such, events can act as catalysts for changing shared perception regarding the ratio between opportunities and threats. They can signify a shifting conjunction of threats and opportunities.

Events mediate between changes in the structure of political opportunities and cycle of contention. Events and/or changes in the structure of political opportunities matter; they can lead social movement activists to engage in reframing processes, which, in turn, can shape their strategy and ensuing tactics. The social construction of opportunity is an indeterminate process, one that is contingent upon historical specificity and sense of opportunity/threat, as they dialectically fluctuate in accordance with other actors in a multi-actor field (e.g., authorities, countermovement, allies, unforeseen external events, etc.).

By applying Social Constructionist tenets and guidelines to the study of collective action, it is possible to ground the effects of events on perceptions of opportunity, and to explore the ways that the reframing of perceptions in turn, influences contention. Only through such an analysis can we situate ourselves in a position to grasp how relative opportunity/threat is, how the dialectic of opportunity and threat affects a social movement's mobilization and the movement's internal dynamics, and learn about the nature of effects of shifts in political opportunities on contention. Such a positioning may be fruitful also in determining when it is that social construction becomes a necessary condition for any effects of shifts in political opportunities, and when it is only facilitative.[1]

*Political opportunity structures*

The Palestinian situation under occupation demonstrates the importance of perceiving political opportunity structures as historically embedded. Opportunity
must be analyzed from the perspective of the specific historical situation in
which a possible challenger is located. Otherwise, existing distinctions and
classifications of POS might be of little use. The applicability of the POS variable in settings that are non-industrialized democracies necessitates careful
adjustments and sensitizing (Boudreau 1996, 2004).

We saw that for specific Palestinian actors (e.g., Islamic Jihad, and hardliners of the Rejectionist Front) the concept of political opportunity structures
within the context of fighting Israel had no relevance. These groups' rationale
for action had little to do with any type of opportunity in the sense of "opening
windows of opportunities." If the concept of opportunity has any meaning for
such actors, it is only in the creation of opportunities for themselves, as was the
case in the 1990s, when they sabotaged the Oslo Peace Process through an
unprecedented wave of suicide bombings against Israeli targets with the result
that the legitimacy of the Palestinian Authority was undermined.

An exception in this regard was the Muslim Brotherhood. Traditionally, the
Brotherhood emphasized social-oriented activity. For them the notion of
opportunity had little utility; they had no political agenda to fight Israel. The
same, however, cannot be said about Hamas which, after its founding in January
1988, represented a politicization of the Brotherhood. In that regard, once
Hamas began participating in the realm of the political struggle the notion of
political opportunity structures became relevant. This raises the need to carefully
distinguish between levels of opportunities and the importance of asking
"opportunity for what?" to avoid a misuse of the concept.

Indeed, the analysis demonstrated also the complex, multi-layered nature of
opportunity structures; blurring the ongoing dichotomy between the national and
the international levels (McAdam 1999), coupled with blurring between the
national level and the movement level. By definition, the Palestinians' political
goals extended far beyond Israel; without doubt, the 1987 Intifada was in many
ways a struggle over international public opinion (Wolfsfeld 1997). Yet, the
Palestinians had, first and foremost, to cope with state-level opportunity structures. I do not mean to imply that social movements are incapable of creating
opportunities. Rather, I suggest that the Palestinians were able to expand the
space of action available for themselves (and possible future opportunities as a
result) only after an opportunity opened up at the Israeli state level. And, in
many ways, just as the international opportunity structure played a role in the
broadening and deepening of the uprising, so did it play a role in its relative
abatement.

Moreover, to make things even more complicated, there were opportunities at
the movement level as well. Once treated as a field of actors, the analysis of
Israel's mixed policy of facilitation and repression of the Palestinian movement
demonstrates that Israel's crackdown on the Fatah-led PLO in Lebanon and the

dismissal of several West Bank mayors acted as an opportunity for the ascendancy of the internally-based organizations. Similarly, in line with Robinson's analysis of Hamas (2004), Israel's policy of undermining the hegemony of Palestinian Nationalism within the occupied territories was accompanied by an informal policy of a "soft hand" towards the Muslim Brotherhood. This policy can be seen as opening opportunity for the Brotherhood to acquire higher influence within the Palestinian movement, as they indeed acquired during the 1980s.

This multi-level analysis of political opportunity has far-reaching implications for future research. It is crucial to know which level of opportunity was central from the point of view of the movement activists, what purposes the opportunity might serve (i.e., opportunity for what), and in what ways the various levels of opportunities interacted. Interestingly, while in our case it was the opening of opportunity at the state level that enabled Palestinian activists to create opportunity in the international arena, in Eastern Europe during 1989–90 the order was reversed, as shown by Oberscahll (1996). It took an opening in the international arena – the "Gorbachev factor" – to trigger pro-democracy challengers to act contentiously in higher magnitude inside the respective Soviet Bloc states.

### Transgressive and contained contention

The distinction between *transgressive* and *contained* contention (McAdam, Tarrow, and Tilly 2001) is also useful in our case. But, while this distinction may provide a useful starting point for analysis, it nonetheless needs further delimitation and sensitizing in a twofold manner. First, it is important to evaluate the applicability of the distinction throughout the life history of a social movement. Our case study illustrated that while this distinction was useful in analyzing the Intifada action phase, it was problematic when analyzing the preceding phases of contentious politics. Specifically, during the Intifada, the Palestinian contention was seen by Israeli authorities as *transgressive* no matter the type of action they engaged in, yet was perceived as *contained* by outside actors. Thus, the distinction holds only from a specific vantage point. Additionally, throughout the twenty years of occupation, *transgressive* contention became the most, if not the only, attractive option for Palestinian grassroots activists and, gradually, for other political actors in the occupied territories.

This point leads me to the second adjustment. It is of importance to unpack the distinction between *transgressive* and *contained* contention as perceived from the standpoint of each actor within the movement and, thus, to account for shifts that take place in each actor's mode of action. Specifically, Palestinian agents whom I called the "moderates" favored *contained* contention; other Palestinian agents saw *transgressive* contention as the only option that would generate any progress; for still other Palestinian actors (e.g., the Islamic Jihad or the Muslim Brotherhood), the distinction between *contained* and *transgressive* contention held no meaning because there was no willingness by these groups to accept societal norms and rules of behavior or to work within existing power relations.

We have seen that changes and shifts took place in the action strategy of each actor within the Palestinian movement. Islamic groups, in our case, contained their action during specific periods of time because of the needs and tendencies of their own base of power – the Palestinian populace within the occupied territories. A further analysis of Islamic activism would unquestionably be an important contribution to the study of social movements and contentious politics. In that regard, works on Islamic movements edited recently by Wiktorowicz (2004) provide an important contribution, showing how a social movement perspective increases our understanding of this specific type and form of contentious politics. An additional contribution would be an analysis of Islamic activism as part of a larger social movement, and further studies of the ways Islamic groups interact with other non-Islamic groups and actors within a movement are also needed. This book took a first step in this direction; other steps would surely benefit the field.

### *The effect of contingencies on contention*

Finally, this book demonstrates how the dynamics of contention might benefit from attention to contingencies, that is, unexpected developments that can have crucial effects on trajectories of contention. While wisely focusing on regularities in the study of social movements and contentious politics, students of collective action have inadvertently paid insufficient attention to contingencies that can disrupt even the most carefully crafted strategy by actors in contentious politics. For Israel, the rise of an Islamic political force such as Hamas in the early stages of the Intifada certainly influenced its short-term and long-term policies toward the uprising. The politicization of the Muslim Brotherhood suddenly made Arafat an "eligible" partner for future negotiation. For the Palestinian activists, the developing crisis in the Gulf profoundly affected their struggle's visibility and unleashed an emotional reaction that threatened to thwart their painstaking endeavor. Although having less impact than the Gulf crisis, the collapse of the Soviet Bloc also affected the dynamics of the Intifada through the loss of influence by the more balanced Russian policy for the region and the ascendancy of the US as the sole dominant superpower. Social movements, more than many social formations live with *serendipity* (Merton 1968). Attentiveness to contingencies and other externalities in analyzing collective action has the potential of providing dynamic, process-sensitive analyses of collective action.

## Task three: the future of the Palestinian–Israeli conflict

When I began the demanding task of writing this book a colleague cynically told me that I need not worry about the marketability of my work as the Israeli–Palestinian conflict would surely outlive us both. It was summer 2002, after almost two years of bloody contention known as the "new" or "second" Intifada and soon after Israel launched operation Defensive Shield following a series of deadly suicide bombings in Israeli cities. Several questions have been occupying the thoughts of many observers of the conflict ever since the aftermath of the "first" Intifada and in a more pressing manner in the wake of the "second" Intifada. Some of these questions are: *Is there any hope for a possible resolution? Is the involvement of the international community beneficial? Does Israel have a partner for peace? Do Palestinians have a partner for peace? Is peace possible in our lifetime? Does the end of Arafat's era in November 2004 open up new possibilities? And, has the Gaza Pullout brought with it a new hope or, at least, some healing to the seriously bruised wagon of peace?*

This book has offered several insights into the dynamics of the conflict, insights that may be useful for future political initiative. On the basis of those insights it is possible to offer several observations concerning the future of the conflict and prospects for its resolution.

First, for Israel, the resolution of the conflict is not a matter of choice, it is a necessity. It is imperative for Israeli policy makers, regardless of ideological orientations, to grasp to the full the devastating damage the occupation has inflicted on Israeli society, and to understand, and act accordingly. Resolution of the conflict is in Israel's genuine interest just as it is in the Palestinians' interest. The system-wide crisis Israel experienced throughout the 1970s and 1980s is still an ongoing, aggravating matter threatening to tear society further apart.

Israel should stop treating the Palestinians as equal partners in negotiation in the sense of demanding reciprocity as a precondition for any progress in possible resolutions. How could such a demand on the part of Israel hold water when, throughout the 1970s and 1980s, Israel did its best to prevent the rise of such an equal partner? This is not a strategy of negotiation! Rather, it is Israel's way to overlook its role as an occupying force, to ignore the devastating results of the military occupation, and to refuse to acknowledge the asymmetric structure and dynamics of the conflict that must be reflected in any type of negotiation. It is not only that the ability of any Palestinian leadership to assume control and legitimacy takes time, but that Israel has been playing a central role in undermining the ability of any Palestinian leadership to do just that. The "separation wall" (labeled by Palestinians as an "apartheid wall" and by Israelis as the "security fence") is not a solution of any kind, but a direct result of such a lack of strategy and failure (or one might say refusal) to acknowledge the asymmetry in the balance of power and to grasp the mutual benefits that a resolution holds for the two parties/societies. The separation wall only perpetuates the conflict, both inside Israel and between Israel and the Palestinians. The actual unilateral Israeli decision on the line of the separation wall perpetuates sources of Palestinian grievance and discontent and continues to neglect the negative implications of the military occupation for Israeli society.

In this regard, the disengagement plan is a step along the lines of the separation wall – a policy of entrenchment. It could be a step in the right direction if and only if it were, first and foremost, based upon an agreement and coordination between the two parties, and, second, accompanied by an equivalent disengagement from the West Bank. In its present form as an Israeli unilateral policy of entrenchment, disengaging from the Gaza Strip threatens to thwart any possibility of reestablishing a dialogue between the two parties and/or of constructing peace constituencies on both sides. It is not only that Palestinians look at the disengagement from the Gaza Strip as an Israeli gesture to the US rather than as a genuine step towards resolution, but it is also understandable why so many Israelis perceive the disengagement as counter-productive rather than as a justifiable and mutually beneficial policy.

Second, any type of resolution of the conflict should be generated from within the parties themselves, through a dialogue between them. International involvement cannot and should not act as a substitute for communication between Israelis and Palestinians. As we have already seen at the beginning of this book, conflict evolves from human interaction and it is a mode of communication, the type of communication that enables conflictants to know the previously unknown about each other. Conflict communication is crucial for de-escalation processes and for the possibility of forming an infrastructure of cooperation. US Secretary of State Rice's decision to let the parties reestablish direct communication in the Sharm-a-Sheikh Summit during February 2005 is an important step in this direction and should act as guidance for future steps.

As we have also seen, the 1987 Intifada was initiated and guided by Palestinians who grew up and lived in the occupied territories, many of whom had served time in Israeli prisons, while many others practically lived as workers inside Israel. They became pragmatic about what could realistically be achieved. They were not particularly driven by ideology or the search for revenge, as was the case with many on the outside, especially the Tunis-based PLO activists. The Oslo accord was generated out of such conflict communication, a product of direct bilateral contact between pragmatist representatives on both sides. It follows, then, that no resolution is viable without communication between the conflictants themselves. The ability of Palestinians to speak to the Israeli public during the 1987 Intifada and the consequent achievements were their own genuine endeavor. Neither side should forget this.

The radicalization process inside the arena of contention is not entirely confined to the Palestinian side; rather it is interactive, affecting both sides. Such a radicalization process is systematically fed by the extremists on both sides. Exploiting the already fragile communicative infrastructure between the Israeli leadership and the ideology-driven Tunis-based Palestinian leadership who had been living in exile during the first Intifada, these groups sought to undermine Oslo by employing lethal tactics aimed at impairing each other, thereby strengthening their respective bases of power. Such forces were strengthened by the repressive Israeli response and the weakening of the infrastructure maintained by the Palestinian Authority. In the process, the strategic insights regarding the nature of the Israeli adversary, so painstakingly developed by the initiators of the first Intifada, some of whom had been pushed aside by the Tunisian-based Palestinian leadership, were lost.

Third, this book has demonstrated that regardless of Israel's expectations and estimations, the needs and interests of the Palestinians in the occupied territories have shaped their strategy and political claims and goals. Social location and daily necessities slowly pragmatized many of the Palestinian activists and leaders. Such was the case with the tempering of the Fatah-led PLO and Hamas. Such tempering did not evolve in a vacuum; rather, it evolved out of the immersion of the Nationalistic and Islamic ideologies in the daily realities of their respective constituents. In practical terms, this means that the prevalent perception inside Israel that there is no partner for peace may be groundless or, at best, rooted in value judgments that may overlook possible venues for resolution. A partner to conflict *is* a partner for peace.

In this regard, unilaterally disengaging from the Gaza Strip does not only mean an Israeli refusal to recognize its responsibility in the situation, but also undermines the potential of pragmatic forces to regain power and influence. Since no deterministic approach should be applied to analyze human history there is a faint chance that Abu-Maazen will bring about a significant change. As of yet, the Tunisian-PLO has failed to genuinely acknowledge the historical role of the local grassroots forces and their political stand. It may well be that the only way out of fanaticism is rooted in Abu-Maazen's willingness to join hands with the grassroots forces. This type of coalition has the potential for encouraging Hamas to fully participate in the political process and to further pragmatize its agenda.

Hamas has been gaining power and zeal as the living conditions of the Palestinians in the West Bank and Gaza continue to deteriorate. It is possible that we will witness further tempering of Hamas's ideological creed as a result of an improvement in the living conditions of the Palestinian populace. The responsibility of Israel – in fact its genuine interest – is to promote and facilitate the infrastructure for such improvements. Foreign intervention may turn out to be detrimental. The Palestinian populace put forth their leadership in the past and will continue to do so. Neither Israel nor the international community can dictate such a leadership, regardless of who they deem fit.

Finally, in this sense, Palestinians should realize and remember the objective and subjective constraints on the Israeli public and leadership, just as Israelis should realize and remember the subjective and objective constraints on the Palestinian public and leadership. Any resolution to the conflict must be attentive to such constraints; discernment and acknowledgment of the wrongs inflicted by both sides on one another are crucial. This is precisely why any political initiative should be introduced and implemented with great care, in an incremental fashion. It may take years and will probably not take place in my generation. Whether or not this will be the case, it is the responsibility of present leaders to delineate and design the conditions for such remote possible resolutions *here* and *now*. I hope this book will provide some insights into how to make my colleague's cynicism untimely.

# Postscript
## The contentious 1990s and the 2000 Intifada

Beginning September 29, 2000 another cycle of contention emerged, introducing two lethal innovations: the Israeli "liquidation" (or targeted killings) policy and the Palestinian suicide bombings (*Istishad*). While early incidents had occurred prior to the 2000 Intifada (e.g., the assassination of PLO second-in-command Halil al-Wasir in 1988 or the assassination of Izz al-Din al-Qassam mastermind, activist Yihye Ayyash, in 1996, and a Hamas suicide bombing near Beit-El in 1993), this time, the two parties developed these deadly tactics into a full-fledged policy. The liquidation of Hussein Abeiat, a member of the *al-Aqsa* Martyr Brigades,[1] on November 9, 2000 in an attempt to end the Palestinian shootings from Bethlehem on the adjacent Jerusalem neighborhood of Gilo, was the start of a series of dozens of liquidations. By the end of 2000, Israel had liquidated ten more grassroots activists using a variety of techniques such as snipers or air-strikes. Beginning in January 2001, it became clear that the Islamic organizations (and the Tanzim in late 2001) had reached the decision to further escalate the fight against Israel, initiating a series of suicide bombings inside Israel, as a result of which hundreds of Israelis died. It took four-and-a-half years of bloodshed for the two parties to reach a ceasefire agreement at Sharm-a-Sheikh in February 2005.

How is it, then, that in spite of the impressive achievements of the 1987 Intifada we witnessed a sweeping deterioration into violent bloodshed in September 2000? And why is it that intra-factionalism was so much more unmanageable during the 2000 cycle of contention compared to the 1987–92 cycle of contention? I have no claim to provide a thorough analysis of the 2000 Intifada. Rather, I intend to discuss aspects of the dynamics in the territories throughout the 1990s in terms of precipitating the reemergence of Palestinian contentious politics and its early phases.

As we know by now, Palestinian grassroots activists within the occupied territories managed to mount and sustain a voluminous wave of contention aimed at shaking off (hence the name *Intifada)* Israeli occupation. As a result, the structure and dynamics of the Palestinian–Israeli conflict went through a significant shift. As of 1992, the development of Palestinian self-rule in parts of the West Bank and Gaza was already apparent; this represented a first stage in what was agreed would become a Final Settlement Agreement (hereinafter: FSA) between Israel and a future Palestinian Authority.

The Madrid peace conference in late 1991, the subsequent elections for Palestinian self-rule, and the Oslo Accords that began in September 1993, became parts of the process through which a would-be Palestinian State was expected to take shape. The embodiment of this political process was the establishment of the Palestinian Authority with partial ruling powers in June 1994. However, in contrast to expectations and popular perceptions that "everything seemed to be going in the right direction," on September 29, 2000 another wave of contention emerged, the remnants of which are still ongoing at the time of this writing.[2]

What were the reasons for the 2000 Intifada? Did we face a "new" Intifada or a "second" Intifada? Was everything indeed going in the right direction throughout the 1990s? In light of the analysis presented in this book, I would argue that throughout the 1990s the situation in the territories was far from ideal and that many of the reasons for the present situation are rooted in the trajectories and results of the 1987 Intifada. I will further suggest that it is more accurate to speak of one Intifada containing two cycles of contention rather than two distinct Intifadas, hence my use of the terms 1987 Intifada and 2000 Intifada.

In the aftermath of the 1987 Intifada, the level of contention between the Palestinians and the Israeli forces decreased significantly. Yet, even during what Wolfsfeld (1997) labeled as the "peace festival," referring to the euphoria that characterized the first eighteen months of the Oslo Accord, the level of confrontation in the arena of contention remained relatively high. As from 1992, the level of confrontation was low compared with the period 1987–91, yet it remained relatively high culminating in the emergence of another voluminous cycle of contention which began September 29, 2000.

Statistics provided by the Israeli Defense Force Spokesperson Department indicate that despite a relative decrease in the number of "public disturbances" in the territories, the overall frequency of "public disturbances" remained higher than, for instance, the pre-1987 Intifada period. Indeed, the "lowest" year between 1992 and 1999 shows approximately 6,000 contentious events, a figure expected to be much higher given the less biased parameters of inclusion and exclusion. True, the Israeli Defense Force Spokesperson defines stone throwing, barricades, rioting, and tire burning as "public disturbances" whereas demonstrations, strikes, mass funerals, etc. are not included and hence are overlooked.

Is the 2000 cycle of contention a "new" Intifada, a "second" Intifada, or, as labeled by many Palestinians, the *al-Aqsa* (i.e., the Temple Mount) Intifada? Following the analysis developed throughout this book it seems that labeling the 2000 Intifada as "new" or "second" is misleading. On the surface, such a label seems to capture the dominant use of deadly weapons and the fact that hardliners on both Nationalistic and Islamic camps practically set the tone and pace of the confrontation. Regardless of which data source is used, the violence and casualties on both sides (including East Jerusalem) during the first year of the 2000 Intifada, as can be seen in Figure 7.1, the data of which is based on B'Tselem report, far exceed those of the 1987 Intifada.[3]

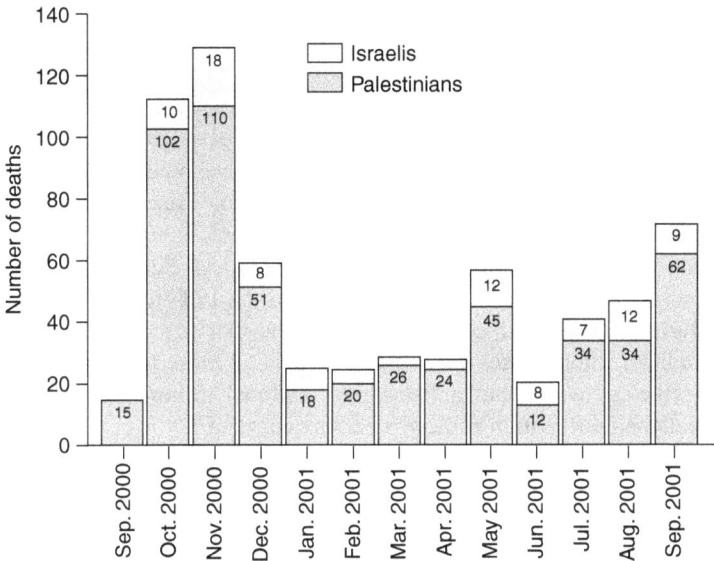

*Figure* 7.1 Palestinians and Israelis killed in the occupied territories (September 2000–September 2001).

Interestingly, the Palestinians named their struggle the "*al-Aqsa* Intifada" (the Intifada of the *al-Aqsa* Mosque), which seems to convey the religious fervor of confrontations especially in light of Sharon's provocative visit to the Haram al-Sharif, but also due to the centrality of Islamic forces in the al-Aqsa cycle of contention (Beitler 2004; Hammami and Tamari 2001). True, Islamic forces are far more dominant in the 2000 Intifada than was the case during the 1987 Intifada. Yet it seems that the terminology of the *al-Aqsa* Intifada is rooted in a misconception, as though the issue of Jerusalem were the only issue left unresolved during the Camp David Summit of July 2000. Whether it was the Israeli or the American representatives who promoted this conception, the fact of the matter was that the Israeli and Palestinian negotiators disagreed on almost every issue discussed (Harel and Isacharoff 2004).

What is undoubtedly true about labeling the *al-Aqsa* Intifada in religious terms is the fact that the forces who dictated the pace and tone of contention were Palestinian hardliners, who not only rejected the Israeli and US attempts to enforce a FSA (as formulated in summer 2000), but who also challenged the Palestinian Authority. Using terminology such as the "new" Intifada implies that throughout the 1990s the situation in the territories was relaxed and suddenly erupted once again on September 29, 2000. Yet, just as with the 1987 Intifada, as demonstrated throughout, there was no sudden outburst.

The 2000 cycle of contention, then, may be "new" in terms of the dominant mode of action employed, that of deadly weapons and suicide bombings, which stands out in contrast to the dominance of a limited form of violence during the 1987 Intifada. The 2000 cycle of contention can also be said to be "new" in terms of the existing Palestinian political and institutional infrastructure, namely an authority, police force, airport, etc., which differ from the situation during the 1987 Intifada (Hammami and Tamari 2001). The existence of a Palestinian Authority has unquestionably generated new dynamics between Palestinians and Israelis and among Palestinians themselves. And, as we will see below, this change in structure, hence dynamics, was a debilitating factor with regard to Palestinian ability to manage intra-factionalism. Nonetheless, when measured by the actors and goals of the struggle, the distinction is less clear-cut. While the 2000 Intifada seemed to lack the popular features of the 1987 uprising (although popular features were present, especially during the first few months), given a deepening radicalization process of which I will have more to say below, the struggle nonetheless was about a Palestinian national minority that seeks to shake off the Israeli occupation and establish its own state.

The continuity between the two cycles of contention also holds when it comes to the actors involved. This mostly consisted of Hamas and Tanzim (Arabic for the organization at the grassroots), which seemed to dictate the pace and tone of contention. While not named as such during the 1987 Intifada, Tanzim actually consisted of grassroots activists who played a central role in the initiation and conduct of the 1987 uprising. The same holds in the case of Hamas. Despite its pan-Islamic agenda, ever since its foundation in early 1988, Hamas has been a Palestinian liberation movement based on Islam. As one incarcerated Hamas terrorist put it, "armed attacks are an integral part of the organization's struggle against the Zionist occupier ... our goal can only be achieved through force, but force is the means, not the end. History shows that without force it will be impossible to achieve independence" (Post, Sprinzak, and Denny 2003: 179).

In this case, it is more accurate to speak of another cycle of contention, although more violent in nature, rather than speaking about a "new" or "second" Intifada. Instead of superficially dichotomizing the two Intifadas it is imperative to ask why was it that after the attempts to establish collaboration between the Israelis and the Palestinians during the Oslo era, we have witnessed the shift towards an episode of collective violence, as has been the case with the 2000 Intifada.

We will not go into an in-depth analysis to account for such a shift. We will, however, attempt to promote an analytical framework for understanding the shift to a cycle of hatred and fanaticism. While the shift towards the dominance of collective violence can be explained by the inherent militant ideologies held by groups on both sides (e.g., Islamic Jihad and Hamas, and militant Jewish Settlers and political parties), or impulsive reactions towards provocative behavior by both parties (e.g., Sharon's visit to the Temple Mount or the violent events of *al-Naqba* day in May 2000), however, we will see that these two possible explanations can be deepened when incorporated in an analysis of interaction and developments *between* the two parties, *within* each party, and *external* to both parties, which brings about a collapse of coordination and a shift from a relatively non-violent mode of contention to a violent one (Tilly 2003).

What follows is a provisional analysis structured according to the three vectors of analysis already used in this book: the *why*, the *how*, and the *when* questions of the 2000 *al-Aqsa* Intifada.

### *The* **why** *question of the 2000 Intifada*

It would be unrealistic to expect Palestinian grievances and discontent to be alleviated quickly and significantly after the Peace Process between Israel and the PLO commenced (Behar 2002). It is one thing to set the ground for ending the Israeli occupation. It is yet a very different and much more complicated matter to eliminate the economic dependency on the Israeli market, for example. The 1987 Intifada may indeed have made considerable political progress, including the promise for a Palestinian State, but its aftermath found the Palestinian market in an even worse condition than before the Intifada. Palestinian self-government was still taking shape, and starting in June 1994, the Palestinian Authority (hereafter: PA) was facing a most pressing and formidable challenge: to cope with the daily financial needs of the population, and, more importantly, to sustain the hope for imminent improvement in their living conditions.

In reality, the Palestinians only partly realized their expectations that their living conditions would improve. A major reason was that various states and international agencies (e.g., the US, Japan, Arab States, and the World Bank) transferred to the PA only part of the funds promised for the development of the economic infrastructure and support for social institutions. An additional reason, no less important, concerned the misconduct and the mismanagement of funds inside the PA.

According to Rekhess and Regavim (2000), accusations were raised by a Palestinian member of the Budget Committee concerning lack of transparency, while other members went further, criticizing the growing nepotistic practice of awarding public company monopolies to relatives of high-ranking officials in the PA, as well as mismanaging the donor countries' funds (p. 476). In November 1999, twenty Palestinian public figures issued the Anti-Corruption Communiqué of the Twenty, which raised a stern criticism of the corrupt conduct of the PA; many of them were arrested by PA security bodies and detained for several weeks.

In fact, criticism of the PA's financial conduct came at a time of relative improvement in the Palestinian economy (see below). During 1994–5 the Palestinian economy faced an additional crisis due to the Israeli policy of implementing ongoing closures over the territories and thus restricting the Palestinians' ability to leave the territories,[4] in addition to placing sharp restrictions on work permits for Palestinians working in Israel. These restrictions followed waves of terrorist attacks initiated mostly by the Islamic Jihad and Hamas military wing Izz al-Din al-Qassam, aimed mostly at undermining the Oslo Accords.

The Israeli polity was far from united over the Peace Process; as we will see below, Palestinian society was far from demonstrating a united front as well. While Israeli Prime Minister Rabin and Yasir Arafat were signing the Declaration of Principles on the White House lawn (Oslo "A") and later the Interim Agreement on September 28, 1995 (Oslo "B"), which gave the PA control over Palestinian cities (with the exception of Hebron), the Israeli government was still utilizing repressive measures such as deportations, house demolitions, and the establishment of new settlements or, as was more often the case, an expansion of existing ones.

Thus, Israeli repression policies were still a major source of concern for the Palestinians in the occupied territories. A report by the Israeli peace movement Peace Now, published in 2000, shows, for example, that whereas the total size of the Jewish population inside settlements in the occupied territories stood at approximately 100,000 people in 1992, by 1999 the number of Jewish population inside settlements rose to 180,000.

Additionally, attacks by Jewish Settlers continued to be a major source of anger and frustration, given the PA's inability to address the attacks while the Israeli army practiced tacit consent when it came to law enforcement against the Jewish Settlers. The worst attack by Jewish Settlers was the massacre at the Cave of the Patriarchs in Hebron on February 25, 1994, when Baruch Goldstein, a religious Jewish zealot, entered the cave, shot dead twenty-nine worshippers, and injured dozens more.

At that point, harsh opposition to the Peace Process was steadily growing, expressing itself both inside and outside the Israeli political system. On November 4, 1995, Israeli Prime Minister Rabin was shot dead by Igaal Amir, a Jewish religious right-wing activist. Facing the ongoing terrorist attacks by Hamas and Islamic Jihad activists, the Israeli public elected Netanyahu, who formed a right-wing coalition, presenting a tougher policy concerning the progress in the Peace Process. In a way, Netanyahu's administration (June 1996 to July 1999) will be remembered mainly for its double-headed policy of reluctantly progressing with the Peace Process while systematically exercising a *de facto* policy of undermining the integrity of the would be Palestinian State.

On the one hand, it was Netanyahu who signed the Hebron Agreement on January 15, 1997, according to which Israel handed over the city of Hebron to the PA, with the exception of the Cave of the Patriarchs, and the Wye Agreement on October 23, 1998, which turned out to be a major factor in his political downfall in 1999. On the other hand, it was the same administration that decided to open the Jewish holy site – the Western Wall Tunnel – in September 1996, and to expand the Jewish settlements around Jerusalem (i.e., the construction on *Har Homa*[5]) in March 1997. Both decisions triggered an outraged response from Palestinians in the occupied territories, expressed by a wide range of protests in which the PA took an active role, accompanied by harsh condemnations by Arab leaders and the international community.

Despite these developments and the economic difficulties the Palestinians experienced during the first half of the 1990s, it should be noted that in a slow, yet consistent, manner the Palestinian economy, according to Rekhess and

Regavim (2002), was on the rise during the years preceding the 2000 Intifada. This consisted in an improvement in trade, a decline in the unemployment rate, and the signing of a natural gas production agreement with British Gas Company. Not surprisingly, the resumption of the Intifada in the fall of 2000 brought about the total collapse of the PA economy.

### The how *question of the 2000 Intifada*

The two central Palestinian collective actors in the wake of the 1987 Intifada were the PA and Hamas. While the PA, dominated mostly by the Fatah-led PLO, acted to form its ruling apparatuses and to substantiate its control, Hamas was the most influential political actor in opposition to the PA. Other oppositional groups included hardliners from within Fatah, coupled with PFLP and DFLP activists. In addition, many grassroots activists opposed the PA who, despite their leading role in the 1987 Intifada, did not enjoy the fruits of its achievements and were pushed aside by the Tunis-based leadership (the "Tunisians") following their return to Gaza as a result of the Oslo Accord (Beitler 2004).

As we will see, some of these activists became members of the Tanzim, set up by Arafat in 1995 as a paramilitary force within Fatah. While the Tanzim was originally meant to act as a militia personally loyal to Arafat and, also, as a counterweight to the Islamic opposition, it was the Tanzim, primarily led by Marwan Barghouti, which, ironically, together with Hamas, raised perhaps the most serious challenge to the PA.[6]

As elaborated in Chapter 5, during the first years of the 1987 Intifada the two rival parties managed to maintain a general consensus vis-à-vis the primary goal the Palestinians were facing. However, as the first signs of political achievements unfolded (especially the commencement of a dialogue between Arafat and the US), Hamas was quick to reject any recognition and acceptance of what had become the Madrid talks of October 1991. Such a rejection was also shared by Nationalist grassroots activists who had already, during the 1987 Intifada, expressed harsh criticism of the Fatah-led PLO for engaging in political accords with the US and expressing willingness for political compromise with Israel.

Indeed, the actual process of peace talks and preparation for self-rule generated a renewal of clashes between the respective Hamas and Fatah-led PLO constituents. During July and August 1992, numerous confrontations broke out between the parties, leading the editor of the daily *a-Sha'ab* to state, "What is happening ... is frightening. It threatens not only the Intifada, but our whole social framework" (Jaradat 1992).

Intimidating as it was, the balance of power was clear. The PLO had established dominance since it held the promise of the desired solution; it thereby enjoyed unequivocal popularity among the Palestinians in the occupied territories. Moreover, as of late 1989, following the heavy Israeli crackdown on Hamas and the imprisonment of many of its key activists and leaders, the PLO was practically the only well-resourced and well-organized political actor within the territories

Facing such an unfavorable balance of power, Hamas acted in two inter-related ways. First, its central leadership core and base of operation was relo-cated to nearby Arab States such as Iran, Syria, Jordan, and also Western countries such as the US, Germany, and England (Mishal and Sela 1999). The externally-based Hamas not only provided most of the funding for Hamas's operations, but also set a more hard-line approach compared to the internally-based core. This approach acted as a manifestation of the total rejection of the political initiatives between Israel and the PA, and led to the initiation of a series of terrorist attacks on Israel aimed at undermining the realization the Peace Process.

Between early 1994 and 1996, a series of suicide bombings initiated by Hamas, resulting in dozens of Israeli deaths and hundreds of injuries, became a major factor in the victory of Benjamin Netanyahu over Shimon Peres and the establishment of a right-wing coalition in the national elections held on May 29, 1996. Throughout this time period, the PA and the internally-based Hamas maintained a tense relationship where the PA, was forced to recognize the growing popularity of Hamas and systematically tried to co-opt it. Hamas, for its part, embraced a pragmatic approach of neither recognizing the PA nor fighting it (Gunning 2004; Mishal and Sela 1999).

A major impetus for this shift in Hamas's approach was the release of Hamas movement's most prominent leader from Israeli prison, Ahmed Yassin. In 1997, after eight years of imprisonment, Yassin managed a quick takeover of the movement's leadership, a move which shifted the leadership's core back to the territories. Highly attentive to its popular base of power, Hamas gradually pre-sented itself as a genuine alternative to the faltering Oslo Accords.

Hamas used the continuing threats from Israeli right-wing groups and government as a justification for its approach. In that context, Hamas's pragma-tism was expressed towards Israel as well. This pragmatism took shape by reviv-ing cultural themes from Islamic history and the Koran and by framing the possibility of peace with Israel as a tactical, temporary pause in the holy Jihad. For that purpose, Islamic concepts such as the *sabr* (patience) and the *hudna* (truce) were elevated from Islamic tradition to legitimize Hamas's religious flex-ibility and to justify such shifts in strategy and tactics. In this way, Hamas was successful in presenting itself as an authentic national alternative to the PA: Islam was still the best and *only* solution, Hamas argued, but one that was inex-tricably entwined with Palestinian Nationalism.

Through such pragmatism, Hamas managed to sustain its tense relationship with the PA. As Arafat's difficulties in delivering on the promise of Oslo increased (difficulties for which Hamas was partly responsible), Hamas's power increased significantly. Still, during the run-up to the 2000 Intifada, Hamas did not enjoy strong public support; surprisingly, at the same time, the popularity of the Fatah and the PA also declined. Hamas's inability to fill the void was due to a systematic crackdown by both Israel and the PA respectively, the relative improvement in the PA's economy, the Israeli–Syrian talks held during the first months of 2000, which meant the possibility of loosing an important ally of Hamas and, perhaps most importantly, the impending promise of a FSA between Israel and the PA (Rekhess and Regavim 2002).

### The **when** *question of the 2000 Intifada*

As we have seen, the causes of the 2000 cycle of contention were, for the most part, to be found in issues unresolved and, to a certain extent, exacerbated by the 1987 cycle of contention. The 2000 Intifada was dominated and guided mostly by Tanzim and the Islamic forces. In the wake of what was considered the most generous offer by Israel to the Palestinians during the Camp David talks in July 2000 by Israeli Prime Minister Ehud Barak, and in reaction to the provocative visit of then Knesset member Ariel Sharon to the Temple Mount, clashes and confrontations broke out throughout the territories, and, soon after, inside Israel. The prevalent question among many Israelis and outside viewers has been: why was it that clashes and confrontations resumed, given such an opportunity for the Palestinians to reach a FSA?

As argued above, tension between the two conflictants gradually increased during the months preceding September 2000, while the collaborative infrastructure formed after the signing of Oslo was seriously damaged during the mid-1990s. This was true on both a formal level, namely, between the military and political officials and negotiators, and on an informal level, that is, between Israeli and Palestinian citizens and security forces throughout the territories.

According to Rekhess and Regavim (2002), senior members of the Palestinian negotiating team warned throughout the year that, given the lack of satisfactory progress in the negotiations, the Palestinians would be forced to turn to another round of violence. In addition, the authors continue, even Arafat himself threatened in June of 2000 to rekindle the Intifada within the Palestinian territories. These warnings came amidst the PLO Central Council decision on February 2, 2000 to unilaterally declare the independence of a Palestinian State on September of the same year, despite Israeli and US objections.

In their detailed account of the 2000 Intifada, Isacharoff and Harel (2004) follow suit and argue that signs of danger were raised when the coordination between Israeli and Palestinian security forces (Defense Coordination Offices – DCO), established in the wake of the Oslo Accord, gradually deteriorated. This consisted, for example, of Palestinian security forces aiming weapons at their Israeli counterparts during joint patrols or a deliberate overlooking of weapons smuggling into the Gaza Strip – a situation that convinced the Israeli commander of the Southern division to recommend that the joint security patrols be stopped.

The situation "on the street" was no less threatening, despite a relative calm during the first few months of 2000. On May 15, during *al-Naqba* commemoration day, massive demonstrations took place, with stones and Molotov cocktails, and shooting incidents broke out throughout the territories. While the action was initiated by Tanzim forces, it became clear that, just as with the Western Wall Tunnel events in 1996, the PA had taken an active role in the fighting. The confrontations lasted for several days, as a result of which eight Palestinians died and hundreds of Palestinians and approximately thirty Israelis were injured.

A week after *al-Naqba* day, a significant development took place outside the arena of contention. Israel decided to unilaterally withdraw from Southern Lebanon on May 22, 2000, after eighteen years of military presence, and created a lasting effect on both conflictants. While no Israeli soldier was injured during the three days of withdrawal, a series of unfortunate military accidents presented Israel's withdrawal as panicky, succumbing to the victorious Hizbollah. Hizbollah's continual shooting at the Israeli forces, the large amounts of military equipment and supplies left behind, and the scenes of thousands of the Southern Lebanese Army's soldiers (Israel's ally in the region) desperately trying to enter Israel, created a poor media impression.

On Israel's part, the fear that the withdrawal from Lebanon was being perceived as a sign of weakness convinced high-rank military officials to prepare a much heavier crackdown should Palestinians in the occupied territories attempt to further escalate the situation. On the Palestinian side, the lesson drawn from the withdrawal was that, given a the sufficient amount of pressure and Israeli casualties, Israel would withdraw from the territories as well. Indeed, as argued by Isacharoff and Harel, Hizbollah's leader, Sheikh Hassan Nasrallah, became a hero in the eyes of many Palestinians. Cited by the authors, a Tanzim activist from Balata refugee camp argued that in retrospect, "Their [Hizbollah's] victory strengthened our faith in the effectiveness of armed struggle and suicide attacks" (2004: 65).

Later, on September 27, 2000, Israeli soldier Sgt. David Biri was fatally wounded near the largest Israeli settlement in Gaza Strip, Netzarim, in the explosion of a roadside bomb. And the next day, in Kalkilya, a Palestinian police officer opened fire and killed his Israeli counterpart during a joint patrol. These incidents were consistent with remarks made by Palestinians officials, demonstrating that portraying the *al-Aqsa* Intifada as a sudden outburst of violence resulting from Sharon's visit to the Temple Mount on September 28, 2000 is far from accurate. According to the Palestinian Facts Organization, Imad Falouji, the Palestinian Authority Communications Minister said that the violence had been planned in July, far in advance of Sharon's provocative act. Additionally, in an interview given to the Palestinian Authority newspaper, Sakhr Habash, a member of the Fatah's Central Committee, contended that Sharon's visit was no more than a spark. Indeed, for Barghouti, Sharon's visit was purely instrumental as it held the potential of demonstrating to the Palestinian public the cost of not acting – what Goldstone and Tilly call *current threat* (2001). In a revealing interview with the London-based Arabic daily *al-Hayat*, Barghouti commented,

> The night prior to Sharon's visit, I participated in a panel on a local television station and I seized the opportunity to call on the public to go to

the al-Aqsa Mosque in the morning . . . After Sharon left, I remained for two hours in the presence of other people, we discussed the manner of response and how it was possible to react in all the cities and not just in Jerusalem. We contacted all (the Palestinian) factions.[7]

Barghouti's attempts at mobilizing the Palestinian population to action involved a visit to the Arab Triangle (i.e., a Mandatory term denoting a triangular-like geographical area in which many of the Israeli Palestinians reside inside Israel) on the same day as Sharon's visit. These attempts did not fall on deaf ears. The deepening frustration and indignation among Israeli Palestinians and signs of rising tension were already felt during the first half of 2000, when confrontations broke out in the city of Sakhnin during the commemoration of the 1976 Land Day.[7a]

Yet, the most severe expression of the cumulative rage among Israeli Palestinians occurred on October 1, 2000. Erupting in the Umm al-Fahm area, the clashes and disturbances were quick to spread throughout the Triangle and spilled into Israeli cities, involving Palestinian and Jewish communities such as Tiberias, Jaffa, and Upper Nazareth. According to Susser and Rekhess (2002), the violent clashes, lasting for three days, came to a halt as a result of an aggressive police response, using tear gas, rubber bullets, and live ammunition. On October 3, 2000, during the harsh response, thirteen Israeli Palestinians were killed, and hundreds of protesters and dozens of police officers were injured.

While a thorough study is warranted, based on the line of argument developed thus far it seems plausible to suggest that, as supposedly generous as Barak's proposal to the Palestinians was, and whether it was an opportunity for Arafat to finally deliver the promise of Oslo, Barak's (and President Clinton's for that matter) insistence on concluding a FSA might have triggered the 2000 Intifada. Indeed, a FSA would have thwarted both Tanzim and Hamas's agendas, perceived as an imminent threat to the opportunity they had created for themselves to acquire domination within the territories throughout the second half of the 1990s.

Tanzim under the leadership of Barghouti was systematically accumulating power within the Nationalist Movement. While carefully refraining from questioning or criticizing Arafat, Barghouti nonetheless raised stern criticisms over the Tunisian-led PA and systematically acted to take over the Fatah's High Committee and the Palestinian "street." An indication of Barghouti's political power and influence occurred in March 1999. Following a harsh repression of public protests against the corruption inside the PA by the latter's security forces, Barghouti called on a general strike in the West Bank, a call which was widely met. The clashes that broke out and the consequent death of a twelve-year-old boy from security force shootings pushed Barghouti to initiate the strike without consulting Arafat, and to refuse to end it despite the heavy pressure exerted by Arafat and PA officials (Harel and Isacharoff 2004). This and other examples of Barghouti's aspirations caused deep concerns among Fatah and PA's high officials, who influenced Arafat limit Barghouti's political power by encouraging rivalries, such as indirectly supporting Barghouti's competitor, Hussein al-Sheikh, as leader of Tanzim, or limiting the flow of funds to Barghouti's grassroots forces. These efforts at limiting Barghouti's power were unsuccessful.

Later on, in March 2000, Barghouti made his grand scheme to rekindle another popular struggle public, warning Fatah members that, "Whoever thinks it is possible to reach a final status agreement through negotiation would better stop fantasizing. In these matters, we must engage in confrontations. We need tens of battles like the *al-Aqsa* Tunnel" (cf. Harel and Isacharoff 2004: 48). Amidst the Camp David Summit it became clear that the Barghouti-led Tanzim gained dominance in setting the pace and tone of the situation, enjoying widespread popularity among the Palestinian populace.

Arafat's rejection of Barak and Clinton's proposal made at Camp David, and the consequent failure of the talks, turned him almost overnight into a hero in the PA. Yet, the Camp David Summit was too late and offered too little; Camp David was doomed to failure before it had begun, as Arafat was fully aware of the growing challenge back home, realizing that any concession or compromise on his part would mean political suicide or even worse (Harel and Isacharoff 2004).

Furthermore, the 2000 Intifada was, simultaneously, a challenge against the PA and Israel. An expression of this is found in an interview given by Hamas Spokesperson in Hebron Abdel Khaleq al-Natshe to the *Palestine Times* in April 2000.[8] When asked about Hamas's relations with the PA, al-Natshe answered, "The Palestinian Authority is our oppressor, but again we don't like to accentuate this too much, since our conflict is with Israel."

In the case of the Tanzim, the PA was not perceived as an oppressor and Arafat was unequivocally considered sacred: the indisputable leader of the Palestinian People. Still, we have already seen the inherent tension between the externally-based PLO and the internally-based PLO resulting from Arafat's being the leader of the Palestinian People writ large, and the evolving unique interests and aspirations of the Palestinians *within* the occupied territories. We have also elaborated on the division of labor made between the symbolic leadership of Arafat and his Tunisian cadre, and the functional leadership of the grassroots activists in the West Bank and Gaza Strip who practically initiated and conducted the 1987 Intifada; as long as the achievements of the 1987 Intifada were realized in a promising fashion, the initiators of the Intifada were willing to put up with the posturing of the Tunisian-based PLO.

Yet, as elaborated above, things were far from going in the right direction. Arafat, upon his return from Camp David in late July 2000, had little control over the situation and his popularity rating was exceptionally low. In attempts to maintain his popularity, Arafat had little choice but to welcome and support the Intifada, going so far as ordering the release of many of Hamas's key political and military activists.

Indeed, according to the results of a public poll conducted by the Palestinian Jerusalem Media and Communication Center in June 2000, administered among

1,200 respondents randomly sampled, Arafat's situation and the PA's popularity were at an all-time low. The main results reveal that only 31 percent of the respondents said they trusted Arafat as their leader (33 percent said they trusted nobody), approximately 40 percent said they were not satisfied with the performance of the PA, and about 90 percent believed there was corruption within the PA's institutions in varying degrees. Still, it seems that Arafat's rejection of Barak and President Clinton's FSA formula significantly inflated his popularity among the Palestinians in the occupied territories.

This did not mean, however, that Arafat fully regained control over the situation. In an interview with Israeli daily *Ha'aretz* following the conclusion of the Sharm-a-Sheikh Summit (October 2000), Barghouti contended that "the current Intifada would not stop with an order, as it did not start with an order . . . insinuating that the 'street' might not obey Arafat should he announce a cease-fire with Israel and a halt to the Intifada" (Rekhess and Regavim 2002: 468). The fact of the matter was that neither Arafat nor the PA had any serious control over the wide-spread clashes, acting more as an "overseer" than as the Intifada's general command (Mansour 2002). And, to make things even more complicated, the attempts to dissociate himself from the violence vis-à-vis the US and EU undermined Arafat's status vis-à-vis Tanzim and Hamas, both of which managed to form a coalition named the National and Islamic Forces (NIF) (including other organizations such as the Islamic Jihad, the DFLP, etc.).

An expression of the underlying challenge to the Tunisian-led PA can be found in a statement drafted by the NIF to President Arafat on January 13, 2001, during the preparations for what became the Taba Talks.[9] The content of the statement is revealing, demonstrating the firm and bold characteristics of the grassroots forces. I have decided to quote from it at length as it provides a glimpse of the double-headed challenge mounted by the NIF:

> In the Name of God, the Forgiving and Compassionate
> Our Brother, the President and Struggler Abu Ammar, god save him The President of State of Palestine. . . . We approach you in the name of the strugglers of the Intifada and their people with greetings and appreciation while affirming the importance highlighted by our people and their national and Islamic forces and their institutions on reinforcing their national unity and continue with the blessed Intifada that consolidated this unity until it achieves its goals in expelling the occupation and extracting our national rights in freedom, independence, and return. This victorious process is subjected these days to a US–Israeli conspiracy that aims to abort our process through the proposals made by President Clinton. . . . We warn of the dangers of the so-called principle acceptance . . . on this poisonous document. . . . We express our confidence in your steadfast position that adheres to the national constants [i.e., freedom, independence, and return]; however, we warn of falling into the trap of dealing with these tricky scenarios. . . . Your Excellency. . . . Our people are not tired. . . . The consensus of our people to continue with the Intifada until it achieves its goals requires from

all of us to be prepared for a long battle ... which requires reconsidering our internal condition and addressing it in a radical manner to secure the components of steadfastness. God help you in your tasks to the best interest of our people and homeland. Together until victory, until liberating Jerusalem, and achieving independence and return.

The State of Palestine
January 13, 2001

This excerpt is telling for several major reasons. First, the opening of the statement with "In the name of God" stands in sharp contrast to the opening phrase in leaflets formulated during the 1987 Intifada, that of "O great people of Palestine!" True, religious aspects were indeed present in the UNCU leaflets during the first cycle of contention in 1987, yet they were secondary to the nationalistic features of the uprising. This change in emphasis represents the zealous characteristics of the coalition formed between the hardliners of the Nationalistic and the Islamic forces during the 2000 Intifada. The Intifada has and continues to be colored as a sacred struggle and every Palestinian must align himself accordingly.

Second, the Palestinian goals are presented, again, in an uncompromising fashion; the goals of freedom, independence, and return are *constant*; meaning, they are invariant and indissoluble. Any deviation from the constants is seen as damaging to the sacred unity of the Palestinians, which, in itself, is preserved by the struggle.

Third, Arafat, while being elevated to the status reserved only for kings, is nevertheless warned not to deviate from the *constants*. He is reminded of his militant past and of his days of armed struggle, being addressed as Abu Ammar the Struggler, to designate the sacredness of the goal, the achievement which justifies the means employed and, equally important, the organic linkage between himself (not the Tunisian-led PA) and the Palestinian People. Thus, in spite of his Excellency, Arafat is still bound by the blessed Intifada and, just as with the NIF members, he is required to act for the fulfillment of the national *constants*.

Fourth, an integral part of the collective endeavor consists of internal reforms, seen as essential for the continuation of the Intifada. Specifically, the continuation of the Intifada and the willingness of the Palestinian People to carry the burden of the struggle are contingent upon a radical restructuring of the Palestinian Authority and a serious attempt to abolish the corruption within the Palestinian leadership. The legitimacy of Arafat as the leader of the Palestinian People is conditioned on such radical "reconsidering of our internal condition."

Last, but not least, the NIF implicitly criticizes both Arafat and the PA by ending with the statement "The State of Palestine," thus demonstrating its disapproval of the Palestinian leadership's impotence in standing up to the PLO Central Council's decision to unilaterally declare independence on September 13, 2000. In signing the statement as such, the NIF practically argues for the irreversibility of what is seen as a "victorious process," that is, telling Arafat and the PA that the Intifada is unstoppable. In addition, the NIF is also claiming its role as the genuine force and voice behind the Intifada, the same force and voice that handed the Palestinian Declaration of Independence over to Arafat in November 1988.

Two indicative examples of the PA and Arafat's lack of complete control over the developments and overall deterioration towards chaotic bloodshed in the arena of contention took place soon after Sharon's provocative visit to the Temple Mount. On September 30, Muhammad al-Durrah, a twelve-year-old Palestinian boy was killed by gunfire. Jamal al-Durrah left home that morning with his son Muhammad al-Durrah to shop for a car. On their return home, they were crossing a main street in the Bureij refugee camp when heavy shooting broke out between Palestinian militiamen and an Israeli Defense Force outpost near the Netzarim junction in Gaza Strip. The two sought sanctuary between a concrete cylinder and a low cinderblock wall as bullets rained down around them for about 45 minutes, of which several minutes were filmed by a French television crew, showing the boy cling to his father as his father tried to shield him from the bullets. Evidently, the boy was hit by four bullets, while his father suffered critical injuries. Although several months later an investigation led by the IDF concluded that al-Durrah was not hit by the IDF's bullets, the incident and the Israeli declaration of a probable hit shortly after the incident triggered massive demonstrations and violent clashes throughout the territories.

As it turned out, the death of Muhammad al-Durrah had been precisely what Barghouti needed to mobilize the population. While Sharon's visit brought with it a somewhat mild response in terms of massive, popular participation, the al-Durrah incident proved successful in that sense. Alas, this time, in comparison to the 1987 Intifada, the massive participation was one of unrestrained fury and vengeance – as subsequent events demonstrated.

On October 12, 2000 two Israeli reservists who made a wrong turn into the West Bank city of Ramallah were arrested by the PA police. Dressed in civilian clothes, one reportedly wearing a Palestinian headdress, they were suspected of belonging to an undercover Israeli assassination squad. An agitated Palestinian mob stormed the police station, beat the two soldiers to death, and threw their mutilated bodies onto the street. The killings were captured on video by an Italian television crew and broadcasted on TV, outraging the Israeli public. The killings, called by Prime Minister Barak "cold-blood lynching," and the alleged involvement of Palestinian policemen, coupled with the tarrying intervention of the PA, brought about a strong military response by Israel. Within hours, Barak ordered the tight sealing of Palestinian towns, deployment of large forces near Ramallah, and unleashing of helicopter gun-ships. Arafat's headquarters in Gaza were hit, missiles destroyed the top floor of the police station, and in Beit Lahia the headquarters of Tanzim was hit by rockets.

These two incidents are also indicative of the international community's attitude towards the 2000 Intifada. As in 1987, the 2000 Intifada was, to a large extent, a struggle over world opinion; both parties made considerable efforts to promote their own frame to the question of "what is it that is going on here?!"

In the main, there had been no significant changes in the interpretations the two conflictants promoted to the international news media during the 2000 Intifada in comparison to the 1987 Intifada. Israel's emphasis on the PA's responsibility for the escalating violence, and the Palestinians' conjuring up of the *al-Nakba* and the refugees' status, together with stressing the issue of Jerusalem as the capital city of the Palestinian State, reflected the changing nature of the political context of contention rather than a change in the framing efforts of either party respectively. Indeed, while Israel consistently argued the illegitimate and unjustified use of Palestinian violence, especially in light of a most "generous offer" given to Arafat in the summer of 2000, the Palestinians repeatedly painted their actions as an act of authentic national defiance in the face of an ongoing, intransigent Israeli repression of their national *constants* (i.e., freedom, independence, and return), this time under the poisonous contours of Oslo.

What, then, were the results of the struggle on world opinion? The reader should know by now that the portrayal of the Palestinians as victims during the first years of the 1987 Intifada by US and European news media went through gradual changes as a result of Arafat's support of Saddam Hussein during 1990, the signing and initial implementation of Oslo, and the Camp David talks of July 2000. The refusal of Arafat to accept the FSA plan offered in Camp David only added to the doubts raised regarding the fit between the frame of Israeli repression and the developments in the arena of contention. Nevertheless, Sharon's provocative visit to the Temple Mount and the miserable al-Durrah incident certainly had an impact on foreign journalists' decision to use the frame of Israeli repression.

As with the 1987 Intifada, there was no question of who was the stronger party, as the heavy shootings between Palestinian and Israeli forces, coupled with air-strikes by Israeli helicopters, became the best show in town. The Palestinians were perceived as the victims despite their frequent use of terrorist acts and deadly weapons, while Israel desperately tried to exert pressure on foreign journalists and news agencies to change their use of words and terms such as "Israeli Settlers" or "Palestinian victims" (Balint 2000). Indeed, whereas Israel tried to promote the issue of the PA's role in instigating violence, the frequent question in the international news media during the first days of the clashes was "Isn't Israel using excessive force?" together with the broader question of "Has Oslo collapsed?"

Yet, as Israeli scholar Yaron Ezrahi argues (2000), while the al-Durrah incident put Israel on the defensive in terms of promoting its own interpretation of the growing clashes, the lynching on October 12, 2000 and the horrendous pictures of the mutilated bodies brought about a significant shift in the international framing of the 2000 Intifada. An example of this shift took place soon after the incident when, during an interview with the BBC, the distinguished Palestinian–American scholar Edward Said was practically "put on the stand" when he was repeatedly asked whether Arafat was in control of the situation and whether the PA was inciting the population towards such barbaric behavior. This shift was also apparent on CNN. In an article appearing on October 13, a day after the lynching, the inability of the PA's forces in face of world attempts to end the bitter violence is emphasized:

> As world leaders scrambled to salvage what little cohesiveness remained of the Israeli–Palestinian peace process after 15 days of violence, gunfire in Ramallah, fiery demonstrations in Gaza and confrontations in Jerusalem's Old City kept emotions high on Friday ... In Gaza, angry demonstrators set fire to buildings housing a hotel, a liquor store and several bars as Palestinian security forces were unable to control the crowds. Leaders of the Palestinian Hamas movement also tried in vain to calm the situation.

The lack of a clear answer concerning who was the victim became even clearer following the attempts towards a ceasefire agreement in Sharm-a-Sheikh on October 17, 2000, the initiative to which the above excerpt refers, and its immediate breakdown. While no actual signing of a ceasefire agreement took place, President Clinton was nonetheless able to extract an oral ceasefire understanding between Barak and Arafat. According to a declaration made by Clinton, the two sides agreed to immediately end the violence of the past weeks and to cooperate with a body that would supervise the ceasefire arrangements.

Alas, violence broke out shortly after the declaration. In what turned out to be an unauthorized tour of Mount Ebal (north of Nablus) by a group of Jewish Settlers, one settler died and four were wounded as a result of a Palestinian shooting on the group. The provocation by the Settlers, the immediate deadly response by Tanzim forces, the developing confrontation between Israeli and Palestinian armed forces as the former were called to evacuate the Settlers, and the subsequent unbending proclamations made by Arafat vowing to continue the Intifada and by the Israeli Government Spokesman accusing Arafat of his unwillingness to take action in order to stop the violence – were all indicative of the growing animosity between the two parties.

From the international news media's point of view it became clear that the answer to the question: who is the victim? – was even less clear than it had been following the al-Durrah incident. A series of articles titled "Whose Holy Land?" by *New York Times* journalists published between October 3 and October 23, 2000 can be seen as a useful indication of the way the international news media dealt with the worsening developments in the arena of contention, recognizing the mutual responsibility of the two parties in the chaotic bloodshed.

# Methodological appendix

The possibility of a developing Palestinian collective attention and construction of domestic Israeli divisions – manifested in a series of crisis-events – as political opportunity was guided by four questions:

1   To what extent were Palestinians in the occupied territories interested in and attentive to domestic Israeli sociopolitical issues and developments?
2   What is the depth and scope of Palestinian familiarity with domestic Israeli sociopolitical issues and developments?
3   How did Palestinians frame these domestic Israeli sociopolitical issues and developments?
4   What meaning did Palestinians give to their confrontation with Israeli forces?

## Conceptualizing Israeli crisis-events

By crisis-event, I mean not just a happening or occurrence, whether private or public, but manifestations of an issue-culture with sociopolitical impacts on the political system specifically and on society as a whole. Such manifestations are assigned with cultural significance and are part of ongoing public discourse that revolves around a specific issue, which, in turn, involves a direct or indirect challenge to authorities.

The below list contains eight Israeli crisis-events. All eight are manifestations of sociopolitical issue-culture that expressed and, simultaneously, affected Israeli democracy during the 1970s and 1980s. The "issue-area" (Azar *et al.* 1972) that links all the crisis-events concerns with domestic Israeli divisions over the occupied territories' future status. These crisis-events are public manifestations of this conflict, reflecting Israel's power deflation situation. The rationale behind focusing on crisis-events that are linked to the occupied territories' issue-culture rests on the importance of concentrating on the historical sequence of events in relation to one another and in particular historical configuration, an "events-in-history" mode of analysis (Tarrow 1996).

In addition to this criterion, the decision of what counts as crisis-event rests on two sources. First, I drew on numerous works conducted on the Israeli polity post 1967. These works cast light on the system-wide crisis Israel was experiencing as a result of the historical decision to maintain its hold over the territories and the Palestinian population inside them.

Second, I used Azar and colleagues' (1972) five parameters for what counts as event, of which one is already elaborated above.

1 The political entity (the *actor*) that initiates an activity. This includes a person and/or a group or organization as long as they gain status within the behavior of the political system or any of its subsystems, and their goals or activities are aimed at influencing the public domain.
2 The political entity to which an activity is directed (the *target*). A target can be the state or the political system, or any of their representatives. A target can also be a social movement or any of a movement's members or representatives.
3 Those actions, reactions, and interactions (the *activity*) which are precipitated by clearly identified actor(s) or directed toward clearly identified target(s).
4 Time – the calendar day on which the source (i.e., *news media*) reports the events. As such, an additional parameter for what counts as event is the recording of the event at least once in any publicly available news media (given the time-period of the study: 1974–86).

The below summary of the chosen crisis-events mostly concentrates on the actor/s, the activity, the time, and the target. The italicized dates denote periods during which the crisis-event was first publicized or regained publicity, thus defined as additional event with its coverage analyzed respectively.

Source: Yedihot Aharonot Almanac, *Those Were the Years: Fifty Years to the State of Israel* (1998), Nissim Mishal (ed.), Tel-Aviv: Mishkal; Israeli dailies *Yedihot Aharonot* and *Maariv*

### Moti Ashkenazi's protest (February 10, 1974)

Reserve officer, the commander of the "Budapest" bastion (the single one that hung on during the Yom Kippur War at the Suez Canal front), preceded its release from hospital to initiate a sit-in strike in front of Prime Minister Golda Meir's office in Jerusalem. Ashkenazi demanded the resignation of Defense Minister Dayan, who was seen as the most responsible for the 1973 war's omission, and immediate changes in the political leadership. Ashkenazi's lone protest campaign expanded within days into a wide wave of unrest among Israeli public opinion, encouraging hundreds of soldiers to join in and collectively promote his demands.

### Gush Emunim's settlement in Sebastia

On *July 25, 1974* several Block of the Faithful activists and constituency, escorted by a few members of parliament, settled in Sebastia (inside the West

Bank), receiving wide-scale media coverage. In order to make their evacuation more difficult, the activists chained themselves with iron chains. After four days during which they consistently refused to evacuate voluntarily, a large military armament was sent in to commence evacuation by force. The evacuation was met by a passive resistance, forcing the soldiers to carry each and every settler out by hand. The Sebastia incident precipitated a deep public debate in Israel between the proponents of territories settlement and their opponents who, on their part, claimed that Israel should make use of the territories to achieve peace. During 1975 the tension between Block and the army intensified when, on *March 6* a violent confrontation took place as a result of a second settlement attempt. Only on December 8, 1975 did the Block accept Minister Galili's compromise proposition to relocate to a nearby military camp.

### The officers' letter (March 7, 1978)

Triggered by the right-wing movement Gush Emunim's (Block of the Faithful) growing influence on Israeli society and government amidst the peace talks in Camp David, the first Israeli peace movement consolidated. A group of combat reserve officers drafted a carefully worded letter to Israeli Prime Minister Begin during his stay at Camp David, with a stern warning that only a peace-seeking Israel, which exhausted all possible means for attaining peace would be able to stand firm and win any future war that might be forced upon it. Although avoiding any signs of disobedience, the officers who later formed Peace Now set a major precedent in which soldiers interfered in politics and latently expressed their objection to fighting any war that was not a threat to Israel's existence.

### Yamit evacuation (April 21, 1982)

During the Israeli evacuation of the Jewish settlements from the Sinai Desert, as part of the implementation of the Camp David Accord (1979), the Yamit evacuation represented the strongest expression of civic opposition to government policy. IDF forces sent to start the evacuation confronted a forceful resistance by hundreds of Settlers entrenched on the house roofs. Trying to approach the houses, the soldiers faced a barrage of stones, bottles, curses, and water buckets. A ferocious, violent confrontation took place when an iron cage was repeatedly lifted onto the roofs to take down the Settlers by force. Confrontation also took place at the town monument, where a group of right wing extremists climbed onto it, refusing to surrender. The evacuation lasted four days when Minister of Defense Sharon gave the order to raze the town to the ground.

### Peace Now demonstrations against the Beirut siege and the Sabra and Shatila massacre

Israeli's largest left-wing movement, Peace Now, organized two unprecedented demonstrations in Tel Aviv expressing the growing public debate over the increasing involvement in Lebanon. The more the "Peace for the Galilee" operation continued, transgressing its declared primary objectives, so did the inner Israeli criticism increase. Growing public unrest and protest were primarily targeted at Prime Minister Begin and Defense Minister Sharon. The first massive demonstration took place after the Israeli military encircled Beirut, on *July 3, 1982*, estimated at 100,000 participants. The protesters expressed their rejection of the continuing and intensifying Israeli presence in Lebanon. The second demonstration (*September 25, 1982*) took place as a result of the Sabra and Shatila refugee camps massacre. This time the protesters demanded a state investigating committee, which would inquire whether Israel was accountable for the catastrophe. It took a few weeks time for public pressure to force the government to appoint an investigating committee on October 1, 1982, which, six months later, found Sharon indirectly responsible for the massacre and recommended his resignation.

### Emil Grinzweig's assassination (February 10, 1983)

During a Peace Now demonstration in Jerusalem in front of Prime Minister Begin's office, a grenade exploded causing the death of Grinzweig a thirty-five-year-old paratrooper officer, together with ten other demonstrators slightly injured. Recruited like many others for service in Lebanon, Grinzweig joined the demonstration to express his protest against Israel's continuing involvement in Lebanon. Together with other protesters, he marched from the center of Jerusalem to the government building. Throughout their march, right-wing group members and proponents harassed them physically and verbally. After a long police investigation, a young man from Jerusalem, Yona Abrushmi, confessed to the deed, claiming that he was influenced by right-wing propaganda, which regarded left-wing activity as illegitimate. Abrushmi was sentenced to life in prison.

### The General Security Service (SHABAK) Affair

On *April 13, 1984* four Palestinian terrorists hijacked a bus number 300 travelling from Tel-Aviv to Ashkelon, and forced the driver to drive all the way to Gaza. Near the Dir-al-Balah area military elite forces took control over the bus and its twenty-five passengers. During the attack, two of the terrorists were killed, together with an Israeli female soldier; the other two were captured alive and were handed over to the security service. In contradiction of the formal report that all terrorists had died during the rescue operation, several cameramen held photos proving that two terrorists were actually captured alive. Despite the censorship prohibition, the photos were published. The exposure of the affair resulted in public demand for an investigating committee. The committee nominated by Defense Minister Moshe Arens put the blame on General Mordechay, who confessed to beating the terrorists during their interrogation. While Mordechay was exonerated by a military court, several security service members turned to the Government Judicial Counselor Zamir, admitting that the security service members who had testified in front of the investigating committee had conveyed false evidence, coordinated their arguments, and also eliminated evidence connecting the head of the service to the killing of the terrorists. The new evidence thus exposed (*May 25, 1986*) led Zamir to demand that the head of the service be put on trial. Facing a deep objection from Prime Minister Peres, who was backed by Foreign Minister Shamir and Defense Minister Rabin, Zamir decided to resign. The new counselor, Harish, who was expected by Peres and Shamir to be more "flexible" also refused to cancel the complaint against the head of the service that Zamir had handed over to the police . The public ravel led Peres and Shamir to tactically accept the head of the service's resignation, only to acquit him through President Hertzog (*June 25, 1986*). This maneuver, when published in the media, caused profound turmoil among the public, expressed most vividly by the former Minster of Law Tzadok saying, "This is the darkest day for Israeli rule of law."

### The uncovering of the Jewish Underground (April 27, 1984)

Following an intensivee secret service investigation, a Jewish Underground that acted in the territories against Palestinian targets was uncovered. Approximately 30 Settlers, some of whom were high-ranking military officers on duty, composed the Underground. Fully equipped with explosives and highly organized, the Underground members were arrested after booby-trapping five Arabic buses. During their interrogation they confessed a series of terrorist attacks, such as the assassination of Palestinian mayors, murder in the Islamic college of Hebron, and also an attempt to organize an attack at the Temple Mount. All Underground members were put to trial and convicted. Three of them were sentenced to life imprisonment and the others to long-term imprisonment (*May 23, 1984*). After a relatively short period in prison, most of the Underground members were released, while President Hertzog pardoned the others a few years later.

## Measuring Palestinian construction of political opportunity

There were two stages to the research: several preliminary in-depth interviews with Palestinian grassroots activists and Israeli journalists and officials, followed by a systematic content analysis of Palestinian print news media published during the 1970s and 1980s. The interviews, although unsystematic, provided useful information about the degree of interest in and familiarity with Israeli society among some Palestinian activists and about how their knowledge was gathered and circulated. Content analysis of news articles was the primary method used. It allowed us to look more systematically at the *amount* and *nature* of coverage of domestic Israeli events and developments, while examining changes among various newspapers over time. Combining the two methods provided a more comprehensive picture of how Palestinian framers and readers constructed meaning about domestic Israeli politics. The interview schedule and coding sheets are presented in their entirety; not all of the results and findings have been discussed in the text.

# In-depth interviews

The interviews were conducted between December 1998 and November 2000. A total of nine interviews was carried out, with five Palestinians and four Israelis, using a semi-structured approach. This approach uses the same core of questions but allows the interviewer to follow up interesting avenues that develop in the course of the session. All five Palestinian interviewees had lived in the occupied territories during the 1970s and 1980s and were present and/or involved in the events and occurrences before and during the Intifada as participants and/or grassroots leaders. The second sub-group, of four Israelis, included three journalists reporting on the occupied territories and a retired security service official who was immersed in the situation in the territories during the several years preceding the 1987 Intifada.

The interviews lasted about an hour with the Israelis and about two hours with the Palestinians. The Israeli interviewees were asked about their perceptions as to how much Palestinians were aware of internal Israeli events and developments. The Palestinian interviewees were also asked about the ways in which Palestinians obtained information about Israeli affairs, the extent to which different newspapers were used in the flow of information in the territories, relationships between groups before and during the Intifada, and whether Palestinians were aware of the division inside Israel between groups favoring the continuation of the occupation and groups that were for ending it.

## *Interviewees (pseudonyms)*

*Halil (January 7, 1999):* In his late fifties, at the time of the interview Halil was a businessman in East Jerusalem. Prior to the Intifada he was the editor of one of the dailies. The interview lasted for roughly ninety minutes and took place in an East Jerusalem hotel.

*Hussni (April 1, 1999):* Age thirty-eight, at the time of the interview was a cook in a Tel-Aviv restaurant and lived in Shoafat, a refugee camp near Ramallah. The interview took place at around 1:00 am in a coffee shop next to his workplace.

*Daud (August 22, 2000):* Age thirty-three, living in Hable, a small town on the outskirts of Kalkilya. The interview took place in his office. During the Intifada Daud was a grassroots Shabiba (Fatah youth) leader. Imprisoned in 1991 and released in 1997.

*Bilal (August 29, 2000):* Age thirty-two, resident in Hable. Between 1990 and 1995 Bilal was in prison. The interview took place in Daud's office and lasted for approximately two hours. Bilal also was a Shabiba leader before and during the Intifada up until he was imprisoned.

*Rahed (September 9, 2000):* Age thirty-nine, resident in Hable. A Democratic Front grassroots activist before and during the Intifada. The interview took place in Daud's office and lasted for two-and-a-half hours.

*Reuben (November 20, 2000):*   In his early seventies, a high-ranking official in the Israeli Ministry of Defense before and during the Intifada. The interview lasted for one hour and took place in Ra'anana where Reuben lives, in a public café.

*Yoram (December 31, 1998):*   In his late fifties, resident in Jerusalem. An Israeli journalist who acted for several years as a reporter in the occupied territories. The interview lasted for two hours and took place in his office.

*Ronen (June 6 and June 17, 2000):*   In his early sixties, resident in Jerusalem. An Israeli reporter for the occupied territories before and during the Intifada. The interview lasted for three hours in two separate sessions, one in his office and the second in a public café.

*Karen (September 6, 2000):*   In her early fifties, living in Jerusalem. Has been acting as a reporter to the Gaza Strip for over a decade. The interview lasted for over an hour at a public café in Jerusalem.

### Interview schedule

*Questions in bold denote questions that emerged within the course of the session.

### General questions

- Was it important for Palestinians to know what was going on inside Israel? Why?
- To what extent were Palestinians attuned to and aware of Israeli politics?
- In what ways did Palestinians obtain such information?
- What were the major daily newspapers distributed within the territories?
- To what extent, if any, were newspapers used in the flow of information within the territories?
- Were Palestinian newspapers the only source of information about domestic Israeli events?
- In cases where Israeli politics received coverage, what type of coverage was it, and what type of events and developments were covered the most?
- Were Palestinians aware of the division inside Israel between groups that favored the continuation of the occupation and groups that were calling for ending the occupation?
- Do Palestinians see any difference between left-wing political parties and right-wing political parties?
- During the second half of the 1970s and 1980s there were several events in Israel that revolved around the issue of the occupation. Were Palestinians aware of events such as the Shabak Affair or the Jewish Underground? **How would you say such awareness affected the public discourse in the territories?**

*Intifada related questions*

- How do you see the Intifada in terms of its meaning and goals?
- Who do you think made the Intifada?
- Would it be accurate to say that the PLO was not deeply involved during the first phases of the Intifada?
- Many people say that the Intifada started on December 9, 1987 because of the truck accident in Gaza. Do you think this is accurate? **What about the numerous organizations that were formed within the territories during the 1980s? Did they have any influence on the Intifada's inception?**
- What was the relationship between the nationalist (e.g., the Shabiba) and religious (e.g., Muslim Brotherhood) groups before the Intifada?
- Would it be accurate to say that the Intifada influenced such a relationship? **Why and how?**
- How did Palestinians cope with the Israeli military before the Intifada, for example, the military policy known as the "iron fist"?
- Could you describe how Palestinians coped and made sense of the fact that before and during the Intifada there were groups inside Israel calling to stop the occupation and, on the other hand, groups like the Settlers calling to expand the settlements as much as possible? **In what ways did Palestinians perceive each camp inside Israel?**

## Content analysis

The goal of the content analysis was to examine how the Palestinian public discourse fluctuated over the various domestic Israeli events in a more systematic fashion, by paying attention to both *quantity* and *quality* of information. The content analysis was based on a sample of news articles obtained from the front page of various West Bank newspapers that were published in the occupied territories during two consecutive time periods: 1974 to 1986 (from which 188 articles were sampled) and 1987 (from which eighty-four articles were sampled). The unit of analysis was a combination of the news article headline, sub-head, and first paragraph. For the first period, articles were selected if they linked, implicitly or explicitly, internal Israeli affairs and Palestinian affairs in the occupied territories; the criterion for including a specific news article for the second period was whether it dealt with the confrontations and their *direct* effects inside and outside the territories.

Separate coders were trained and given a sample of articles in order to test the reliability of the coding sheet. Questions which received insufficient level of agreement (below 70 percent) were either re-tested to increase reliability or simply dropped from the final version. The reliability results for coding questions used in the book are presented below:

| Variable | Agreement percentage | Scott's Pi |
|---|---|---|
| Israeli cohesion** | 75 | 0.69 |
| Prognosis of Palestinian situation** | 81.5 | 0.77 |
| Type of Israeli sociopolitical issue covered** | 84.9 | 0.77 |
| Linking Israeli sociopolitical issue with Palestinian situation** | 85.5 | 0.78 |
| Nature of link between Israeli sociopolitical issue and Palestinian situation** | 79.2 | 0.73 |
| Reference to Israeli crisis-event** | 96 | 0.89 |
| Type of reference to Israeli arena* | 88.6 | 0.76 |
| Promoted solution to occupation* | 85.7 | 0.76 |
| Type of rhetoric* | 90 | 0.82 |

Note
*Based on thirty articles randomly sampled for the period 1987.
**Based on fifty articles randomly sampled for the period 1974–86.

### Coding sheet – time period: 1974–86

1    Article issue date
    1    February 1974
    2    July 1974
    3    March 1975
    4    March 1978
    5    April 1982
    6    July 1982
    7    September 1982
    8    February 1983
    9    April 1984
    10    April 1984B
    11    May 1984
    12    May 1986
    13    June 1986
2    Newspaper
    1    al-Fajr
    2    Al-Quds
    3    a-Sha'ab
3    Does the article refer to Israeli society as united?
    1    Yes
    2    No
    9    Unclear
4    What is the location of the article?
    1    Margins
    2    Bottom
    3    Center of page
    4    Main article

5     What is the relative size of the article?
      1     Small
      2     Mid
      3     Big

6     Is there a photo added to the article? (if 1, go to 7)
      1     No
      2     Yes

6(b)     What party does the photo show, concentrate on or relate to?
      1     Foreign party
      2     Foreign and Israeli party
      3     Foreign and Palestinian party
      4     Palestinian party
      5     Both Palestinian and Israeli
      6     Israeli party

7     Which party/event is the article's direct object(s)? (if not 3, move to 10)
      1     Palestinians
      2     Palestinians/Israelis
      3     Israelis
      9     Not applicable

8     To which Israeli party(s) or event(s) does the article mainly relate? (A party can be an individual as well as a group or institution, whether private or public.)
      1     Pro-occupation army party(s)
      2     Pro-occupation political party(s)
      3     Pro-occupation social party(s)
      4     Anti-occupation army party(s)
      5     Anti-occupation political party(s)
      6     Anti-occupation social party(s)
      9     Not applicable

9     Which of the party(s) above is being directly quoted?
      1     No party
      2     Pro-occupation army party(s)
      3     Pro-occupation political party(s)
      4     Pro-occupation social party(s)
      5     Anti-occupation army party(s)
      6     Anti-occupation political party(s)
      7     Anti-occupation social party(s)
      9     Not applicable

10     Is there a reference to inner critique/challenge of Israeli policy regarding the Palestinian issue? (if no, go to 14)
      1     No
      2     Yes

11     What type of critique does the article concentrate on?
      1     Pro-occupation/anti-Palestinian
      2     Anti-occupation/pro-Palestinian
      9     Not applicable

12     In what ways is Israeli authorities' reaction to such critique/challenge covered?
  1     Reaction in disfavor of Palestinian issue
  2     Reaction in favor of Palestinian issue
  9     NA
13     Who is the criticizer/challenger of Israeli policy regarding the Palestinian issue in the article?
  1     Foreign party(s)
  2     Jewish Diaspora party(s)
  3     Israeli right-wing political party(s)
  4     Israeli left-wing political party(s)
  5     Civic right-wing party(s)
  6     Civic left-wing Party(s)
  7     Military party(s)
  8     Investigating committee
  9     Not applicable
14     Is there a reference to Israeli sociopolitical issue(s)?
  1     No
  2     Yes
15     What type of sociopolitical issue does the article mainly refer to?
  1     Foreign policy
  2     Economy
  3     Cultural
  4     Political
  5     Social cleavages
  6     Social control
  7     Legitimacy and trust
  8     Other
  9     Not applicable
16     Does the article relate to previously connected or similar Israeli sociopolitical issues?
  1     No
  2     Yes
  9     Not applicable
17     Does the article link Israeli issues with the Palestinian situation? (if yes, go to 17b)
  1     No
  2     Yes
  9     Not applicable
17(b) In what ways is the Israeli issue considered in regard to the Palestinian situation?
  1     Discouraging
  2     Encouraging
  3     Informative
  9     Not applicable

18   Does the article relate to an Israeli crisis-event?
   1   No
   2   Yes
   9   Unclear
19   How would you consider the article's coverage regarding the Palestinian situation?
   1   Discouraging
   2   Informative
   3   Encouraging
   9   Not applicable

## *Coding sheet – time period: 1987*

1   Article issue date
   1   May 1987
   2   October 1987
   3   December 1987
2   Newspaper
   1   Al-Quds
   2   Al-Fajr
   3   A-Sha'ab
   4   Al-Ahad
3   In what ways does the article cover/view Palestinian activism?
   1   Reluctant
   2   Informative
   3   Supportive
   9   Not applicable
4   Whose activity does the article emphasize?
   1   Israeli
   2   Israeli/Palestinian
   3   Palestinian
   4   Not applicable
5   If Israeli: action is being described as...
   1   Initiative action
   2   Reactive action
   9   Irrelevant
6   If Palestinian: action is being described as...
   1   Reaction to Israeli act
   2   Initiation of action
   9   Irrelevant
7   Where there is a reference to the Israeli arena, what type of reference is it?
   1   Disfavor of Palestinian
   2   In favor of Palestinian
   8   Unclear
   9   Not applicable

8    In what ways does the article frame solutions to the occupation?
    1    Extremist (i.e., armed struggle/no compromise)
    2    Radical (i.e., end to the occupation through Palestinian popular struggle)
    3    Moderate (i.e., diplomatic initiative)
    4    Unclear
    9    Not applicable

9    Who is the main actor in the article?
    1    Israeli
    2    International
    3    Palestinian
    8    Unclear
    9    Other

10    What type of Palestinian activity is covered?
    1    Diplomatic/political act
    2    Terrorist/armed act[1]
    3    Disruptive populist act[2]
    4    Peaceful populist act
    9    Not applicable

11    Is there a reference to the possibility of change? (if 1 or 9, disregard question 12)
    1    No reference
    2    Reference
    9    Unclear

12    What type of reference is it?
    1    Change is desired but can be negative
    2    Change is possible yet remote
    3    Change is possible and within reach
    9    Not applicable

13    Would you classify the article as promoting action?
    1    No
    2    Yes
    3    Unclear

14    Does article refer to Israeli activity/policy in regard to the territories?
    1    Yes
    2    No

17    Does article present Israel as united?
    1    Yes
    2    No
    9    Irrelevant/unclear

# Notes

## Introduction

1 For clarity, I am using Mitchell's model (1981) of conflict structure constituting three distinct dimensions: conflict *situation* dealing with perceived incompatible interests or worldviews or values; conflict *attitudes* dealing with mutual perceptions of the parties involved and, conflict *behavior* of both parties to further their goals.

2 No systematic attempts will be made to integrate the role played by other segments of the Palestinian people in the Intifada's inception, such as the Palestinian population within Israel, known as the Israeli–Palestinians. I shall refer to these actors in so far as they are inextricably connected to the analysis of the Intifada's dynamics. For a systematic and comprehensive treatment of Israeli–Arabs in Israel see: A. Ghanem, *The Palestinian–Arab Minority in Israeli, 1948–2000* (State University of New York Press 2001).

3 West Bank print media differ from PLO print media (e.g., *Filastin al-Thawra* [The Palestinian Revolution] or *Shu'un Filastiniya* [Palestinian Affairs]) that were based outside the occupied territories and tended to reflect issues and concerns of the PLO in specific and the Palestinian people (writ large) in general.

## 1 Constructing political opportunity

1 See: *Economy and Society*, p. 305.

2 Here I am referring to Gramsci's distinction between hegemony and domination (dominio). Such a distinction does not imply that the operation of hegemony forecloses the operation of dominio. We should view Gramsci's distinction as an analytical one, and that in reality the two poles interact.

3 Perrow makes an important distinction between the above-mentioned versions of resource mobilization, usually identified with McCarthy and Zald (1977), labeled as Resource Mobilization-2, and previous works by Gamson (1968, 1975), Oberschall (1973), and Tilly (1978), which he names Resource Mobilization-1. Resource Mobilization-1 emphasizes the contentious dynamic between challengers and authorities, i.e., the structural conditions that affect challengers' strategy. The Political Process Model, which evolved out of Resource Mobilization-1 is the one promoted here with a few adaptations, as will be elaborated below.

## 2 The *why* question of the Intifada

1 According to Morris (1987), who studied the history of the Palestinian refugees, there is a lack of agreement among scholars in regard to the exact number of the 1967 displaced people. Estimations range between 200,000 and 300,000, of whom 17,000 displaced people were allowed to return to Israel within the framework of family reunification appeals.

2 There is a lack of agreement among Israeli and Palestinian scholars regarding the exact number of Palestinian residents in the territories in June 1967. According to a 1970 estimation conducted by the Israeli Central Bureau of Statistics, 370,000 people populated the Gaza Strip and 608,000 people populated the West Bank. By comparison, the 1987 numbers show a significant increase in the overall Palestinian population divided by Gaza, the West Bank, and East Jerusalem: 630,000 people in the Strip, approximately 900,000 on the Bank, and 130,000 in East Jerusalem.

3 The 1945 Emergency Defense Regulations was enacted by the British Mandate in order to deter Jewish resistance. Israel upheld the regulations as of May 1948 and used them as legal basis for the military rule over the Palestinians. The executive arm can revive the regulations whenever there is an imminent threat, or the perception of such, to Israel's security.

4 The expansion of violent acts in the territories, coupled with the growing awareness by Israel of the state of lawlessness among Jewish Settlers, resulted in a decision by the Israeli Government Judicial Counselor to appoint a special committee for investigating suspicions against Israelis inside the West Bank. This report, the Karp Report, revealed a gloomy picture regarding to the level of violence initiated by Jewish Settlers against Palestinians.

5 B'Tselem Report, "Disputed Waters: Israel's Responsibility for Water Shortage in the Occupied Territories," September 1998.

6 According to Gilbar (1992), between 1983 and 1986, an average of 4,600 Palestinians migrated from the West Bank to neighboring Arab States for jobs, whereas between 1970 and 1982 the average stood on 9,300 per year. In the Gaza Strip, it is possible to discern a similar, although less sharp, pattern. For Gilbar, such a pattern is indicative of the deepening economic grievances experienced by the Palestinians in the occupied territories.

7 B'Tselem Report, "Demolitions and Sealing of Houses as Punitive Measures in the West Bank and Gaza during the Intifada," Jerusalem, 1989. No systematic data exists on the demolition of houses prior to 1979. According to another report, however, between 1967 and 1972, approximately 1,000 houses were demolished, and an additional 200 between 1972 and 1978.

8 During the 1950s and 1960s many young Palestinian activists joined Pan-Arabic organization, such as the Socialist Arab *Baath* party and *al-Qawmyyun al-Arab* (the Arab Community/Nation). The political agenda of such organizations involved the principle that a solution to the Palestinian question would come about only through an Arab State's joint effort.

9 The term comes from *Fiday*, which refers to a person who dedicates his/her life for the sake of the national cause.

10 This distinction parallels the one made above between naturalism (i.e., man as object of historical changes) and voluntarism (i.e., man as subject of historical change). A revolutionary movement would not wait for circumstances to be ripe, waiting for signs of salvation, but rather would make circumstances ripe.

## 3 The *how* question of the Intifada

1 The Rejectionist Front adopted the line of absolutism with regard to Israel, that is, a total refusal of any recognition of and/or compromise with Israel. The Rejectionist Front had broadened during the early 1980s, especially after further tempering of the PLO following the Lebanon War, and included other groups, such as a militant wing of the Fatah led by Abu-Musa, and the General Command of the PFLP led by Ahmed Jibril. All groups were influenced by Syria and Libya and supported by the Soviet Union.

2 One should also bear in mind the Lebanon civil war of 1976–7, during which the PLO

was defeated by the Syrian army and the Christian-Maronite militias, and the following Lebanon War against Israel in summer 1982, two developments that unquestionably influenced the PLO's policy.
3 An unsuccessful attempt to revive the PNF took place during the Camp David Accord in 1978. By 1979, the PNF was formally outlawed by Israel.
4 "HATZAV," a special report, October 29, 1985, p. 45.
5 See, for example, Hiltermann (1991) for an outstanding analysis of the Women's movement; Frisch (1989) for a useful analysis of the youth movement, and a series of articles published in *Journal of Palestine Studies* by Penny Johnson during the second half of the 1980s for a systematic analysis of the students and campuses under occupation. In my analysis of the Labor Movement, I am largely drawing on Hiltermann's work.
6 "Statement by the Preparatory Committee for the first General Conference of the Workers Unity Bloc in the Occupied Territories," July 5, 1985.
7 I shall return to the long-lasting impact of the mayors' dismissal from office by Israel in the following chapter, dealing with the *When* question of the Intifada.
8 Here I am referring not only to the Israeli repression but also to Israel facilitation of the Muslim Brotherhood's activity in the hope that the latter would act as a counterforce to the growing nationalist camp within the territories during the mid-1980s.

**4 The *when* question of the Intifada**

1 Data on "public disturbances" is taken from A. Shalev, *The Intifada*, Tel-Aviv: Papirus, 1990; Israeli Central Bureau of Statistics Annual Publications for the West Bank and Gaza, 1988 vol. 18; and Israel Government Yearbook. Common to the three sources are the criteria for what counts as "public disturbances," which is stone throwing, illegal demonstrations, mounting barricades, distribution of leaflets, terrorist activities, and hoisting PLO flags. Data on demolition of houses is taken from B'Tselem Report "Sealing and Demolition of Houses," Jerusalem, September 1995; and data on deportees is taken from J. Hiltermann, *Israel Deportation Policy*, Ramallah: Al-Haq, 1988. No systematic data exists on demolition of houses prior to 1979.
2 For details see methodological appendix.
3 I use the labels "right" and "left" wing only as they refer to the issues of peace and security within the Israeli context.
4 It should be noted that the fall of the Labor Party and the rise to power of the Likud in the 1977 elections was more than a mere change of administration. In fact, the ending of over 20 years of Labor political hegemony was another major manifestation of the Israeli public's estrangement from and lack of legitimization of the Labor Administration, those same developments that further escalated to affect the stability of the political system during the proceeding years.
5 The founders of the Block were in fact members of the Ma'fdal who seceded from the party in March 1974, primarily by reason of the party's willingness to compromise over the future of the occupied territories.
6 In 1985 Israel brought back most of its military forces from Lebanon, while establishing a "security zone" in the southern part of Lebanon. In 1983 Israel's economy collapsed following an unstoppable rise in stock values, massive demand by the public, and consequent, unprecedented devaluation of the Israeli currency.
7 It should be remembered that the interviews were meant primarily to provide a general sense of how, if at all, Palestinians were interested in Israeli society. A more systematic and deeper sense was obtained through an analysis of various Palestinian newspapers. For more details see Methodological Appendix.
8 Such as *Radio Monte Carlo* in Arabic, *Baghdad Voice* of the PLO, and *Sanaa Voice of Palestine*.
9 Thus the lower class would tend to attend the town quarter while the more well-to-do would attend the teahouse.

10 Previous to 1987 the Islamic voice within the occupied territories can be said to have had insignificant political influence. In a later stage of the research a fourth newspaper was added: *al-Ahad* (The Covenant) a news organ of the Islamic organization, the Hizbollah. I shall have more to say on the decision to include *al-Ahad* below.

11 In terms of statistical significance, the association among the three time periods in the case of *al-Fajr* came out to be on the verge of insignificance (0.048), whereas with the other two newspapers the significance test values came out to be statistically significant at the level of 0.05.

12 "Hamanit," the Israeli Intelligence Force Publication, No. 17, April 1991, p. 63.

13 I chose the December wave, commonly dated as the outburst of the Intifada, as a key date, to examine whether there was a significant difference in comparison with the previous waves.

## 5  The Intifada: tactics for expanding political opportunities

1 According to Israeli Yearbook and Almanac, this includes Molotov cocktails (3,732 between 1988 and 1991), throwing of grenades (111 between 1988 and 1991), or the planting of explosive devices (374 between 1988 and 1991).

2 For clarity, *repertoire of actions* is seen here as a type of menu for choice from which movement activists *tactically* choose during episodes of contention. The specific combination employed constitutes the movement's *mode of action*, and the ability to generate and sustain such mode of action is a central *power* of the movement. I shall use the concepts interchangeably according to the specific context.

3 According to Mishaal and Sela (1999), during the first three years of the Intifada the Hamas initiated 66 terrorist acts against Israeli targets in and outside the occupied territories: ten during 1988, thirty-two during 1989, and twenty-four during 1990. Hamas's activity during 1990 included also acts inside Israel and other types of action such as arson and stabbings.

4 It should be noted that the local level, that is the United National Command of the Uprising, addressed the Israeli Palestinians on several occasions throughout 1988, calling for their participation in days of strike. To the best of my knowledge, such calls were significantly lessened between 1989 and 1990, only to rise again towards the second half of 1990, during which a process of radicalization developed at both levels of the Palestinian leadership. I shall return to this process below.

5 A Personal Diary of the Israeli Palestinian Conflict, edited by Nigel Parry, www.birzeit.edu/diary/intifada/localorg (11/7/00).

6 This is the first leaflet in which the UNCU named itself as such. The first leaflet was published in Gaza in December 1987, signed by the National Forces in the Gaza Strip.

7 Palestinians were allowed to open accounts in Israeli banks and legally receive funds transferred to them from abroad.

8 *Al-Adha* is the day of the victim during which Muslims offer sacrifice to Allah for instructing Abraham to sacrifice the Oryx and not his son Ishmael.

9 I shall focus primarily on Hamas and its relationship with the Nationalist Movement. While the Islamic Jihad was, and still is, an important actor, nonetheless Hamas acquired a far greater social and political influence during the uprising. It is also true that the Islamic Jihad, although highly active in the early phases of the uprising, did not substantially and/or distinctively affect the course of the Intifada. I will inter-changeably use the term Hamas and Muslim Brotherhood according to the specific context under analysis.

10 Succinctly, Resolution 242 (November 22, 1967) calls for the withdrawal of Israeli armed forces from territories occupied in the recent conflict, and respect for and acknowledgment of the sovereignty, territorial integrity and political independence of every State in the area and their right to live in peace within secure and recognized

borders. Resolution 338 (October 22, 1973) calls upon all parties to the present fighting to cease all firing and terminate all military activity immediately, in the positions they now occupy, and to start immediately after the cease-fire the implementation of Security Council resolution 242 (1967), and for negotiations to start between the parties concerned under appropriate auspices aimed at establishing a just and durable peace in the Middle East.

11 It should be noted that Hamas used deadly weapons on several occasions during early 1988, against Israeli targets, yet no responsibility was taken. Still, the dominant mode of action during the first half of 1988 focused on religious rituals such as fasting and prayers, which, in a way, helps to explain the Israeli "soft hand" policy in regard to the Hamas.

12 Jewish settlement on the Arabian Peninsula, which was attacked and conquered in 628 CE, after Muhammad accused its inhabitants of treachery against Muslims. The remaining Jews were allowed to hold on to their land on condition that half of their crops would be given to the Muslims.

13 The army of the Jihad, the holy war against the people who refuse to accept Islam.

14 Inhabitants of Ribat, Settlers in the frontiers of the Muslim world during the initial period of Muslim conquests, who were seen as fulfilling the religious precept of defending the kingdom of Islam.

15 Shamir's plan, presented in Washington in April 1989, included the idea of free elections in the occupied territories as a first step towards peace, with the elected Palestinian delegates going on to participate in negotiations on an interim settlement. No reference to the PLO was made. Baker's first peace initiative, from November 1989, consisted of five concessive points, which were based on Shamir's election plan. The only new element of the plan was the emphasis on direct talks between Palestinians and Israelis, under the auspices of Egypt, for a final settlement. Baker's plan was not implemented and in June 1990 Shamir put together an Israeli right-wing government.

16 *Middle East Report*, May–June 1988, p. 43.

17 It should be noted, however, that Palestinians attended the talks as part of a joint delegation with Jordan and without Arafat's participation, as insisted upon by Israel and the US. The Palestinian decision to participate in the Conference was approved by the Palestinian National Council in Algeria on September 23, 1991. Moreover, during the Intifada there had been other attempts at diplomatic initiatives, some of which were informal and secret between Israelis and Palestinians (e.g., talks between Labor Party member of Knesset Ephraim Sneh and PLO members during August and September 1988 in Paris), and some under the lead of international actors (e.g., Mubarak's Proposal of January 1988 or the Shultz Plan of March 1988).

## 6 Conclusion and the future of the Israeli–Palestinian conflict

1 I thank Chuck Tilly for stimulating my thoughts on this issue.

## Postscript: the Contentious 1990s and the 2000 Intifada

1 A Fatah offshoot formed after September 2000, consisting of hundreds of members that are under the direct control of the Tanzim. We will say more on the Tanzim below.

2 I will nonetheless use past tense in referring to the 2000 Intifada. This is so given the formal declaration made by Ariel Sharon and Abu-Maazen to mutually stop all violent actions during the Sharm-a-Sheikh Summit in February 2005.

3 Between 1988 and 1991, fourteen Israeli soldiers were killed by Palestinians compared to 798 Palestinians killed by Israeli forces (of whom eight were killed inside Israel). See: "Fatalities in the al-Aqsa Intifada, Data by Month," (www.btselem.org/English/Statistics/Al_Aqsa_Fatalities_Tables.asp accessed October 22, 2004).

4 Based on the Declaration of Principles of September 1993, the PA was allowed to establish a strong police force and to enjoy authoritative powers and responsibilities. However, Israel continued to maintain the right to defend itself against external threats, as well as the responsibility, for the overall security of Israelis, for safeguarding internal security and public order. In practical terms, this meant that Israel was still the sole and ultimate ruler in large areas of the West Bank and Gaza Strip.

5 In English "the Wall Mountain," Palestinian lands south to Jerusalem confiscated in 1991.

6 While more will be said on the relationship between the Tanzim, Hamas, and the PA below, for a fuller analysis of this aspect and the ways it affected the dynamics within the Palestinian movement see Alimi (2006).

7 "Start of the al-Aqsa Intifada in 2000" (www.palestinianfacts.org accessed October 22, 2004).

7a In early 1976 the Israeli government decided to expropriate more Arab lands in the Galilee. As a response to the Israeli plan it was decided to initiate a general strike throughout the Arab sector to protest against the yet another land seizure. On March 30 the strike began and lasted for a day. During that day, the Arab residents faced heavy repressive measures by Israeli security forces that had begun surrounding the "explosive" areas the day before. As a result of the confrontations six Israeli-Arabs were killed and dozens injured. From that day on, it has become customary to commemorate the Land Dead every year as emblematic of the ongoing neglect and discrimination against the Arab citizens of Israel.

8 *Palestine Times*, issue 106, April 2000 (www.ptimes.org/issue106/index accessed February 29, 2004).

9 JMCC Documents: "Letter addressed to President Arafat from the Palestinian National and Islamic Forces," (www.jmcc.org/banner/banner1/bayan/aqsabayan3.htm accessed October 22, 2004).

## Methodological appendix

1 Armed activity refers to the use of deadly weapons, such as guns, grenades, or rockets. I do not consider the Molotov cocktail as a deadly weapon despite its possible fatal results. Such results can come about by other means or tools such as sticks and stones, which here, together with Molotov cocktails, are considered as "cold weapons." The crucial point in such a distinction lies in the mode of production of the specific means, and the type of ingredients used, whether they are "homemade" or manufactured, coupled with the likelihood of death.

2 I purposely use the terms "peaceful" and "disruptive" instead of alternative terms such as "violent act." Would a Palestinian demonstration, say, in Hebron during which stones were thrown against Israeli soldiers be considered by a Palestinian journalist or editor as violent? It is unlikely, since for Palestinians any such demonstration or protest is justified in face of the occupation and, alternatively, any action that disturbs the public order is considered violent by Israel. For that reason, the distinction between disruptive and peaceful is more valid as it stresses the Palestinian viewpoint.

# Bibliography

Abu Shakrah, J. (1986) "The 'Iron Fist' October 1985 to January 1986," *Journal of Palestinian Studies*, 15:120–6.

Abu-Amr, Z. (1988) "The Palestinian Uprising in the West Bank and Gaza Strip," *Arab Studies Quarterly*, 10:384–405.

Adler, P. and Adler, P.A. (1980) "Symbolic Interactionism," in J.D. Douglas, P.A. Adler, P. Adler, A. Fontana, R. Freeman, and J.A. Kotarba (eds) *Introduction to the Sociologies of Everyday Life*, Boston: Allyn and Bacon.

Alimi, E.Y. (2003) "The Effects of Opportunities on Insurgencies," *Terrorism and Political Violence*, 15:111–38.

—— (2006) "Re-Contextualizing Political Terrorism: A Collective Action Perspective for Understanding the Tanzim," *Studies in Conflict and Terrorism*, 29(3):263–83.

Alin, E.J. (1994) "Dynamics of the Palestinian Uprising," *Comparative Politics*, 26:479–98.

Aminzade, R. and McAdam, D. (2001) "Emotions and Contentious Politics," in R.R. Aminzade, J.A. Goldstone, D. McAdam, E.J. Perry, W.H. Sewell, Jr., S. Tarrow, and C. Tilly (eds) *Silence and Voice in the Study of Contentious Politics*, Cambridge: Cambridge University Press.

Aminzade, R., Goldstone, J.A., and Perry, E.J. (2001) "Leadership Dynamics and Dynamics of Contention," in R.R. Aminzade, J.A. Goldstone, D. McAdam, E.J. Perry, W.H. Sewell, Jr., S. Tarrow, and C. Tilly (eds) *Silence and Voice in the Study of Contentious Politics*, Cambridge: Cambridge University Press.

Arian, A. (1999) *Bitahon Be'tzel Iyuem* [Security Threatened], Tel-Aviv: Papirus.

Ashrawi, H.M. (1978) "The Contemporary Palestinian Poetry of Occupation," *Journal of Palestinian Studies*, 7:77–101.

Awad, M. (1984) "Non-Violent Resistance: a strategy for the occupied territories," *Journal of Palestinian Studies*, 52:22–36.

Ayalon, A. (2000) *Historia shel Ha'tikshoret Ha'aravit* [The History of the Arab Press], Israel: Ministry of Defense Press.

Azar, E.E. (1986) "Protracted International Conflict: Ten Propositions," in E.E. Azar and J. Burton (eds) *International Conflict Resolution: theory and practice*, Essex: Wheatsheaf.

Balint, A. (2000) "Word Rockets," *The Seventh Eye*, 29:6–9.

Bar-On, M. (1985) *Shalom Achshav* [Peace Now], Tel Aviv: Hakibutz Ha'meuchad.

Barzilai, G. (1987) "Democrtia Be'milhama" [Democracy at War], unpublished thesis, Tel-Aviv University.

Bassiouni, C.M. and Cainkar, L. (1989) *The Palestinian Intifada – December 9,*

*1987–December 8, 1988: a record of Israeli repression*, Database Project on Palestinian Human Rights, Chicago, Illinois.

Behar, M. (2002) "The Peace Process and Israeli Domestic Politics in the 1990s," *Socialism and Democracy*, 16:34–48.

Beitler, R.M. (1995) "The Intifada: Palestinian adaptation to Israeli counterinsurgency tactics," *Terrorism and Political Violence*, 7:49–73.

—— (2004) *The Path to Mass Rebellion: an analysis of two intifadas*, Lanham: Lexington Books.

Benford, R.D. (1997) "An Insider Critique of the Social Movement Framing Perspective," *Sociological Inquiry*, 67:409–30.

Benford, R.D. and Snow, D.A. (2000) "Framing Processes and Social Movements: An Overview and Assessment," *Annual Review of Sociology*, 26:611–39.

Benvenisti, M. (1989) *The Shepherds' War*, Jerusalem: Jerusalem Post Press.

—— (1992) *Mahol Ha'Haradot* [Fatal Embrace], Jerusalem: Maxwell-Macmillan-Keter.

Bernard, M.A. (1980) "Stasis in Thucydides: Narrative and Analysis of Factionalism in the Polis," unpublished thesis, University of North Carolina.

Bishara, A. (1993) "Al Sheelat Ha'miut Ha'palestini Be'israel" [On the Palestinian Minority Question in Israel], *Teoria Ve'bikoret*, 3:7–35.

Brockett, C.D. (1991) "The Structure of Political Opportunities and Peasant Mobilization in Central America," *Comparative Politics*, 23:253–74.

Fireman, B. and Gamson, W.A. (1979) "Utilitarian Logic in the Resource Mobilization Perspective," in M.N. Zald and J.D. McCarthy (eds) *The Dynamics of Social Movements*, Cambridge, MA: Winthrop.

Cohen, A.A. and Wolfsfeld, G. (eds) (1993) *Framing the Intifada: people and media*, Norwood, NJ: Ablex.

Creswell, J.W. (2003) *Research Design: qualitative, quantitative, and mixed methods approaches*, 2nd edn, Thousand Oaks: SAGE.

Daqqaq, I. (1983) "Back to Square One: A Study in the Reemergence of the Palestinian Identity in the West Bank 1967–1980," in A. Schölch (ed.) *Palestinians across Both Sides of the Green Line*, London: Ithaca Press.

Davis, J.C. (1962) "Toward a Theory of Revolution," *American Sociological Review*, 27:5–19.

Della-Porta, D. (1995) *Social Movements, Political Violence and the State*, Cambridge: Cambridge University Press.

Della Porta, D. and Diani, M. (1999) *Social Movements: an introduction*, Oxford: Blackwell.

Diani, M. (1996) "Linking Mobilization Frames and Political Opportunities: insights from regional populism in Italy," *American Sociological Review*, 61:1053–69.

Donati, P.R. (1992) "Political Discourse Analysis," in M. Diani and R. Eyerman (eds) *Studying Collective Action*, London: SAGE.

Eisinger, P. (1973) "The Conditions of Protest Behavior in American Cities," *American Political Science Review*, 67:11–28.

Ezrahi, Y. (1997) *Rubber Bullets*, Berkeley: University of California Press.

—— (2000) "Give them Cameras!" *The Seventh Eye*, 29:12–13.

Falloon, V. (1986) *Excessive Secrecy, Lack of Guidelines*, West Bank: Al-Haq.

Farsoun, S.K. and Landis, J.M. (1989) "Structure of Resistance and the 'War of Position,'" *Arab Studies Quarterly*, 11:59–86.

Feige, M. (2002) *Shtey Mapot La'Gada* [One Space, Two Places: block of the faithful, peace now, and the construction of Israeli space], Jerusalem: The Hebrew University Magnes Press.

Ferree, M.M. (1992) "The Political Context of Rationality: Rational Choice Theory and Resource Mobilization," in A.D. Morris and C.M. Mueller (eds) *Frontiers in Social Movement Theory*, New Haven, CT: Yale University Press.

Flacks, R. (2004) "Knowledge for What? Thoughts on the State of Social Movement Studies," in J. Goodwin and J. Jasper (eds) *Rethinking Social Movements: structure, meaning, and emotion*, Oxford: Rowman & Littlefield.

Frisch, H. (1992) "Me'maavak Mezuian L'gius Politi" [From Armed Struggle to Political Mobilization], in G. Gilbar and A. Susser (eds) *Be'ein Ha'conflict: ha'intifadah* [At the Core of the Conflict: the intifada], Tel Aviv: Hakibutz Hamehuad.

—— (1996) "From Repression to Facilitation: The Effect of Israeli Policies on Palestinian Mobilization in the West Bank, 1976–1987," *Terrorism and Political Violence*, 8:1–21.

Gamson, W.A. (1968) *Power and Discontent*, Homewood, IL: Dorsey Press.

—— (1985) "Goffman's Legacy to Political Sociology," *Theory and Society*, 14:605–22.

—— (1988) "Political Discourse and Collective Action," in B. Klandermans, H. Kriesi, and S. Tarrow (eds) *From Structure to Action: comparing movement participation across cultures, international social movement research Vol. 1*, Greenwich, CT: JAI Press Inc.

—— (1990) *The Strategy of Social Protest*, 2nd edn, Belmont, CA: Wadsworth Publishing Company.

—— (1992) *Talking Politics*, Cambridge: University of Cambridge Press.

Gamson, W.A., Fireman, B., and Rytina, S. (1982) *Encounters with Unjust Authority*, Homewood, IL: The Dorsey Press.

Gamson, W.A. and Lasch, K.E. (1983) "The Political Culture of Social Welfare Policy," in S.E. Spiro and E. Yuchtman-Yaar (eds) *Evaluating the Welfare State*, New York: Academic Press.

Gamson, W.A. and Modigliani, A. (1989) "Media Discourse and Public Opinion on Nuclear Power: A Constructionist Approach," *American Journal of Sociology*, 95:1–38.

Gamson, W.A., Croteau, D., Hoynes, W., and Sasson, T. (1992) "Media Images and the Social Construction of Reality," *Annual Review of Sociology*, 18:373–93.

Gamson, W.A. and Wolfsfeld, G. (1993) "Movements and Media as Interacting Systems," *Annals of the American Academy of Political and Social Science*, 528:114–25.

Gamson, W.A. and Meyer, D.S. (1996) "Framing Political Opportunity," in D.J. McAdam, J.D. McCarthy, and M.N. Zald (eds) *Comparative Perspective on Social Movements*, Cambridge: Cambridge University Press.

Gerner, D.J. (1991) *One Land Two Peoples*, San Francisco: Westview Press.

Ghanem, A. (2001) *The Palestinian–Arab Minority in Israeli, 1948–2000*, New York: State University of New York Press.

Gilbar, G. (1992) "Defusim Economim Ve'demografim ke'sibot La'intifadah" [Economic and Demographic Patterns as Causes of the Intifada], in G. Gilbar and A. Susser (eds) *Be'ein Ha'conflict: ha'intifadah* [At the Core of the Conflict: the intifada], Tel Aviv: Hakibutz Hamehuad.

Goffman, E. (1974) *Frame Analysis: an essay on the organization of experience*, New York: Harper Colophon Books.

Golan, G. (1991) "Soviet Policy in the Middle East," in A. Ayalon (ed.) *Middle East*

*Contemporary Survey, Vol. 15, 1990*, The Moshe Dayan Center for Middle Eastern and African Studies and The Shiloah Institute and Tel Aviv University: Westview Press.

Goodwin, J. and Jasper, J.M. (1999) "Caught in a Winding, Snarling Vine: the structural bias of political process theory," *Sociological Forum*, 14:27–54.

—— (eds) (2004) *Rethinking Social Movements: structure, meaning, and emotion*, Oxford: Rowman & Littlefield.

Goldstone, J.A. and Tilly, C. (2001) "Threat (and Opportunity): Popular Action and State Repression in the Dynamics of Contentious Action," in R.R. Aminzade, J.A. Goldstone, D. McAdam, E.J. Perry, W.H. Sewell, Jr., S. Tarrow, and C. Tilly (eds) *Silence and Voice in the Study of Contentious Politics*, Cambridge: Cambridge University Press.

Goodwin, J., Jasper, J.M., and Polletta, F. (2000) "Return of the Repressed: the fall and rise of emotions in social movement theory," *Mobilization: An International Journal*, 5:65–84.

Gramsci, A. (1971) *Selection from Prison Notebooks*, trans. Q. Hoare and G. Nowll Smith, London: Lawrence and Wishart.

Gunning, J. (2004) "Peace with Hamas? The Transforming Potential of Political Participation," *International Affairs*, 80:233–55.

Gurr, T.R. (1970) *Why Men Rebel*, Princeton, NJ: Princeton University Press.

Hammami, R. and Tamari, S. (2001) "The Second Uprising: end or new beginning?," *Journal of Palestine Studies*, 30:2–25.

Harel, A. and Isacharoff, A. (2004) *The Seventh War*, Tel-Aviv: Yedioth Ahronoth Books and Chemed Books.

Harkabi, Y. (1986) *Hachraot Goraliyot* [Fateful Decisions], Tel Aviv: Am Oved.

—— (1997) "Ha'Palestinim: me'tardema le'hitorerut" [Palestinians: from hibernation to awakening], in M. Ma'oz and B.Z. Kedar (eds) *The Palestinians National Movement*, Tel Aviv: Mishrad Ha'Bitahon.

Hass, A. (1996) *Li'Shtot Me'Hayam shel Aza* [Drinking the Gaza Sea], Tel Aviv: Hakibutz Hameuchad.

Hatina, M. (2001) *Islam and Salvation in Palestine*, Tel Aviv University: The Moshe Dayan Center for Middle Eastern and African Studies.

Hiltermann, J.R. (1988) *Israel's Deportation Policy: in the occupied West Bank and Gaza*, 2nd edn, Ramallah: Al-Haq.

—— (1991) *Behind the Intifada*, Princeton, NJ: Princeton University Press.

Hoffer, E. (1989) *The True Believer: thoughts on the nature of mass movements*, New York: Harper Perennial.

Hofnung, M. (1991) *Israel: bithon ha'medina mul shilton ha'hok 1948–1991* [Israel: security needs *vs.* the rule of law 1948–1991], Jerusalem: Nevo.

Horowitz, D. (1977) "More than a Change of Government," *The Jerusalem Quarterly*, 5:3–19.

Horowitz, D. and Lissak, M. (1990) *Metzukot Ba'utopia* [Grievances in Utopia], Tel-Aviv: Am Oved.

Hunter, R.F. (1991) *The Palestinian Uprising*, Berkeley: University of California Press.

Jaradat, M. (1992) "Islamic Resistance Movement (Hamas) in the Territories Occupied in 1967," *News from Within*, 8:7–11.

Jasper, J. (2004) "A Strategic Approach to Collective Action: looking for agency in social movement choices," *Mobilization: An International Journal*, 9:1–16.

Johnson, C. (1982) *Revolutionary Change*, 2nd edn, Boston, MA: Little, Brown and Co.

Johnson, P. (1986) "Palestinian Universities under Occupation," *Journal of Palestine Studies*, 15:127–33.

Johnson, P., O'Brien, L., and Hiltermann, J. (1988) "The West Bank Rises Up," *Middle East Report*, 152/18:4–12.

Kaminer, R. (1996) *The Politics of Protest*, Sussex: Sussex Academic Press.

Kaufman, E. (1990) "The Intifada's Limited Violence," *Journal of Arab Affairs*, 9:109–21

—— (1991) "Israeli Perceptions of the Palestinians' 'Limited Violence' in the *Intifada*," *Terrorism and Political Violence*, 3:1–38.

Khalidi, R.I. (1988) "The Uprising and the Palestinian Question," *World Policy Journal*, 5:497–518.

Khawaja, M. (1991) "Collective Violence and Popular Gatherings in the West Bank 1976–1985," unpublished thesis, Cornell University.

—— (1993) "Repression and Popular Collective Action: Evidence from the West Bank," *Sociological Forum*, 8:47–71.

—— (1994) "Resource Mobilization, Hardship, and Popular Collective Action in the West Bank," *Social Forces*, 73:191–220.

Kimmerling, B. (1983) *Zionism and Economy*, Cambridge, MA: Schenkman Publishing.

Kimmerling, B. and Migdal, J.S. (1999) *Palestinim: am be'ivatzruto* [Palestinians: the making of a people], Jerusalem: Keter.

Kitschelt, H.P. (1986) "Political Opportunity Structure and Political Protest: anti-nuclear movements in four democracies," *British Journal of Political Science*, 16:57–85.

Klandermans, B. (1988) "The Formation and Mobilization of Consensus," in B. Klandermans, H. Kriesi, and S. Tarrow (eds) *From Structure to Action: comparing movement participation across cultures, international social movement research Vol. 1*, Greenwich, CT: JAI Press Inc.

—— (1997) *The Psychology of Social Protest*, Oxford: Blackwell.

Korn, D. (1994) *Zman Be'Afor* [Time in Gray], Tel Aviv: Zmora-Bitan.

Kornhauser, W. (1959) *The Politics of Mass Society*, Glencoe, IL: The Free Press.

Kurzman, C. (1996) "Structural Opportunity and Perceived Opportunity in Social Movement Theory: The Iranian Revolution of 1979," *American Sociological Review* 61:153–70.

—— (2004a) *The Unthinkable Revolution in Iran*, Cambridge, MA: Harvard University Press.

—— (2004b) "The Poststructuralist Consensus in Social Movement Theory," in J. Goodwin and J. Jasper (eds) *Rethinking Social Movements: structure, meaning, and emotion*, Oxford: Rowman & Littlefield.

Kuttab, D. (1988) "The Palestinian Uprising: self-sufficiency," *Journal of Palestine Studies*, 17:36–45.

—— (1988b) "A Profile of the Stonethrowers," *Journal of Palestinian Studies*, 17:4–23.

Lederman, J. (1992) *Battle Line: the American media and the intifada*, Boulder: Westview Press.

Lesch, A.M. (1990) "Prelude to the Uprising in the Gaza Strip," *Journal of Palestinian Studies*, 20:1–23.

Levine, D.N. (ed.) (1971) *Georg Simmel: On Individuality and Social Forms*, Chicago: The University of Chicago Press.

Lissak, M. (1990) "The Intifada and the Israeli Society," in R. Gal (ed.) *Ha'milhama Ha'shviyt* [The Seventh War], Tel-Aviv: Hakibutz Hamehuad.

Litvak, M. (1990) "The West Bank and the Gaza Strip: The Intifada," in A. Ayalon (ed.) *Middle East Contemporary Survey, Vol. XV, 1990*, The Moshe Dayan Center for Middle Eastern and African Studies and The Shiloah Institute and Tel Aviv University: Westview Press.

—— (1991) *Palestinian Leadership in the Occupied Territories*, Tel Aviv: Moshe Dayan Center for Middle East and African Studies.

Lockman, Z. and Beinin, J. (eds) (1989) *Intifada: the Palestinian uprising against Israeli occupation*, Washington: A MERIP Book, Between the Lines.

Lombard, M., Snyder-Duch, J., and Campanella Bracken, C. (2002) "Content Analysis in Mass Communication – assessment and reporting of intercoder reliability," *Human Communication Research*, 28:587–604.

Longrigg, S.H. and Stoakes, F. (1970) "The Social Pattern," in L.M. Abdulla and C.W. Churchill (eds) *Readings in Arab Middle Eastern Societies and Cultures*, The Hague and Paris: Mouton.

Lustick, I. (1993) "Writing the Intifada," *World Politics*, 45:560–94.

Makhul, M.K. (1988) "This is Not a Revolt – This is a War," *Journal of Palestine Studies*, 17:91–9.

Mansour, C. (2002) "The Impact of 11 September on the Israeli–Palestinian Conflict," *Journal of Palestine Studies*, 31:5–18.

Ma'oz, M. (1984) *Palestinian Leadership on the West Bank*, London: Frank Cass & Co. Ltd.

McAdam, D. (1999) *Political Process and the Development of Black Insurgency, 1930–1970*, 2nd edn, Chicago: The University of Chicago Press.

—— (2001) "Harmonizing the Voices: Thematic Continuity across the Chapters," in R.R. Aminzade, J.A. Goldstone, D. McAdam, E.J. Perry, W.H. Sewell, Jr., S. Tarrow, and C. Tilly (eds) *Silence and Voice in the Study of Contentious Politics*, Cambridge: Cambridge University Press.

McAdam, D., Tarrow, S., and Tilly, C. (2001) *The Dynamics of Contention*, Cambridge: Cambridge University Press.

—— (1996) "To Map Contentious Politics," *Mobilization: An International Journal*, 1:17–34.

McAdam, D. and Sewell, W.H. (2001) "It's About Time: Temporality in the Study of Social Movements and Revolutions," in R.R. Aminzade, J.A. Goldstone, D. McAdam, E.J. Perry, W.H. Sewell, Jr., S. Tarrow, and C. Tilly (eds) *Silence and Voice in the Study of Contentious Politics*, Cambridge: Cambridge University Press.

McCarthy, J.D. and Zald, M.N. (1977) "Resource Mobilization and Social Movement: a partial theory," *American Journal of Sociology*, 82:12–41.

Mead, G.H. (1999) "The Self, the I, and the Me," in C. Lemert (ed.) *Social Theory: the multicultural and classical readings*, 2nd edn, Boulder, CO: Westview Press.

Melluci, A. (1995) "The Process of Collective Identity," in H. Johnston and B. Klandermans (eds) *Social Movements and Culture*, Minneapolis: University of Minnesota Press.

—— (1996) *Challenging Codes: collective action in the information age*, Cambridge: Cambridge University Press.

Merton, R.K. (1968) *Social Theory and Social Structure*, New York: Free Press.

Meyer, D.S. (1990) *A Winter of Discontent*, New York: Praeger.

—— (2004) "Protest and Political Opportunities," *Annual Review of Sociology*, 30:125–45.

Meyer, D.S. and Minkoff, D.C. (1997) "Conceptualizing Political Opportunity," paper presented at the ASA in Toronto, Canada, August.

Mills, W.C. (1963) *Power, Politics and People*, New York: Oxford University Press.

Mishal, S. (1989) "'Paper War' – Words Behind Stones: the intifada leaflets," *The Jerusalem Quarterly*, 51:71–94.

Mishal, S. with Aharoni, R. (1989) *Avanim Ze Lo Hakol* [Speaking Stones], Tel Aviv: Hakibutz Hamehuad.

Mishal, S. and Sela, A. (1999) *Zman Hamas: alimut ve'pshara* [The Hamas Wind – Violence and Coexistence]. Tel Aviv: Miskal.

Mitchell, C.R. (1981) *The Structure of International Conflict*, London: St. Martin's Press.

Morris, A.D. (1984) *The Origins of the Civil Rights Movement*, New York: The Free Press.

—— (2000) "Reflections on Social Movement Theory: Criticisms and Proposals," *Contemporary Sociology*, 29:445–54.

Morris, A.D. and Staggenborg, S. (2002) *Leadership in Social Movements*, Online. Available www.cas.northwestern.edu/sociology/faculty/files/leadershipessay.pdf (accessed December 18, 2003).

Morris, B. (1987) *The Birth of the Palestinians Refugee Problem: 1947–1949*, Cambridge: Cambridge University Press.

Najjer, O.A. (1994) "Palestine," in Y.R. Kamalipour and H. Mowlana (eds) *Mass Media in the Middle East*, Westport: Greenwood Press.

Nassar, J.R. and Heacock, R. (eds) (1990) *The Intifada: Palestinians at the crossroads*, New York: Preager.

Negbi, M. (1987) *Me'Al Ha'Hok* [Above the Law], Tel Aviv: Am Oved.

Neuman, L.W. (2000) *Social Research Methods*, 5th edn, Boston, MA: Allyn and Bacon.

Oberschall, A. (1973) *Social Conflict and Social Movements*, Englewood Cliffs, NJ: Prentice Hall.

—— (1996) "Opportunities and Framing in the Eastern European Revolts of 1989," in D.J. McAdam, J.D. McCarthy, and M.N. Zald (eds) *Comparative Perspective on Social Movements*, Cambridge: Cambridge University Press.

Oliver, A.M. and Steinberg, P. (1993) "Information and Revolutionary Ritual in *Intifada* Graffiti," in A.A. Cohen and G. Wolfsfeld (eds) *Framing the Intifada: people and media*, Norwood, New Jersey: Ablex.

Olson, M. (1968) *The Logic of Collective Action*, New York: Schocken.

Park, R.E. (1967) *On Social Control and Collective Behavior*, ed. R. Turner. Chicago: University of Chicago Press.

Paz, R. (1992) "Ha'gorem Ha'islami Ba'intifada" [The Islamic Factor in the Intifada], in G. Gilbar, and A. Susser (eds) *Be'ein Ha'conflict: ha'intifadah* [At the Core of the Conflict: the intifada], Tel Aviv: Hakibutz Hamehuad.

Peled, Y. (1993) "Zarim Be'utopia: ma'amadam ha'ezrchi shel ha'falestinim be'Israel" [Strangers in Utopia: the civic status of Palestinians in Israel], *Teoria Ve'bikoret*, 3:21–35.

Peleg, S. (1996) "A Group Dynamics Model for Political Success," *International Journal of Group Tensions*, 26:123–44.

—— (1997) *Le'hafitz et Zaam Ha'el* [Spreading the Wreath of God], Tel Aviv: Hakibutz Hamehuad.

—— (2000) "Peace Now or Later?: movement–countermovement dynamics and the Israeli political cleavage," *Studies in Conflict and Terrorism*, 23:235–54.

Peretz, D. (1990) *Intifada: the Palestinian uprising*, Boulder, CO: Westview Press.

Perrow, C. (1979) "The Sixties Observed," in M.N. Zald and J.D. McCarthy (eds) *The Dynamics of Social Movements*, Cambridge, MA: Winthrop Publishers.

Piven, F.F. and Cloward, R.A. (1979) *Poor People's Movement: why they succeed, how they fail*, New York: Vintage.

Playfair, E. (1987) *Demolition and Sealing of Houses: as a punitive measure in the Israeli-occupied West Bank*, Ramallah: Al-Haq.

Polletta, F. (1998) "Contending Stories: narrative in social movements," *Qualitative Sociology*, 21:419–44.

—— (1999) "Snarls, Quacks, and Quarrels: culture and structure in political process theory," *Sociological Forum*, 14:63–70.

Poloma, M.M. (1979) *Contemporary Sociological Theory*, New York: Macmillan.

Post, J.M., Sprinzak, E., and Denny, L.M. (2003) "The Terrorists in Their Own Words: interviews with 35 incarcerated Middle Eastern terrorists," *Terrorism and Political Violence*, 15:171–84.

Pressberg, G. (1988) "The Uprising: Causes and Consequences," *Journal of Palestine Studies*, 17:38–50.

Raanan, Z. (1980) *Gush Emunim* [Block of the Faithful], Tel Aviv: Sifriat Ha'Poalim.

Rekhess, E. (1975) "The Employment in Israel of Arab Laborers from the Administered Areas," *Israel Yearbook on Human Rights Vol. 5.*

—— (1987) "Media Ktuva Ba'shtahim: profil politi" [Written Media in the Territories: political profile], *Monthly Report Vol. 1*, General Staff Press, 1215.

—— (1989) "The West Bank and the Gaza Strip," in I. Rabinovich and H. Shaked (eds) *Middle East Contemporary Survey, Vol. 11, 1987*, The Moshe Dayan Center for Middle Eastern and African Studies and The Shiloah Institute and Tel Aviv University: Westview Press.

—— (1992) "The West Bank and the Gaza Strip," in A. Ayalon (ed.) *Middle East Contemporary Survey, Vol. 15, 1991*, The Moshe Dayan Center for Middle Eastern and African Studies and The Shiloah Institute and Tel Aviv University: Westview Press.

—— (1992b) "Arviey Israel VeHa'Intifada" [Israeli Arabs and the Intifada], in G. Gilbar and A. Susser (eds) *Be'ein Ha'conflict: Ha'intifadah* [At the Core of the Conflict: The Intifada], Tel Aviv: Hakibutz Hamehuad.

Rekhess, E. and Regavim, R. (2002) "The Palestinian Authority," in B. Maddy-Weitzman (ed.) *Middle East Contemporary Survey, Vol. 24, 2000*, The Moshe Dayan Center for Middle Eastern and African Studies and The Shiloah Institute and Tel Aviv University: Westview Press.

Resheff, T. (1996) *Shalom Achshav* [Peace Now], Jerusalem: Keter.

Ritzer, G. (1988) *Contemporary Sociological Theory*, 2nd edn, New York: Alfred A. Knopf.

Robinson, G.E. (1997) *Building a Palestinian State*, Bloomington, Indianapolis: Indiana University Press.

—— (2004) "Hamas as Social Movement," in Q. Wikrorowicz (ed.) *Islamic Activism: a social movement theory approach*, Bloomington, Indianapolis: Indiana University Press.

Rubenberg, C. (1983) *The Palestine Liberation Organization: its institutional infrastructure*, Belmont, MA: Institute of Arab Studies.

Rubinstein, D. (1998) "Palestinians and Israelis: an uneven curiosity," *Palestine-Israel Journal*, 5:34–9.

Ryan, C. (1991) *Prime Time Activism*, Boston, MA: South End Press.

—— (2005) "Building Theorist-Activists Collaboration in the Media Arena: A Success Story," in D. Croteau, B. Hoynes, and C. Ryan (eds) *Rhyming Hope and History*. Minneapolis: University of Minnesota Press.

Ryan, C., Anastario, M., and Jeffreys, K. (2005) "Start Small, Build Big: negotiating opportunities in media markets," *Mobilization: An International Journal*, 10:111–28.

Sahliyeh, E. (1986) *In Search of Leadership: West Bank politics since 1967*, Washington D.C.: The Brookings Institute.

Sandler, S. and Frisch, H. (1984) *Israel, the Palestinians and the West Bank: a study in inter-communal conflict*, Lexington, MA: Lexington.

Schattschneider, E.E. (1975) *The Semisovereign People*, New York: The Dryden Press.

Segal, H. (1987) *Ahim Yekarim* [Dear Brothers], Jerusalem: Keter.

Sewell, W.H. (1992) "A Theory of Structure: duality, agency, and transformation," *American Journal of Sociology*, 98:1–29.

Shalev, A. (1990) *Ha'intifadah* [The Intifada], Tel Aviv: Papirus.

Shamir, S. (1974) *Communications and Political Attitudes in West Bank Refugee Camps*, Tel Aviv: Shiloah Center.

Shiff, Z. and Yaari, E. (1990) *Ha'intifada* [The Intifada], Tel Aviv: Shoken.

Shinar, D. (1987) "The West Bank Press and Palestinian Nation Building," *The Jerusalem Quarterly*, 43:37–48.

Shinar, D. and Rubinstein, D. (1987) *Palestinian Press in the West Bank: the political dimension*, Jerusalem: The Jerusalem Post (The West Bank Database Project Series).

Simmel, G. (1955) *Conflict*, trans. R. Bendix, Glencoe, IL: The Free Press.

Siniora, H. (1988) "An Analysis of the Current Revolt," *Journal of Palestinian Studies*, 17:3–13.

Skocpol, T. (1979) *States and Social Revolutions*, Cambridge: Cambridge University Press.

Smelser, N. (1962) *Theory of Collective Behavior*, London: Routledge and Kegan Paul.

Snow, D.A. and Benford, R.D. (1988) "Ideology, Frame Resonance, and Participant Mobilization," in B. Klandermans, H. Kriesi, and S. Tarrow (eds) *From Structure to Action: comparing movement participation across cultures, international social movement research Vol. 1*, Greenwich, CT: JAI Press Inc.

Snow, D.A., Rochford, E.B., Worden, S.K., and Benford, R. (1986) "Frame Alignment Processes, Micromobilization, and Movement Participation," *American Sociological Review*, 51:464–81.

Sprinzak, E. (1981) "Gush Emunim – Model Ha'Karhon shel Kitzuniyut Polltit" [Block of the Faithful – The Iceberg Model of Political Extermism], *Medina, Memshal Ve'Yahasim Beinleumyim*, 17:22–49.

—— (1986) *Ish Ha'yasher Be'eynav: illegalism ve'extra-parliamentarism be'israel* [Every Man Whatsoever: illegalism and extraparliamentarism in Israel], Tel-Aviv: Poalim.

—— (1995) *Alimut Polltit Be'israel* [Political Violence in Israel], Jerusalem: Jerusalem Institute.

Susser, L. and Rekhess, E. (2002) "Israel," in B. Maddy-Weitzman (ed.) *Middle East Contemporary Survey, Vol. 24, 2000*, The Moshe Dayan Center for Middle Eastern and African Studies and The Shiloah Institute and Tel Aviv University: Westview Press.

Tamari, S. (1988) "What the Uprising Means," *Middle East Report*, 152:24–30.

Taraki, L. (1990) "The Development of Political Consciousness Among Palestinians in the Occupied Territories, 1967–1987," in J.R. Nassar and R. Heacock (eds) *Intifada: Palestinians at the Crossroads*, New York: Preager.

Tarrow, S. (1989) *Democracy and Disorder*, Oxford: Clarendon Press.

—— (1996) "The People's Two Rhythms: Charles Tilly and the study of contentious politics," *Society for Comparative Study of Society and History*, pp. 586–600.

—— (1998) *Power in Movement*, 2nd edn, Cambridge: Cambridge University Press.

Tashakkori, A. and Teddlie, C. (eds) (2003) *Handbook of Mixed Methods*, Thousand Oaks: SAGE.

Tessler, M. (1990) "The Intifada and Political Discourse in Israel," *Journal of Palestinian Studies*, 19:43–61.

Tilly, C. (1978) *From Mobilization to Revolution*, Reading, MA: Addison-Wesley.

—— (2003) *The Politics of Collective Violence*, Cambridge: Cambridge University Press.

Tinder, G. (1995) *Political Thinking*, Boston, MA: Harper Collins.

Tucker, R.C. (1978) *The Marx-Engels Reader*, 2nd edn, New York: W.W. Norton and Company.

Urban, K.J. (1993) "Theories of Conflict and the Palestinian Leadership during the First Two Years of the Intifada," unpublished thesis, University of Tennessee.

Vitullo, A. (1988) "Uprising in Gaza," *Middle East Report*, 152/18:18–23.

Weber, M. (1978) *Economy and Society*, Guenthar R. and C. Wittich (eds), trans. E. Fischoff, H. Gerth, A.M. Henderson, F. Kolegar, C.W. Mills, T. Parsons, M. Rheinstein, G. Roth, E. Shils, and C. Wittich, Berkeley: University of California Press.

Weimann, G. and Winn, C. (1994) *The Theatre of Terror: mass media and international terrorism*, New York: Longman.

Welchman, L. (1993) *A Thousand and One Homes: Israel's demolition and sealing of houses in the occupied Palestinian territories* (Al-Haq's Occasional Paper No. 11), Ramallah: Al-Haq.

Williams, R. (1977) *Marxism and Literature*, London: Oxford University Press.

Williams, R.H. and Benford, R.D. (2000) "Two Faces of Collective Action Frames: a theoretical consideration," *Current Perspectives in Social Theory*, 20:127–51.

Wolfsfeld, G. (1988) *The Politics of Provocation*, New York: State University of New York Press.

—— (1996) *The Central Arena*, unpublished manuscript, The Hebrew University of Jerusalem.

—— (1997) *Media and Political Conflict – news from the Middle East*, Cambridge: Cambridge University Press.

### Documents, reports, and newspapers and magazines articles

"*A Joint Manifestation by 'Yesha' Council and Gush Emunim*," A letter to Israeli Government, May 30, 1989.

Al-Haq (1990) *A Nation under Siege: Al-Haq Annual Report on Human Rights in the Occupied Palestinian Territories, 1989*, Ramallah: Al-Haq.

—— (1988) *Twenty Years of Israel Occupation of the West Bank and Gaza.* Ramallah: Al-Haq.

—— (1991) *Protection Denied: Continuing Israeli Human Rights Violations in the Occupied Palestinian Territories, 1990*, Ramallah: Al-Haq.

Alternative Information Center (1996) *The Situation in the Occupied Territories in the Wake of the Suicide Bombings*, Jerusalem: Alternative Information Center.

*An-Najah Newsletter*, "Interview with Dr. Sofian Sultan, Chairperson An-Najah Employees Union," April 1985.

"Arafat: Without the U.S. There Will Be No Achievements," *Jerusalem Post*, February 17, 1988, p. 5.

"*Hamanit*," the Israeli Intelligence Force Publication, No. 17, April 1991, p. 63 (in Hebrew).

"*Hatzav*" – Special Publication: An Interview with Yassar Arafat. October 29, 1985.

"*Meyda – On developments and Occurrences in Judea and Samaria and the Gaza Region*," Various issues: No. 1/1983, No. 2, 3, 4, and 5/1984. Published by Israeli Consultant for Arab Affairs – Department of Coordination for Judea and Samaria and Gaza Region (in Hebrew).

"Odai: How We Organized Locally," *Intifada Diary: Ten Years After*, Online. Available at: www.birzeit.edu/diary/intifadah/locaorg.html (accessed November 7, 2000).

"Something was in the air all of 1987" (Interview), *Middle East Report*, No. 152, Vol. 18, No. 3, (May–June 1988), pp. 43–4.

"Statement by the Preparatory Committee for the First General Conference of the Workers Unity Bloc in the Occupied Territories," 5 July 1985.

"Statement of the Unified National Command of the Uprising in the Occupied Territories on the Assassination of Khalil al-Wazir, Baghdad, 17 April 1988," *Journal of Palestinian Studies*, 17/3:169.

"The Palestinians' Fourteen Demands," *Journal of Palestinian Studies*, 17/3:63–6.

B'Tselem (1989) *Annual Report 1989: Violations of Human Rights in the Occupied Territories*, Comprehensive Report, December 1989. Jerusalem: B'Tselem.

—— (1989a) *Demolitions and Sealings of Houses as a Punitive Measure in the West Bank and Gaza Strip During the Intifada*, Comprehensive Report, September 1989. Jerusalem: B'Tselem.

—— (1994) *Law Enforcement vis-a-vis Israeli Civilians in the Occupied Territories*, Comprehensive Report, March 1994. Jerusalem: B'Tselem.

—— (1995) *A Policy of Discrimination: Land Expropriation, Planning and Building in East Jerusalem*, Comprehensive Report, May 1995. Jerusalem: B'Tselem.

—— (1998) *1987–1997: A Decade of Human Rights Violations*, Information Sheet, January 1998. Jerusalem: B'Tselem.

—— (1998b) *Disputed Waters: Israel's Responsibility for the Water Shortage in the Occupied Territories*, Information Sheet, September 1998. Jerusalem: B'Tselem.

—— "Fatalities in the al-Aqsa Intifada, Data by Month," Online. Available at: www.btselem.org/English/Statistics/Al_Aqsa_Fatalities_Tables.asp (accessed October 22, 2004).

FACTS Information Committee (1988) *Towards A State of Independence – The Palestinian Uprising: December 1987–August 1988*. Jerusalem: FACTS.

Galili, L. (1989) "Local Residents Led by Hamas Activists Disrupted an Israeli–Palestinian Conference in Beita," *Ha'Aretz*, March 26, p. 3.

Gangath, H. with Assaily, N. (1989) "Intifada: Palestinian Nonviolent Protest – An Affirmation of Human Dignity and Freedom," *The Palestinian Center for the Study of Nonviolence*, East Jerusalem, Occupied Palestine. Unpublished manuscript.

International Center for Peace in the Middle East (1983) *Human Rights in the IDF-held Territories: 1979–1983*, Tel Aviv.

Jerusalem Media and Communication Center (1989) *The Intifada: An Overview: The First Two Years*, East Jerusalem: JMCC.

—— (1991) *The Stone and the Olive Branch: Four Years of the Intifada – From Jabalia to Madrid*, East Jerusalem: JMCC.

—— "*JMCC Public Opinion Poll No. 37: On Palestinian Attitudes Towards Final Status Negotiations and the Declaration of the State – June 2000*," Online. Available at: www.JMCC – Public Opinion Polls4.htm> (accessed November 28, 2004).

—— "Letter addressed to President Arafat from the Palestinian National and Islamic Forces," Online. Available at: www.jmcc.org/banner/banner1/bayan/aqsabayan3.htm (accessed November 22, 2004).

*Palestine Times*, issue 106, April 2000, Online. Available at: www.ptimes.org/ issue106/index.html (accessed February 29, 2004).

Palestinian Academic Society for the Study of International Affairs. *PASSIA Diary 1998 – 10 Years*, Jerusalem: Al-Quds.

Palestinian Human Rights Information Center (1988) *The Cost of Freedom – Palestinian Human Rights Under Israeli Occupation*, A Special Report. Chicago, IL: The Palestinian Human Rights Information Center – International.

—— (1989) *The Cost of Freedom: 1989 – Palestinian Human Rights Under Israeli Occupation*, Annual Report. Chicago, IL: The Palestinian Human Rights Information Center – International.

—— (1994) *Human Rights Update*, 8/7 (July 1994), Jerusalem.

Parry, N. (ed.) *A Personal Diary of the Israeli Palestinian Conflict*, Online. Available at: www.birzeit.edu/diary/intifada/localorg.html (accessed November 7, 2000).

Peace Now & Israelis by Choice (1988) "A Taste of Peace," Press release, December 15.

Prisoner's Friends Association in Israel (1995) "List of General Demands by the Palestinian Prisoners in Jenin Prison," December 6.

Ratz – The Israeli Civil Rights and Peace Movement (1988) "A letter to Minister of Defense Yitzhak Rabin," Press release, February 16 (in Hebrew).

Shaked, R. (1989) "Radio Intifada" (Intifada Radio), *Yediot Ahronot*, September 18, p. 27.

"Start of the al-Aqsa Intifada in 2000," Online. Available at: www. palestinianfacts.org.html (accessed October 22, 2004).

The Islamic Association for Palestine (1990) *Charter of the Islamic Resistance Movement (HAMAS) of Palestine*, Dallas, TX: USA.

Workers Unity Bloc Central Bureau (1985) "All Efforts should be Exerted to Hold the Bloc's First General Conference," Press Release. July 5.

## Governmental sources

Israel Central Bureau of Statistics (1988) *Statistics on Judea, Samaria, and Gaza Strip*, Vol. 18. Jerusalem.

Israel Defense Force Spokesperson Department and Ministry of Information (1992) *Five Years to the Uprising – data*, IDF Spokesperson, Jerusalem.

Israel Defense Force Spokesperson Department (Undated) *Terrorist Activities in Judea and Samaria and Gaza Strip – Data: December 1987–October 1994*.

Israel Ministry of Education and Culture, Ministry of Information, Publication Service, *Israel Government Yearbook*, Vol. 1979, 1980, 1981, 1982, 1983, 1984, 1985, 1986, 1990, 1991, 1993. Jerusalem, Israel.

Israel Yearbook and Almanac 1991/2 (1992) Event of 1991. Volume 46. Jerusalem: IBRT Translation/Documentation Ltd.

Israeli Defense Minister Spokesman (1992) *The Hamas and the Islamic Jihad*, special publication 18 December.

# Index

References to figures are in **bold**. References to tables are in *italic*.

For Product Safety Concerns and Information please contact our EU
representative GPSR@taylorandfrancis.com
Taylor & Francis Verlag GmbH, Kaufingerstraße 24, 80331 München, Germany

www.ingramcontent.com/pod-product-compliance
Lightning Source LLC
Chambersburg PA
CBHW050423280326
41932CB00013BA/1977